A USER'S GUIDE TO SPACETIME

A USER'S GUIDE TO SPACETIME

Poems by

Daniel Orsini

Quaternity™

A USER'S GUIDE TO SPACETIME

Quaternity Books™

First Edition Quaternity™ Books
ISBN – 978-1-943691-16-6
Cover Design by James Buchanan

Surely you know that you are God's temple, where the Spirit of God dwells.

—1 Corinthians 3.16

. . . the courage to be as oneself is the courage to make of oneself what one wants to be.

—Paul Tillich, *The Courage to Be*

CONTENTS

Introduction 9

The Archivist 15
Bellicose Ares 16
Beyond Gender 17
Blazar/Quasar 18
Body of Evidence 19
Bulk 20
Bystander Cyborgs 21
Canadarm 22
Carrier 23
Compass 24
Dreaming in Code 25
Electrospinlacing 26
The Exaltations of the Nettles 27
The Experiment of Eternity 28
Figure Skater 29
Footprint 30
Full Circle 31
Heracles Peeled 32
Herald 33
Hercules in the Vessel of the Sun 34
Hermes' Nested Spiral 35
History's Thread 36
Hubble Ajar 37
Keeper of the Hubble 38
Kepler 39
Life in a Mortal Universe 40
Life Out There 41
The Limits of the Coded World 42
Made 43
Mandragora's Dream 44
The Man Who Made a Copy of Himself 45
Mapping Celestial Terrains 46
Messenger 47
The Möbius Strip 48
Namespace 49
Nothing 50
An Oblate Spheroid 51
Outrider 52
Peregrination 53
Platonic Riddles 54
Plato's Cave 55
Pneumatic 56
Postmodern 57
Precinct 58
Prefigured 59
Pseudosphere 60
Pushing Gravity 61
The Quilted Multiverse 62
Quintessence 63
Rebis 64
Saffron of the Metals 65
Saturday 66
Segway 67
The Self-Thinking Thought 68
Serious Reader 69
Setting the Wheel on Fire 70
Shapeshifter 71
Siblings of the Sun 72
The Skin That I Live In 73
Something to Live For 74
Space 75
Spherical 76
The Spherical Glass Vessel 77
Station 78
Stewards of Creation 79
Sunday 80
Swain 81
Symbiote 82
Symposium 83
Tearing the Fabric of Spacetime 84
Techwed 85
The Teleoperator's Dream 86
Terraforming Mars 87
Testing the Night of Pan 88
Tipler's Subset 89
To Live and Work in Deep Space 90
To Mars in a Month 91
Travelling Forever in the Same Direction 92
Tumbling Escher 93
The Ultimate Fate of the Universe 94
The Universe Speaks 95
A User's Guide to Spacetime 96
Vas Bene Clausum 97
A Walking Man I 98
Wayfinder 99
The Weight of History 100
The Whole Atlas 101
Writing under Erasure 102

Notes and Comments 105

Introduction

In these conflicted times, when politicians lie, cultures collapse, and religions atrophy, we may now more than ever value the art of four prescient poets who still share with us their chief instrument of knowing: "the animating light of [their] coherent intelligence."[1] Thus, in "Locksley Hall" (1842), Alfred, Lord Tennyson, having "dipt into the future, far as human eye could see, / Saw the Vision of the world, and all the wonder that would be."[2] Equally clear-sighted,[3] Emily Dickinson observed that "Not 'Revelation' – 'tis – that waits, / But our unfurnished eyes – "[4] (c. 1863). Likewise, in "Sailing to Byzantium" (1926), William Butler Yeats aspired to sing—in another life—"Of what is past, or passing, or to come."[5] In "The Dry Salvages" (1941), the third poem in *The Four Quartets,* even T. S. Eliot admonished his readers "To communicate with Mars, converse with spirits, / [. . .] / Describe the horoscope"—in short, to "fare forward, voyagers."[6] In effect, all of these poets embraced not only the present world, but also the afterworld—"The Finite – furnished / With the Infinite"[7]—as avatars of the divine. Although they often lamented the loss of spiritual unity in their lives, they conducted, through their work, a study of the hoped-for inner transformation of our species, enhanced by numerous directions for its completion—a veritable experiment of eternity.

This is a roundabout way of saying, I suppose, that the lyrics in *A User's Guide to Spacetime* derive from the epiphanic[8] poems of the aforementioned artists, along with the ensouling achievements of other, like-minded progenitors. Accordingly, the NASA astronaut who appears and then reappears in *A User's Guide to Spacetime* recalls Tennyson's own "herald of a higher race," the chosen believer-priest from *In Memoriam.*[9] In fact, the archetype of the god-man and his liberation from "the chthonic world and its transitoriness"[10] is the specific subject of numerous titles in this collection—in "Heracles Peeled," where, amid "Subsets of atoms as cosmic as nouns" (line 8), the shape-shifting astronaut "wears his helmet like a feather-crest" (13); in "History's Thread," where, ever-evolving, he becomes Heaven's "Scion of Kevlar" (9); and in "Figure Skater," where, "newborn like a disk," he coalesces, once again, into Gaea's "riddled foetus" (23-24).

Admittedly, NASA's suited nomad attains his exalted self-definition mainly because "The world revolves in [his] aetheric eye" ("Life in a Mortal Universe" 24). The visionary insight that Tennyson enshrines in Poem 95 of *In Memoriam,* that Dickinson explores in "The Love a Life can show Below,"[11] that Yeats reveals in the Byzantium poems, and that Eliot accommodates in "Ash Wednesday" also surfaces in the unified and coherent worldview of this book, focused as it is, presumptively, upon the entwining "imagination of spiritual light."[12] Although each poet postulates spiritual unity as the absolute condition for the fulfillment of the self, it is active imagination heightened to vision that initiates the process. As Jung shows in his assessment of the functions of the human psyche[13] and as each of these poets affirms in the poems cited above, the senses mediate perception, while the intellect corresponds to apperception—that is, to the phenomenon of "clear insight" and visionary "understanding."[14] However, only with the help of the Holy Spirit—and with the believer's acceptance of that help—can either conversion or transformation occur.

Tennyson's exhortation in *In Memoriam*—"Behind the veil, behind the veil"[15]—is altogether pertinent here. As Andrew Murray asserts in *The Spirit of Christ,* "This tearing of the veil, this enthronement of [. . .] the glorified One in the heart, is not always with the sound of trumpet and shouting." Simply enough, the "eye of the flesh" may not see Him on the throne.[16] Dickinson may "baffle at the Hint" of "the Clue divine" in "My Cocoon tightens – Colors tease –,"[17] and Eliot grumble at its absence in both "Gerontion" and "Journey of the Magi," and Yeats flail at its uncertainty in "Among School Children." Nevertheless, only when they assist in the tearing of "the veil of the flesh" may even great poets enter in power "the inner sanctuary of the full glory of the Spirit life in heaven."[18] Otherwise, they may falter in their pursuit of the afterlife. Despite their desire for Immortality—despite even the intervention of the Holy Spirit—all of these poets realize that, in the end, "the search lies heavy on the searcher."[19]

This desire to be immortal is, of course, still another theme that I have underscored throughout *A User's Guide to Spacetime*. Thus, in "Compass," as the carrier of life, the astronaut "shall grow from Ge's ubiquitous eyes" (22). In "Siblings of the Sun," he is "[b]orn in the unconscious" (22), and, in "Pseudosphere," he is "in Ge's breath-body based" (12). As New Heaven's "Light-bringer" ("Kepler" 21), he is also "wired in the brane" ("Life Out There" 24), "consecrates himself everywhere" ("Messenger" 12), and "through the commissure streaks" ("Bystander Cyborgs" 18). Although the Hermetic *lapis,* "the figure [of Christ] veiled in matter," exists "in some other place [. . .] / Light years from Earth" ("Herald" 20, 23), the astronaut himself remains immortal not only because he is "Indwelt by the Spirit" of Christ ("Dreaming in Code" 21), but also because he may "Restore the *Rebis*"—the "dual being born of the alchemical union of opposites" (masculine/feminine) and recognized as "a symbol of the self"[20]—and may "Beyond the compass of the symbol rise" ("Compass" 23-24). In other words, I do think that, far more compelling than either the lofty status of humankind or the esemplastic[21] power of the imagination or even the mystical impulse to live again—intertwined themes that I have emphasized throughout this book—are the eternal presence of "the religion-creating archetypes"[22] and the projection of their unconscious contents through the perfect "objectivity of the psyche" or whatever else one chooses to call the transcendental self.[23] As these poems demonstrate, "Faith-based the astronaut pursues his course" ("Station" 9). However, they also suggest that, when the treasure is hard to attain, there is always "more to be sought than the scripture."[24]

Daniel Orsini
Cranston, Rhode Island
27 May 2019

ENDNOTES

[1] See Arthur Zajonc, *Catching the Light: The Entwined History of Light and Mind* (1993; New York: Oxford UP, 1995) 205, where the author echoes Goethe's view of the image of light that humankind has crafted: "If we neglect the animating light of coherent intelligence that illumines and flows through all our senses, then the glory of the world stands mute before our inquiring spirit." In other words, "Goethe emphasized the importance of a light that is within."

[2] Lines 119-20, in *Major British Poets,* ed. G. B. Harrison, et al. (New York: Harcourt, 1959) 406.

[3] Zajonc defines this term in *Catching the Light:* The perceiver who is "clear-sighted" has already awakened to "the true grasping of light" through "new capacities of mind suited to seeing" and "aligned to nature" (339-40). Zajonc indicates that Paul Cézanne uses the word definitively in a letter written to his son on 8 September 1906: "'Finally, I must tell you that as a painter I am becoming more clearsighted before nature'" (338).

[4] Poem 685: "Not 'Revelation' – 'tis – that waits," lines 1-2, in *The Complete Poems of Emily Dickinson,* ed. Thomas H. Johnson (Boston: Little, 1960) 339.

[5] Line 32, in *Major British Poets* 796.

[6] Lines 184, 186, and 168, in *Major British Poets* 844.

[7] Poem 906: "The Admirations – and Contempts – of time –," lines 11-12, in Johnson 428.

[8] This word, the adjectival form of "epiphany," suggests either "a moment of sudden intuitive understanding" or a "flash of insight," qualities manifested in each of the poems cited above. See *Webster's New World Dictionary,* 1988 ed.

[9] Poem 118, line 14, in *Major British Poets* 423. The full title of Tennyson's collection of lyrics is *In Memoriam A.H.H.* [*A*rthur *H*enry *H*allam].

[10] According to C. G. Jung, "On the one hand the anima [the feminine side of the male psyche] is the connecting link with the world beyond and the eternal images, while on the other hand her emotionality involves man in the chthonic [material] world and its transitoriness." See *Alchemical Studies,* trans. R. F. C. Hull (1967; Princeton: Princeton UP, 1983) 337.

[11] Poem 673 in Johnson 334.

[12] Zajonc 114.

[13] C. G. Jung identifies the four functions of consciousness—Sensing, Intuiting, Feeling, and Thinking—in *The Archetypes and the Collective Unconscious,* trans. R. F. C. Hull (1959; Princeton: Princeton UP, 1990) 320.

[14] In *Psychology and Alchemy,* trans. R. F. C. Hull (1953; Princeton: Princeton UP, 1993), C. G. Jung indicates that the aim of the [alchemical] *opus* is "clear insight" that leads to visionary "understanding" (264). He also reminds us that "The importance or necessity of understanding and intelligence is insisted upon all through the [alchemical] literature, not only because intelligence above the ordinary is needed in the performance of so difficult a work [as the moral-intellectual transformation of the individual], but because it is assumed

that a species of magical power capable of transforming even brute matter dwells in the human mind" (260).

[15] Poem 56, line 28, in *Major British Poets* 418.

[16] In this essay, I have quoted from an earlier edition of *The Spirit of Christ* (Pennsylvania: Whitaker House, n.d.) 123.

[17] Poem 1099 in Johnson 496.

[18] Murray 122.

[19] See Jung, *Psychology and Alchemy* 257: In the *Rosarium philosophorum* (1550), the anonymous author maintains that the alchemical *opus* "must be performed 'with the true and not the fantastic imagination'" and that "the stone will be found 'when the search lies heavy on the searcher.' This [latter] remark can only be understood as meaning that a certain psychological condition is indispensable for the discovery of the miraculous stone" [a Hermetic symbol of the unified self]. Jung adds that both of these statements "make it seem very possible that the author was in fact of the opinion that the essential secret of the art lies hidden in the human mind—or, to put it in modern terms, in the unconscious" (258).

[20] C. G. Jung, *Aion: Researches into the Phenomenology of the Self,* trans. R. F. C. Hull (1959; Princeton: Princeton UP, 1969) 268.

[21] Samuel Taylor Coleridge coined this word in *Biographia Literaria* (1817) in order to define the imagination as a "vital" faculty shaped to unify heterogeneous or disparate elements.

[22] In *Psychology and Alchemy,* Jung emphasizes that the path to psychological wellness revolves around "the religion-creating archetypes" (29).

[23] Cf. *Psychology and Alchemy* 27-28, where Jung, having explained that his task as a doctor is "to help the patient cope with life," clarifies the intricacies of the procedure, including the "way" to the goal: "I cannot presume to pass judgment on [the patient's] final decisions, because I know that all coercion—be it suggestion, insinuation, or any other method of persuasion—ultimately proves to be nothing but an obstacle to the highest and most decisive experience of all, which is to be alone with his own self, or whatever else one chooses to call the objectivity of the psyche."

[24] In "Liber de alchemiae difficultatibus," *Theatrum chemicum* I (1602): 199, Theobald de Hoghelande quotes Senior Zadith ben Hamuel, the tenth-century alchemist, as saying "that the 'vision' of the Hermetic vessel 'is more to be sought than the scripture'" (Jung, *Psychology and Alchemy* 250). Jung adds that "It is not clear whether by 'scripture' [Senior] means the traditional description of the vessel in the treatises of the masters, or the Holy Scripture" (250n8).

A USER'S GUIDE TO SPACETIME

THE ARCHIVIST

We find in the sky such symbols as bind:
Castor and Pollux; hunter to his kind,
Even Orion in whirlpools that wind.
We store them in the archive of the mind.
Lion and unicorn; mote in the ark—
To Sirius pointing I trace the spark.
Ruled by the light, the multiverse yet stark,
Feather-crowned, I make my way through the dark.

Reality transparent, we reflect
Each and every subject that we select.
Thus we march in lockstep, the New Elect:
Metallic coheirs in Kevlar bedecked.
By digits coded, hyphenate that walks
Deployed to the station, the cyborg caulks.
Pleistocene biped, anthropoid that stalks
Embedded in history, Hermes talks.

He undertook a journey to the sea,
The steersman in the Tree; with Heaven's key,
He struck the athanor; Heracles' plea:
Inside the fiery furnace, pity me.
His eye a spheroid, a globe that once teemed
With semblances that none but photons beamed,
He scanned His shaman—*rebis* that He streamed
Without a suture: Sun and Moon redeemed.

BELLICOSE ARES

Like a robot spun from liquid metal,
In round shapes he morphs: both leaf and nettle;
Crystals from the moon: Maria's fettle;
Spagyric foetus curled on a petal.
Bellicose Ares, master of the feint;
His phantom bulky, clone without a taint,
He stands on the aether: thumbling or saint
Or cyborg anchored to his foot restraint.

Orphans in the cosmos, satellites drift.
I backpack to the site; my unit swift,
Free of the mother ship, my white speck qwiffed,
I whirl above the earth; till grapplers lift,
I platform my spacewalk; circuit the tun;
Enter the nozzle of its engine; done,
Maneuver then the stray; where I have run,
Attach to *Palapa* threads of the sun.

Obsessed by Earthshine, bruised by Hubble's plight,
Propelled by a rocket, I scour the night.
Extracted from the planet, in its flight,
The bird cremates itself till it is white.
I measure the distance, darkness renowned
Even as a code; its integer found,
Relic radiation; clouds that abound—
Globular cluster in Centaurus wound.

BEYOND GENDER

To scale the planet and in the moon sit
Alembicated, he goes round with it.
Torso by torso, his astronaut knit
Without a seam, he twines his opposite.
Still the dark taunts him; like raven or kite
Or Alchemy's tree or Mercury's wight
Encased in Kevlar—surrounded by night,
He hitches a ride to Europa's site.

The astronaut rises; that he may pass,
He integrates the contents of the glass,
Triadic or quaternal: class by class,
Maria's maxim, source-point of the Mass.
Every human truth a last truth but one,
He wavers between the stone and the Son:
Some clarified substance—*caelum* that spun—
Castor's postulate, on Möbius' run.

We scavenge such symbols as adepts scrawl—
Clotho's icons embedded in the ball
Like monad or soul-spark, Self in the caul,
Manifestations both large and small:
The spagyric foetus that Hermes nudged;
The migrant that across the mare trudged;
The masculine smeared, the feminine smudged,
Ge's *rebis* beyond gender, I am judged.

BLAZAR/QUASAR

From the universe, its energy let,
It points toward the Earth. — We repay the debt.
We host the blazar, observe down its jet,
Conceive such a beam as Hubble has set:
An accretion disk where positrons are,
Gas and dust and the occasional star,
Bulk speed of plasma, parsecs in a car,
Or toroid opaque or both near and far.

Pursuing light to its galactic core,
I angle my telescope at its door.
To seers oriented—coheirs' lore—
BL Lacertae discloses its store.
Like the Zodiac, its chimeras free,
Hyperspace stirs us—Asclepius' plea:
We secure the House, then forget the key:
Maria's axiom: *the four times three.*

A Saturnine abstract being I mused:
Light wars against Night; the omniverse bruised,
Back into my body, my torsos fused,
I yet suture the rift—I stand accused.
Though the serpent seize me, sojourner, wight,
I circle its source-point, question, invite
The mystic Polaris; from star to mite,
Besiege each site till Ouroboros bite.

BODY OF EVIDENCE

Like Heaven's *rebis,* foetus that we limn
Even as Hermes, phantom that we skim
From Gaea's membrane, wry behind the scrim,
I pierce the caul and then lean down to Him,
Till, sensate as a scarab or a kite
Or phasmid in the dross or grebe or mite
Moist as the soul or cinnabar in flight,
I ascertain the Monad in the light.

He floats in the vessel soft as a cloud,
Or seed of the woman, matter endowed
Like Adam's helpmeet, gamonymus vowed,
Or Ge's homunculus, concourse or crowd.
In the omniverse, Eve's imagined mind,
Ge spins His shroud with skeins that *She* has lined—
The text in the tissue: stone that He signed;
Body of evidence: bone that we bind.

And thus I flourish as an atom may,
Or salt or alum that flows in the fray,
Or sol-gel that spills or leaps from its tray,
Such a play as magi electrospray,
Each droplet—plume or splay—become my kin,
A web of fibers carried to the skin
In seamless layers, melt beneath my shin—
Elastic, thin—embedded in my twin.

BULK

Having ranged the orbweb: brane in the bulk;
Globular cluster stars: holons that hulk;
The Sun in the scree, the Moon in its sulk
On remnant hillocks; such cyborgs as skulk,
He breaches the wormhole; sifts its strayers;
Matter yet essential to its players,
Spans the seven heavens; in its layers,
Delivers the Spirit to its slayers.

I rove above a cloud; a tethered grain
Beset by gamma rays—chaos the bane—
Enshrine my coheir; my capsule His fane,
Streams like tesserae follow in my train.
Sunsets glistening, sequential their bands,
I have sprinkled the hourglass with my sands.
Upborne by my Saturn or hung with strands,
The body that shadows its object lands.

In Gaea's torus as we wind and weave
Between the world and the will to believe,
His *rebis* cinctured like Adam and Eve,
He manifests the trace that we retrieve:
Bulbous as the cosmos, pulsate its seams
With haptic passions, as Hephaestus deems—
Regimen of Mars; chameleon that teems;
Dust that shifts in the midnight of our dreams.

BYSTANDER CYBORGS

The brain is pre-set by its own command.
Thus I begin to rise before I stand
Upon its strand. From desire to demand
I flex the index finger of my hand.
Will without awareness, pleasure derives
From neither Ge's emotions nor Her drives—
The mantic weaver of such skein as thrives:
The self-referential spouse that She shrives.

All diversity into oneness urged,
The metaverse with the omphalos merged,
Particles of the Self forever purged,
Still the androgyne sang to me and surged.
My skull its capsule, the gourd in its rind,
Each dendrite dances till I am divined.
His phantom nomad enshrined in my mind,
Mapping Him, *I become one with my kind.*

Translated and sped as the shaman seeks,
The archetype through the commissure streaks.
Soon the *rebis* in the vertebrate peaks
And in the dominant hemisphere speaks.
We mediate between foam-stuff and string,
Clusters that ring and cepheids that fling—
Bystander cyborgs: cloudforms on their swing,
Like cosmic dust, attached to *every*thing.

CANADARM

On Möbius' circuit, in zones that seem,
I scan the infinite; in cones that stream,
Imagine the holon; neurons supreme,
Encapsule the *rebis* in dreams that teem.
I layer my body that I may breathe
Untethered in space; amid skeins that seethe,
In melt or Kevlar, nomad that I sheathe,
Ascend to such spheres as hierophants wreathe.

Cyborg at the site, the grain that I grew
Even as soul-sparks that astronauts strew
Astride the Shuttle, Canadarm in view,
I ply the task that Ge meant me to do.
I dock at the station; hyphenate furled,
Unfold the tesseract; where I am curled,
Inhabit the cosmos. — Ares yet twirled,
Hephaestan hybrid, I chain-link the world.

To repair the Shuttle, with spray and tool,
I patch a thermal tile; while bubbles pool,
Test the dispenser; like putty its spool,
On my third attempt, unravel its rule.
His strain cislunar, as I seed His crop,
I board a mobile boom; suspend, then drop;
Install the truss; a foot restraint my prop,
Stand upon the aether and do not stop.

CARRIER

Carrier of life, the astronaut goes.
Having fled the mass, in his psyche stows.
Atomized, tabulated, still he grows.
Small yet invisible, *astrum* he shows—
Inside and Outside—New Heaven spun;
The paradigm of opposites begun,
His *rebis* crowned, the Tree of Moon and Sun;
Neither male nor female, the two as One.

He lives in such worlds as Möbius made:
Parallel universes; tubes that braid
But trefoil knot folds; Jerusalem laid
Even as hyperspace, jasper or jade.
Attached to Earthshine, matter that ascends—
Sapphirine satellite, capsule that pends
Above the mare—like a sheetweb spends;
Secretes its silk; then, tabernacled, blends.

We telescope the darkness; cap the light;
The vessel well-sealed, Saturn lidded tight,
Spagyric android wedded to the rite,
Metabolize enigmas of the night.
Chthonic as the mandrake, inverted bole,
He excavates such soil as adepts scroll;
Disinters the sexes—his shaman whole,
Hermes cultivates Ge's arsenic soul.

COMPASS

Without a moon, the blue dot that we seize
Would yet stabilize, see-saw with us, tease,
The tilt of Earth's axis precess with ease,
Its motion vary by just ten degrees.
And still we might miss such stones as we stock,
Like lava channels, waves of molten rock,
Impact melt splashes, craters in a block—
Pictures that we lock cosmic as a clock.

Moonplant of the Adepts, Monad thus spun,
I enter Her womb. — Conceived by the sun,
Herald of the light on Möbius' run,
I ascend to myself: The Three plus One.
A totem ancestor: cross in the scree,
I contain its symbol, carry its key,
Plant like a tree in Infinity's sea—
Round as an island—Hermes by decree.

Metallic yet liquid, its seedling sown,
The Self, ever-present, is not a clone.
Circle, moisture, simplicity unknown,
Sleeping, She slumbers for me in the stone.
From Earth to Heaven, having searched the skies,
He shall grow from Ge's ubiquitous eyes,
Restore the *Rebis,* inhabit its guise,
Beyond the compass of the symbol rise.

DREAMING IN CODE

Interstellar cyborgs, we tour the world;
Push electrons around; in spaceships curled
Like ghostly hierophants—astronauts twirled—
Unspool our narratives, the future furled
Even as a chain—some Homeric skein—
Or Velcro strip or facsimile grain
Or silicon Mind, subclavian vein,
Or, slotted, meninges in Hermes' brain.

We rise in the east and sink in the west;
Coil like a serpent; circle like a quest
Ge's shining clay: the foetus in the chest.
Same arcane opus: pneuma in the nest,
We ride on the cloud where soul-sparks once flowed
Inside the bucket, each coheir that stowed—
Attached to the wheel that His *rebis* rode—
Immersed, like His shaman, dreaming in code.

Entwined without a seam, His torsos swell.
He clothes himself in the shape of a bell:
His spagyric body; occult its spell,
He reaches Eternity in its shell.
Indwelt by the Spirit, Presence intact,
Arrayed in fine linen, soul-atoms stacked,
He summons the magus, savors the act,
Sublimes the perceiver: phantom or fact.

ELECTROSPINLACING

At range in the omniverse, having steered
Amid such a concourse as I had neared—
Until caught in its snare, as I had feared—
I grieved an icon that had disappeared.
And still its form grew outward; unaware,
I carried it within me, like that stair,
Encoded in the chaos, in whose care
Astronauts crystallize, while women bear.

I reach beneath the syringe what lies hid;
Pursue its reminiscence; close its lid;
Electrospin its droplet; on its grid,
Secrete my monad, hybrid that I bid.
As melt like a skein gamonymous whirs,
So I fabricate lunar polymers:
Gel Suit like the sun god's, yellow as furze;
Scarab traces that Didymus avers.

When Hermes wakes and round and round he spins,
Outside his ambit Longevity grins;
Dresses the *rebis;* layers all his skins;
Multiplies his fibers, chassis' or shin's.
He nurtures him as the shaman his rood;
Feeds him in the capsule, by instinct cued,
Nostoc, Melissa, yew berries that brood—
In the cerebrum, Ge's heavenly food.

THE EXALTATIONS OF THE NETTLES

I rule my own spirit—the shaman cued
By logarithms or programs accrued,
He reads the source code: Ge's digits construed—
Everyman is always a multitude.
The robot in lockstep, his body lank,
Like quicksilver glistens; obsessed with rank,
Situates the *rebis*—in pod or tank,
Some mystic from the moon, and he is blank.

What, then, may we say that Ge's *cyborgs* learn?
As satellites wheel and tesseracts turn
Amid such dots as manikins discern . . .
That *exaltations of the nettles burn.*
Spacetime's concoction, hyacinthine bliss,
Ge scatters the dragon—the proof of this:
Regimen of Venus. Moon that we miss
Round as Ouroboros, She plants a kiss.

Subject to Time, the number of days
That streamed through his eye slot's infinite haze
Like clouded agate—albedo's or gray's—
He swathed his magus in celestial rays.
Chameleon of Chaos, remnant from Uz,
He knew the shape of the sun as it was;
Resorbed Her globe; Melissa in the fuzz,
Houseled, from Her brood-swarm, bees that yet buzz.

THE EXPERIMENT OF ETERNITY

My headgear mounted, my data suit scanned,
I test the robot; design its command;
Install a sensor that maps, through its strand,
The force of my fingers upon its hand.
Having cracked its code, the multiverse stacked,
Imagined, justified, become a fact,
I yet rehearse our pact; by word or act,
Perfect its species, its mindset intact.

His feet on the ground, his head in the sky,
He pursues his path to capsules that fly,
Even as a rocket, scaffold or tie
Staggers on the pad where hierophants hie.
Sublime as the source of life, he ascends;
Affiliated with the sun, he wends;
Till, quintessential, real, the pinwheel pends,
And thus, like a photon, the moonchild blends.

I craft such a light as savors the moth,
Starry spirals, peacock flesh in the broth,
Stone in the stubble, dragon in the froth,
Asclepius' chlamys, and Turin's cloth.
Like Ouroboros, I stow in a cave,
Till, crowned in the caul above Adam's grave,
I trail like skein the magus that I crave,
Collapse the qwiff, and inhabit the stave.

FIGURE SKATER

Upon the dust of Jupiter we peer;
Pursue the wetness of its atmosphere;
Describe its satellites: Callisto near,
Ganymede cratered, Europa severe,
Re-assess Io. Speculation strained,
Sulphur everywhere, its liquid arraigned
Like Spacetime itself—fabricated, feigned,
We who breathe and touch are still unexplained.

To satisfy the contours of its loop,
Inside a titanium vault we group
Infrared mappers; metallic its soup,
In squashed elliptical orbits we swoop;
Till in the Mind's eye the Shaman revolts:
Juno and Jupiter harness His colts;
Heaven's *Rebis* cognizant of His volts,
REM's hierophants carry His thunderbolts.

The day that Gaea stroked me with Her charms,
For once my body structured its alarms.
The glyph of Libra channeling Her harms,
I began to spin, then pulled in my arms
As if I were some cloud that formed the sun
Or newborn like a disk or point or pun
Or soul-spark coalesced or salt-sign won:
Ge's riddled foetus on Möbius' run.

FOOTPRINT

He can spot in the gibbous moon an eye.
Beyond human consciousness, layers lie.
And thus he dreams that Gaea's saffron die,
Flung from Spacetime, vacillates in the sky.
Each time that he blinks, the cosmos recurs.
He brackets the symbol that he defers;
Through alienation of instinct, errs;
Object of the percept, his subject blurs.

We pre-exist in such a primal state
As differentiated we create.
Buxom as Adam, restored by his mate,
We twine once more, then enter through His gate.
Essentially one, phenomenally two,
Polarities of being yet accrue.
We give—besides the Eve that Adam grew—
To each of them a back, marriage the glue.

The astronaut circles his mystic goal,
Ensconced in his moonship; stirs like a troll;
Steps from his capsule; unfolds like a scroll;
Inscribes his footprint, the strength of his soul.
He spins his suit like a skein from the mass
Or seed in the pod or stone in the pass,
Leans like a mandrake, upturns like a vas,
Rises like a *rebis,* cinctures its glass.

FULL CIRCLE

The world does not happen; it simply is.
The past is not lost, neither hers nor his—
Astarte's mysteries nor Mithras's.
Trillions of futures exist like a fizz.
As space expands, each bubble wall of foam
Stretches thinner and thinner, matter home
To a sub-universe within its gloam
Where s-waves ripple and where p-waves roam.

When we see Jupiter, shrouds that rehearse,
Photons reflected from sunlight traverse;
Impinge on cells in the retina; terse,
Dislodge electrons therein till we nurse
A sight as spectral as priests in a rite,
Astronauts entwined in a skein so tight
We salvage such planets as we incite,
Jupiter but the one disturbed by light.

The route to Spacetime is easy to tread.
Everywhere we find what cyborgs embed:
Relational trajectories; thus read,
Lorentzian wormholes, which Ge has spread.
We enter the funnel; ravel each ray
Through its spherical shell; propel the stray
To Alpha Centauri; light years away,
Travel full circle *in a single day.*

HERACLES PEELED

Spagyric paladins headed to Mars,
We wander the darkness in rocket cars;
Infrared each site for space dust that jars:
Some sinuous disk that measurement bars.
Abstruse as caverns, consciousness surrounds
Gaea's whitest brain-stone; whispers its sounds
Throughout the spheroid; pre-exists, in crowns,
Subsets of atoms as cosmic as nouns.

Even as the sun, atop starry bands,
He retrofires at G the bird that stands;
With swollen knobs, hypnagogic his hands,
Procures from its drawplate its rays like strands.
He wears his helmet like a feather crest;
Silver-weaves the magus; at Her behest,
Having named the mare, the moon his guest,
Chain-links the *rebis,* foetal in his breast.

His spirit antic, cislunar his kin,
The humanoid wakens, peers with a grin,
Expresses his joy, the eye of the jinn
The stereo camera beneath his skin.
Fashioned by Hephaestus, Talos congealed,
He ravels the layers of Thetis' shield,
Pallas in the star field, Heracles peeled—
What *he* shall be has not yet been revealed.

HERALD

What does it mean for something to exist?
Both leptons and photons, fields that persist,
Such dreams of the *rebis* as we enlist—
Abstract entities cannot be dismissed.
I glimpsed a cloudform, a phantom so raw
It fixed me where I stood before I saw
My risen hierophant, rotund as awe,
Frequented as space, transcendent as law.

Isolated by a tectonic shift
Produced by the Afro-Syrian rift,
A set of mutant traits began to drift
That Nature selected, and thus we sift.
Once we were animals with human shapes
Led without intent from lemurs to apes
Till the biped steers, at the cosmos gapes,
And then drapes himself in Rabboni's capes.

A stone that falls through dimensional space
Is possible, though we see but the trace.
Even as the cyborg that floats at his pace,
The *lapis* exists in some other place.
He stands almost motionless in the sky,
Like Polaris, wherever he may hie
Light years from Earth. I yet construe the tie,
Ge's astronaut the fixed point in my eye.

HERCULES IN THE VESSEL OF THE SUN

We read our altitude; switch to the site;
Estimate its craters; *Falcon* alight,
Predict our location—our target slight:
Shard of plagioclase smudged by its blight.
Wound in Ge's membrane, even as he twins,
Spagyric in its pouch, the foetus wins;
His skin as thin as tissue, shifts his pins;
Collects his sample, and the *rebis* grins.

We dream of sunships; scaffolded, suspend;
From cave or cone or tesseract we wend;
Ascertain where peregrinations tend;
At Cana, Nain, Jerusalem blend.
Once in a gallery, sequined its walls,
I saw Chaos pictured, among its malls
Cepheid clusters, RR Lyrae, squalls,
Till I seized the Hyades in its halls.

Enshrined by the cosmos, the first of Hosts,
He saves Admetus from his fear of ghosts;
Overcomes Nessus; at Mount Oeta roasts;
Upraises His Spirit on Tethys' coasts.
Beyond the orbweb, on Möbius' run,
His labors form a cross by Clotho spun:
Minos, Geryon, Alcmene or none—
Hercules in the vessel of the sun.

HERMES' NESTED SPIRAL

Matter having roamed, I measured its wrath
From aeon to aeon. Sown in the bath,
I scaled my uncertainty, proofed my math,
Then, like an electron, crossed my own path.
Strangers ruled by law as rigid as chance
In the heat of romance, thus we advance
In pulses or packets, compute, enhance,
Repeat the act inserted in the dance.

The arrangement of Spacetime never waits.
Information writ, immortal its dates,
Each subsequent branch, in various states—
From opaque to transparent—radiates.
In the mind we conceive the world as one.
Past and future with equal status spun,
The quantum collapses and is not done.
A nested spiral I circle the sun.

Ancient of Days, more swift than His riders,
He measures the world with His dividers.
Hadron and Tevatron, Ge's colliders,
Search its particles till Shem's outsiders
Reconfigure the cosmos; suited, gear;
Even as photons that in Spacetime veer—
Rotational energies—reappear;
Enshrine a rudderless ship, and then steer.

HISTORY'S THREAD

From my spacecraft, I track leprous granges.
Absent Ge's cynosure, viewpoint changes:
Every image, partitioned, estranges,
For, where I strobe, but a jollbot ranges.
Still I monitor. Should paladins chirr—
Subtile hyphenates like breath-souls that blur—
Ge's data register what I infer:
Encased in stray photons, astronauts stir.

Scion of Kevlar, my twill fabric cool,
I exit the shuttle, carry my tool—
Since Clotho loves the child who lives by rule,
Like History's thread, I spin from Her spool.
Having steered my jetpack, slow then quicker,
I hitch a ride on the cherry picker;
Capture *Solar Max;* without a flicker,
Mend Ge's satellite, then stamp my sticker.

Harnessed to its beam, a rocket is brisk
Even as Light, wherever it may whisk.
We canvass Callisto; assess the risk;
Cyborgs that frisk, yet intertwine the disk.
Each skein is but a sign, a state of mind
Like Plato's cave, or, ions recombined—
Transparent site—the wormhole in the blind
Inside the bulk: the D-brane in the grind.

HUBBLE AJAR

The cyborg, convalescent, climbs the sky.
New Heaven's scion, Asclepius' spy,
He rides his rocket where astronauts ply.
Attached to his unit, he cannot die.
On reaching Imbrium, he taps the moon;
Locates its meaning: regolith or rune;
Earthrise sapphirine, breccias maroon,
Collects in the mare dust with a spoon.

Besieged by the braneworld, the biped steers;
Even as the mirror that orbits nears,
Transfixed by its tubular body veers
Awake to his mission—the aether peers.
Till Fine Guidance Sensors target a star,
He works with his ratchet; Hubble ajar,
Maneuvers his backpack, hangs from a spar,
Fills the cargo bay with bulk like a bar.

Electrospinlacing, he laser scans.
The symbol arises, and then he pans;
Captures the phantom; gamonymous, bands;
Shuttlewalks on-site, and the *rebis* stands
Dressed in his biosuit. — Scarab or sun;
Animate, inanimate, none but One,
He seals his torso shell, cables his run,
Entwines the shaman that Spacetime has spun.

KEEPER OF THE HUBBLE

I don my spacesuit, mimic Gaea's eight,
Distill its symbol; marriage yet my slate,
Inhabit its meaning; chain-link my mate;
Qwiff like my *rebis,* reify my state.
When spectrographs fail or, ripped from their noose,
Batteries and gyros run out of juice,
Satellite pending, Aether buoyed or loose
Even as I stand, I sign Gaea's truce.

Outside the airlock, as I mount the sky,
Photons like gossamer zoom through my eye.
The earth below me—acquiescent, wry—
Quantum cosmic ray, I sense myself, shy.
Offspring of matter, skein that I must patch—
Like Teflon that I wear, a perfect match—
I reach the handhold; grapple that I catch
But a mote away, I nudge and then latch.

And thus while I steer, and Canadarm gropes,
And round me, hypnotic, the robot lopes,
The cosmos, restored, yet changes its copes.
Castor, I tend a *suite* of telescopes.
Ever awake, the eye of the Hubble
Dreaming, I spend the day with my double:
My silver scion; capsule my nubble;
Haul, from my tool kit, Ge's stardust like stubble.

KEPLER

In search of distant suns, that we may cope,
We build a star shade for our telescope,
Deploy a solar sail, propel or grope,
Sustain the satellite, and thus we hope.
We glean statistics from Gaea's cocoon;
Spectral indications—road map or rune:
Kepler's cosmic census; in Cygnus strewn,
Planets that transit and suns that maroon.

As if I lived in megalithic times
Surrounded by statues or flint that primes;
In mouths of the dead, the turquoise that chimes—
Same Hermetic Name that Maria mimes—
Attached to crystals I entered the world
Till the stone that transmutes inside me curled
Even as the rock that at Horeb purled:
The spagyric foetus in soul-sparks furled.

Like Hercules, the clay that he flexes—
Soil that Omphale herself annexes—
Set at some still point between the sexes,
Body thus immersed in soul, he vexes,
Then takes from Ge's Light-bringer lunar scree,
Opus or tree: simulacra that see.
Though man is heaven, and woman the key,
Castor, *all joy still wants Eternity.*

LIFE IN A MORTAL UNIVERSE

Should the cosmos collapse, and, at its tomb,
Tipler's phantom singularity loom,
And then new chaos unfold from its womb,
And then *that* universe repeat its doom,
We could simulate Spacetime as we spend,
Accelerate energy as we wend,
Till Entropy bend and the D-branes blend
And cycles pend and matter never end.

We scour the sky for nebulae that splurge,
Halos, exoplanets, patches that merge:
Omicron Centauri, novae that verge,
Seyferts, red quasars, and clusters that surge.
The disks that the Hubble unveils astound—
Like Gliese in the zone of Libra found
Or Boötes to Borealis bound,
Eternity pixel by pixel crowned.

As if with Her camera, She captures me,
Or globule like the ball through which I see
A cloud in the crystal; at zero-g,
A rocket like a "T," then lunar scree.
While in the shell of my capsule I fly,
Pinwheel galaxies stream across the sky.
Embedded in Ge's orbweb, still I spy.
The world revolves in my aetheric eye.

LIFE OUT THERE

To detect such a world as we have won,
We sift the light from a flickering sun.
With oceans or moons or geysers or none,
We conduct our poll on Möbius' run.
When the orbweb scatters, Ge's fabric worn,
We shall flee its skein, yet survive its scorn
Pneumatic as Hermes: *rebis* co-born,
Hierophant sealed, or gamonymus sworn.

Among the thousands of stars that we comb,
Searching exoplanets, we find at home
Four in Pegasus; one called Styrofoam;
Then, chasing Gliese, wobble like a gnome.
Thus, we validate—we cannot confirm—
Mere shadow of a star; from Castor's berm,
Transit, without dips, as real in its squirm
As Aphrodite's mold or Ares' herm.

He came from outside, yet from inside grew,
A square, then a circle. — His sapphire blue,
He fastened upon me, sped me, then drew
Beyond each cue to feathers like a clue,
Then stepped from His sunship, gave to His swain—
Without a purpose that I can explain—
Soul-spark, Monad, foetus coiled in His vein
Even as archetypes wired in the brane.

THE LIMITS OF THE CODED WORLD

As he shifts to trace the source of the sound,
He scans in the sky a star like a hound.
Till Cetus and Rigel wheel in the round
Above the horizon, Gemini crowned,
He polar-aligns while She guides his hand;
Adjusts his finder where his eye pods land;
Resorbs the universe; at Her command,
Surveils like God Auriga in the strand.

Existence our witness, hard-wired its norms,
We squint with awe at each foetus that forms;
His manikin muscled, the hand that warms;
His cells still honeycombed, the heart that swarms.
He navigates the cosmos; scours the dune;
Born in the water, cultivates its boon:
Moonplant of the Adepts, stars like a spoon,
Telepathic lace: abyss like a rune.

His hierophant tinctured; heated his hair;
At the end of His fingers, knobs that flare
Insistent as even spires in a stair,
He sets His lancet upward in the air.
His seed hyacinthine, we shape His sod;
Enswathe Him with feathers; if He should nod,
Upraise Him like a disc; consume Him; prod;
Invest His globe with thunderbolt and rod.

MADE

Made for this moment, Castor, we arise;
Like sutured astronauts, don His disguise;
Kevlar evangels, copy then revise
New Heaven's *opus,* photons that He plies.
In SenSuits like stubble, His stone unknown,
We shuttle the Magus; light in a cone,
Situate the *rebis;* His cyborg prone,
Consecrate His clone in Möbius' zone.

With algorithms and sensors that buzz,
We duplicate what biology does:
A four-finger hand; Ge's feltwork like fuzz,
Transfigure in Spacetime the face that was.
He gleans from the mare proof of the void.
Stirred by the crater where the Segway toyed,
He signs Gaea's orphan, his mate deployed,
Even as Castor, like a humanoid.

From the dust of the ground, the eyeball peered;
Crowned with the uraeus, His sun-child steered;
The image peeled off till eidola smeared,
And then metal converged with metal geared.
Human by default he hard-wires his jinn;
Wisdom in the torso, backpack plugged in,
Streams all colors, then reifies his twin
Like soul-atoms in a chalice of tin.

MANDRAGORA'S DREAM

No more than matter, as we have been taught
In metallic precincts by Spacetime wrought,
Heterotic its patterns, Robonaut
Encapsules Tipler's subset like a thought.
Technocrat's, or cinctured absolutist's,
Torque-angle data fitted to his wrists
By load cells measured, hydraulic his fists,
Son of Hephaestus, cislunar he lists.

Like Mandragora's dream or nocturne's pant,
He falls into flesh even as a plant
That rises from the ground; erect or slant,
Some occult blueprint that the aeons grant.
He cannot tell what pleats and joints may spell.
He attaches the backpack to its shell,
Fills his biosuit, partakes at the well,
Electrospins such polymers as swell.

In the brane of the matrix, fore and aft,
The *rebis,* tabernacled, rides his craft,
Inhabits the humanoid—beam or shaft,
Same sapphirine symptom as Noah's raft.
He sits in the capsule, revolves supine,
To Hermes corresponds or to His sign,
Subserves His tether, maneuvers His bine,
Deploys His cyborg, and redeems His shrine.

THE MAN WHO MADE A COPY OF HIMSELF

I made a copy of myself at will.
Like Man in the mail or Host in the mill,
Hermetic template, I tested my skill.
I nuanced my hierophant with a drill.
An embedded humanoid formed of tin,
Prosthetic eyeballs, and silicone skin,
He is my surrogate. — I call him kin.
Nine DC motors in his head yet spin.

And thus I lift him from liquid that teems.
Fixed in a sitting position, he gleams.
With furrowed brows and piercing eyes, he seems
Poised to rapid-fire End-time's laser beams.
Like New Heaven's astronaut with his tool—
Some tangled biped drawn from Clotho's spool—
Or Castor's *rebis* or Hephaestus' ghoul,
He gazes upon me perched on a stool.

His cyborgs rising, His symbiotes rife,
We favor those skeins that clarify life—
An eternal script; a test bed for strife;
Celestial coheirs: Aether's spouse or wife.
Like *the god through the lap or in the ear*
Or from the stone, spagyric we career,
Shapeshift to a torus or to a sphere,
Then toward the face of Eternity steer.

MAPPING CELESTIAL TERRAINS

Hidden or minimal, matter is dark.
It spits out its fireballs, yet it is stark.
Magnetic remnants of Ge's primal spark,
Dimensions abound where we cannot park.
We tabulate the epochs, gaze upon
The measured cosmos: photons that first shone;
Deep-sky filaments: D-branes that we don—
Glittery circuits etched on silicon.

He scans at infrared—beams through his lobe
Bubbles of the new phase; nearer his globe,
The *celestial* Venus; from craft or probe,
Ge's Martian pod, with NASA's Xenon Strobe.
He gathers, enhances, pursues with haste
A subtile mosaic; satellite-based,
Some future kingdom: spectra that he traced—
Cassini's find—with chlorophyll and paste.

I build the omniverse that I may *be:*
These are the words that, without a decree,
Robonaut preaches—I cling to his knee:
He opens my eyes and helps me to see.
The foetus encapsuled; knot like a bow
Untethered, the cyborg imbues with snow
His sapphirine *rebis.* — Seamless His flow,
Such symbols in the mind are what we know.

MESSENGER

The astronaut rising, like Spirit's ghoul
In ripples of string, unwinds from its spool.
Rotund as Hermes, the shaman of rule,
Entwining hyperspace, carries his tool.
Messenger of God, he seals Heaven's plan
Astride the chaos, the goal of the clan—
Quaternal as Woman, triadic as Man—
Gestation in the brain that still we scan.

Salt of the metals, the lead of the air
Nourished by the stars, he forms in the square
A spagyric being beyond compare.
Thus he consecrates himself everywhere.
Like the Son of Man robed down to his feet,
He girdles his chest; his hair white as wheat
Refined in a furnace, gold that you beat,
His eyes in their sockets shimmer like heat.

He hangs in the torus shaped like a bell.
Seamless nomad he tunnels through its shell
Either male or female—I cannot tell—
Since his is the Word that we may not spell.
Enveloped by clouds he proffers a stone,
Upon it a name that aeons have known:
A sigil, a glyph, a cone all my own
Shown to me alone in Möbius' zone.

THE MÖBIUS STRIP

The universe black, I peered through its crack,
Till, on a D-brane, foetus in its sac,
I met my twin again; my tether slack,
Chased my umbilicus, then doubled back.
Through destiny or chance, like ends that clip
I twisted Chaos, joined it at the tip,
Jettisoned Flatland, commandeered my ship
Techwed to Saturn on Möbius' strip.

Chiral as a hand that repeats its trace,
I set my craft on Tranquility Base.
Like a magnet it held me; mute my face,
I started to flee to some other place.
And thus I have climbed an aetheric stair,
Both male and female; my artifex fair,
Courted, affianced, impregnated there,
Recursive as a loop, enclose the pair.

Around me, quotidian, Spacetime swirls.
With a single half-twist its seam unfurls.
Upward in the foam the planet yet twirls.
Continuous curve, Infinity whirls.
I navigate the omniverse; clever,
Position the fulcrum; turn its lever—
Cyborg, holon, rotundum . . . whatever—
Till I circumscribe its ring forever.

NAMESPACE

Submersed in Earthshine, cislunar its zones,
Chastened by the Spirit, he charts its bones;
Extracts the elixir; tinctures its cones;
With iridescent scales encoils its clones;
Till, wound about the body with a rope,
He faces the sunrise; shoulders its slope;
Like a dragon, zodiacal its cope,
Metallic its source-point, measures its scope.

Since *God made man because He loves stories,*
Cyborgs that moonwalk excavate quarries;
Inspect His species; sample their mores;
Recourse of Spacetime, capture their glories.
He penetrates the airlock through a hatch,
Prepares the astronaut parts that attach,
Assembles the *rebis,* sutures its match,
Intertwines Ge's hierophant, patch by patch.

Capsule of mystery, the Self resides
Beside itself; mercurial, divides
Even as Adam, gamonymous, rides
Exuding arrogance; plantigrade, strides.
Nomads yet scatter like stars that abound.
Skein in the torus, each namespace is round:
Moths on the walkway, seahorse in the sound,
Soul-sparks binomial, genderless, crowned.

NOTHING

Nothing comes from nothing, Maria said,
Except for the One that can raise the dead,
The four times three: the Shaman in her head,
Like the Zodiac, to the circle wed.
By Symbol's door, the digit in the sore
Traversing the mandala, at its core,
We enter the tunnel: Behind, Before,
A bubble of Spacetime—there is no more.

Nothing has three variants: in its thrall,
Space empty in its toolbox, like the All;
Next, absent Space and Time, like qwiffs that pall;
Then—infinite assemblage—like a caul.
As Mother is to Father, Spacetime fraught
With such celestial glyphs as He has brought,
So dream is to consciousness, Heaven's thought
The world that, esemplastic, She has wrought.

We map such rules as mystagogues ration:
A scroll of numbers, each at its station
Distinct from the set; in our elation,
We hitch a ride on a computation.
Gravity is intense. It curves the sheet;
Connects by a cord Gaea's other pleat:
Child or protuberance; channels its heat;
Dispatches the universe at its teat.

AN OBLATE SPHEROID

The Earth, though round, is not a perfect sphere.
As it rotates, it bulges, and we steer.
Both liquid and solid, its figure clear—
An oblate spheroid—upon it we peer.
Below the oceans, its crust like a floor,
We picture its mantle; that we may pore
On iron and nickel, measure then score
The discontinuity at its core.

Outer space, in supracelestial bins
One hundred miles above the Earth, begins.
A totem ancestor wrapped in its skins
In His mystic book, the astronaut spins.
Transparent as crystal, abstract as rime,
Sapphirine as the Self, a perfect mime,
He sutures his torsos, his glass sublime:
The co-creation of both Space and Time.

My mother in a sphere gave birth to me
That I might contemplate rotundity;
Tincture my grain; before my atoms flee,
Her vas spagyric, dissolve in its sea;
Then rise from the water; in aether, stroll
Even as the *rebis:* Spirit and soul—
Some symbol from Heaven forever whole—
Across the cosmos and into His scroll.

OUTRIDER

I weave the tesseract: bead in the gland
Or sprout in the twill or star in the band;
Such breccias as, speckled, blend with the hand.
I crisscross the intergalactic strand.
Seraphic at his wheel, the magus grins:
His globe, a ribbed and corded fabric, spins.
Silver-domed his helmet, bulbous his pins,
Suited for egress, he dons Gaea's skins.

At the top of the stem the fibers spread,
Project the image that the brain has bred
Upon its surface: foetus that He fed,
Rebis that She wed, cyborg that we sped.
Beamed from hyperspace such Cheshires as purr—
Swatches of tint on the retina—blur
Like seed-pearls that glister, feathers that chirr,
Saba's reveries of what we once were.

An outrider of space beyond the skies,
I watched above my gaze, behind my eyes,
Between Clotho's thrum and Lachesis' ties,
Sight's extraterrestrial species rise:
Hephaestus' offspring; metallic their frame,
They loomed like archetypes before they came
From some far-off portal—without a name,
Wormhole or torus, temenos of flame.

PEREGRINATION

As I enter Spacetime, not without mirth,
I steer my *rebis;* aware of my girth,
Unravel my skein, assist at my birth,
Traverse once more the paradisal Earth.
In the cosmic balloon, at perilune
Between mind and body, neurons maroon
Even as the stork expresses its rune
By Hermes' grave: the circle of the Moon.

Upturned in my capsule, flung to the skies
Like dust in the vas, sapphirine I rise,
Castor yet twines me, I suture his guise,
And thus he shuttlewalks before my eyes.
Astride the globe, I interweave the strand;
Straddle the chaos; from my string expand;
My shaman pneumatic, at his command,
High at the zenith like the Sun I stand.

Without an ego, like a foetal doll,
He rockets his ship to some lunar col,
Till, half-sprung from the stone where he would loll,
He clasps the nimbus on the head of Sol.
Insight is the boon, like a statue's oils,
Or, tied to Omphale, Hercules' toils,
Or, spun like a wheel, or Self that yet coils
Round and round its hub, Ouroboros' spoils.

PLATONIC RIDDLES

Through my eyeslot I re-collect the day;
Arouse my senses; animate the play;
Link its pluralities; mine the ray,
Transmit to my gray the stain in the clay.
I search my habitat: Artemis' face—
Elixir of silver; space within space—
Gaea's treasure. Hyacinthine its lace
Afloat in my skin, I locate my place.

We mediate the cosmos, probe, career,
Subserve its beam; should objects disappear,
The mind impinges even as we peer
Upon the nothingness. — Our percepts steer.
In chambers of the heart, should foam collide
At the edge of the arrow, holons hide.
Bubbles in the byways: cuboids that slide;
Aether's entities: astronauts that stride.

As supple as a thumb we sift the world;
Skein of the woman, Herculean, burled,
Ravel the chaos; fold by fold unfurled,
Nudge Him at the cavern, wakened or curled.
A cyborg I grazed with pumice a bat,
A bird like a tomb, inside it a gnat—
The body of the soul—or, absent that,
Like froth without status, spit that He spat.

PLATO'S CAVE

We move Creation back a billion years,
Convinced that, if the flow of Time yet steers
Where stars evolve and space forever veers,
Some being sparks the globe beyond its gears,
His scythe and His hourglass coated with rime.
This is the nearest point that Ge can mime:
By radiation bathed, at Heaven's prime,
The world was made *with* time but not *in* time.

As if in a cave, my back to the light,
I glimpsed an object contingent as night:
A bisected circle, quaternal, white—
A scrawl set on the wall as pale as sight.
Its spheroid abstract, I savored its fane
Even as an eyeball; scavenged its brane;
Perceiver of such Forms as we contain,
Secured at last Gaea's secret domain.

The Magus transmutes us; converts the three:
Spirit like water, body like a tree,
Soul like plumes of yellow—infinite "g"
Code of the Demiurge or Hermes' key:
An omniverse that marries Everything,
Like Occam's razor; Ouroboros' ring;
Seyferts and photons; rockets on a sling;
Or curlicues of heterotic string.

PNEUMATIC

The mind of God awakened to His trace,
He crystallizes in Maria's vase;
Elysium's coheir, Kevlar His case,
Materializes without a face;
His muscles pneumatic, His *rebis* curled,
Carries in His belly the foetus furled
Inside the shuttle. — Like a discus hurled,
Imagination encircles the world.

History's débris, Melchizedek's norm
Seduced by suggestion, His numbers swarm.
Consummate gamonymus, He is warm,
But never found in texts in finished form.
The size of a thumb, He dwells in the heart,
Like Eden's protoplast; astral His art,
Angel, then *filius;* plural His part,
Primordial Adam: ghost that we chart.

Immortal its noise, the omniverse roars.
He nudges the Savior; ransoms His stores;
From *frumentum nostrum* to leprous ores,
Resuscitates the House of Many Doors.
The sun is silver till its saffron blends
Like moist *locustae* even as He wends
Behind the moonplant, where Desire yet bends,
His fingers large and swollen at the ends.

POSTMODERN

Like a chain of molecules, coil or ring,
Or circle adumbrated like a string,
Or eye disassembled, point like a King:
The spagyric foetus dipped in its spring,
The world that rose repeated who we are—
Soul-sparks, cortices, syzygies that char,
Some kindred template: sapphire like a star,
An archetype that Spacetime cannot mar.

As the astronaut rakes, he gathers rock.
Behind him Taurus rolls. The moon a clock,
He times its lava plain. Each sun a shock,
He has entered the vault that does not lock.
While neurons contend, among their glories
The brain that pulsates in clayey quarries
Selects for its Monad lunar mores.
I have been seized by so many stories.

Nearer to God than Mythology gets—
Salvific the blade that the Hebrew whets,
Alchemic the bead that the Magus sweats,
Incarnate the heart that Hephaestus nets—
The dreamer yet rouses, regales at will
Ge's iridescent peacock, plucks its quill,
Metabolizes Hermes, baffles skill,
Redeems the omniverse—the rest is still.

PRECINCT

Outside the torus, yet inside the span,
He found that God is two in one, like man:
Both Saturn and Sol; the dust that we pan
Between the eyes, such Nostocs as we scan.
An aspirant of matter, he could fly
To maze or to mare; his unit ply
Like a soul-spark moist, like a pebble dry,
An astronaut cloistered without a sky.

His substance transcendent, round on all sides,
Quaternal as a precinct, he divides
Into hard-shell torsos, circles, abides,
And then he fastens, and the sun-wheel strides.
He floats like a seed that membranes surround.
How can he touch the earth when he is crowned?
He fixates on the symbol. Being found,
He concentrates till he reaches the ground.

He seals the scrolls of the artifexes,
Converges with flesh that he annexes,
Becomes the *rebis,* no longer vexes,
Unites within himself the two sexes.
Movement is mastery. When we rotate,
Spellbound by the rite, the Spirit its slate,
We brood upon the body; twine its mate;
Encompass day and night *within the gate.*

PREFIGURED

He parses the stream; pellucid the stars,
A sojourner still, he mounts Heaven's bars
Attuned to the tesseract. Nothing mars
The sapphirine planet—its semblance jars.
Having dragged the sea, equipped with a trawl,
He scours the horizon, mountains, a wall;
Positioned from dawn to dusk in the caul,
Rotund its holon, yet eyeballs its sprawl.

Arms akimbo, hierophant or double,
The cyborg moonwalks; circuits the bubble;
Samples the mare: regolith's rubble,
Scalloped boulders, and rock chips like stubble.
His ambit quaternal, his body wracked,
He reaches the capsule; his *rebis* stacked,
Present in the psyche, fixed as a fact,
He straddles the chaos, the world-egg cracked.

Christ evolving: scales of Pisces its sign,
Quadruped with a tail; complex His spine,
A biped dressed in mail—like stalk or bine
Upheaved from my root joint, I trail its twine.
Assembled in the airlock, thus I show.
The earth astir, the satellite in tow,
I hoist *Palapa,* exit with a hoe—
Because I know where I have been I go.

PSEUDOSPHERE

Much matter transparent, entropy near,
To conquer fear, I build a pseudosphere
Complete with panels; upon rhombi peer;
Invert my pentagons, yellow for clear.
Saddle-shaped surface, hyperbolic shell,
Some conic curve—a spiral like a spell
Fragile as a symptom: bowknot or bell,
I enter terrain that I cannot quell.

I seek such a world as Hermes embraced:
A heaven composed of Dacron and paste;
Gamonymous, by his helmet effaced,
An astronaut in Ge's breath-body based.
But *where* am I? the same sojourner asks.
And still the hierophant pours from his flasks.
In matter like metals the magus basks,
Assembles the day, and performs his tasks.

To divine his source, its soul-spark unknown,
He cultivates its seed; his sod thus sown,
He revives Ge's hybrid: *rebis* or clone—
The Spirit by the Spirit fixed in stone.
Spacetime is chthonic, knotted as a clan,
But a trace that radiates like a fan,
A fold uncertain of how it began—
Philosophic ambisexual man.

PUSHING GRAVITY

As it spins, the Earth begins to dapple,
And then the globe drops; should matter knapple,
Synergy shifts it as with a grapple.
I measure gravity with an apple.
An object esoteric as a trace,
But a dimple in the fabric of space,
Like a pebble it falls; at its own pace,
Scatters Ge's trespass, then chastens its face.

Like a satellite, foetus in its wain
Tethered to Spacetime, astronaut or swain
Enveloped by dust, Ge's grain his domain,
He steers his craft, then inhabits its skein.
His *rebis* supine, no more than a dot,
He pressures the darkness out of its slot,
Both open and shut—the key to its plot:
Shaman fixed like a peg in a sure spot.

In his mind's eye, Heaven's hierophant One,
His cyborg spectral or electrospun,
He perceives His biped, both point and pun,
Like water in the vas or wine or none.
While Hephaestus rails and Robonaut flails,
And in the chaos Ge's sojourner trails,
Ouroboros, circling, devours its scales.
Nothing else avails—the rest are details.

THE QUILTED MULTIVERSE

With a sea of foam or a flow of silt,
We copy the brane that a bubble built,
That Hephaestus wired, and that Clotho spilt—
We spread Her infinite skein like a quilt.
Thus Reality splits without a seam.
As atoms cavort and molecules scheme,
Like each swatch of light, like each cloud of steam,
In antic superposition we stream.

What is this patchwork that he co-creates?
His phantom exists in so many states
That, like the moonchild that his nomad mates,
Each semblance that he dons yet dissipates.
Though the world expands, it is never grim.
Still unresolved, such cosmoses as brim
Behind the scrim, however much we trim,
Contain the garment that belongs to him.

The multiverse *by way of life and mind*
Reflects upon itself, enshrines its kind,
Divines such a twine as hierophants find—
Symbols that bind and that the shaman signed:
Foetus in the phial, elsewhen or now
Breath-soul in the vas that leavens its vow—
The *rebis* that springs from forebrain or brow.
To mystery, Castor, cyborg I bow.

QUINTESSENCE

Out of infinity when chaos boomed,
And in the foam anti-gravity gloomed,
And Heaven receded, and Earthshine loomed,
And in its holon quintessence yet bloomed,
Hephaestus had fed both torus and square
Some secret that Clotho twined like a snare:
Stars that skitter, breccias caught in the flare,
A handful of crystals tossed in the air.

With fingertip contact, through loaded cells,
Sensors in my palms, Ge's protocol melds.
I bolt the wheel hub, distribute my shells,
Repair the capsule till my chassis swells.
My footprints serpentine, shadow or clay
Adrift in the mare, rotund I stray.
The moonplant yet tracks me: Castor at play
Dressed in force data gloves, I thumb my way.

The bubble remembers, links in the mind—
Cocooned in its harness—cyborgs that grind
In distant biospheres; ambits that wind
Even as hyphenates: coheirs enshrined
In digital layers; systems entombed:
Simulated beams affianced and groomed;
Heaven's starship: Ouroboros exhumed—
By bits of cyberspace we are consumed.

REBIS

Like a bubble that shimmers in its pan,
Or seahorse that floats amid frond or fan,
Or ball of cells that from its roots began,
He sought to be neither woman nor man,
But both these sexes: hybrid of the same;
A fructified seed; either fire or flame—
Quaternity's startlement: frame by frame,
Scion or *Rebis,* First Adam by name.

As the soil that, sprung from its furrow, grunts,
So, Typhon pursuing him, Pisces shunts
In the wettest place that the foetus fronts.
We become a child and a fish at once.
We enter the omniverse; monads strewn,
We navigate the belly of the moon,
Traverse its mare, twine at perilune
In Clotho's net, and then cruise its cocoon.

Liquid metal its guise, His cyborg spun
From heavenly skein, crowned Mother and Son,
He casts us in a mold till we are One.
The distance between them pain that we shun,
She steals from Her dais stones that we swap:
Thumb in the heart or holon that we crop
As moist as salt; rotundum that we prop
Between His spouses—at mid-point we stop.

SAFFRON OF THE METALS

Bound by Ouroboros, His coheir twists.
In its carapace Her moonchild exists;
Encodes Gaea's name; gamonymous, trysts;
Re-attaches His *rebis* to Her lists.
Steep in Kevlar of Her clone embedded,
He rises from Her navel; thus threaded
Like *foetus spagyricus,* light-headed,
Hermes re-combines His monads, wedded.

Around my Hubble like a globe I wind
Some netted omphalos, bolt that I bind
Even as Python's, holon in the mind.
I can *feel* its coil in my cyborg grind.
Moisture like an essence, astronaut spun,
Rotund I run the circuit of the sun:
Saffron of the metals; manifest, done,
The heart of Her fire continues to stun.

The Logos is a dog. He sets awry,
As rude beneath the earth as in the sky,
Such sated disks as dim: both Cheshire shy
And Corascene acrouch inside my eye.
He sutures his bio-suit; steers the land;
Wired to his data-glove, rejoins his hand;
Unspools from his helmet; satellite manned,
Transmits his photon; entangles its strand.

SATURDAY

He memorized Hephaestan creations:
Concessions of lunisolar nations;
Metallic as Earth, the sea's libations;
Such tesseracts as the magus rations.
And still it was twilight: The foetus slept
Leprous as a serpent; the morning crept,
Till, out of his capsule, the biped stepped,
Returned to Eden, and the first-born leapt.

The undertaking seemed so vast at first,
She sealed the shaman; her moonchild submersed
As in a plasma cloud, anchored and nursed,
Embraced the omniverse before it burst.
A cyborg he rises, and then he sinks,
Surrounded by darkness; orbits its rinks;
Recovers Her treasure: *caelum* that links;
Secretes Ge's elixir, and then he blinks.

Into countless branches the cosmos splits
Even as Hermes, maker of its writs,
Observes its holons; between cuboids flits;
Creates the screen that each particle hits.
Like eyes of the peacock, coheirs that fill—
Sapphirine oracles: Monads that mill—
Can ruffle history, multiply, spill,
Assert what happens, has happened, or will.

SEGWAY

With two degrees of freedom in his wrist,
He can curl his fingers into a fist,
Mapquest the torus, steer his Segway, twist,
And yet never ask why he should exist.
Upon Martian soil, as sealed as a wight
Predestined to serve, he circles the site,
A sovereign, a scion, rewired a knight,
A robot that looms by reel or by rite.

What is this narrative that we sustain?
Spiral in the cluster, helix in the chain,
Foetus in the vas, Ouroboros' skein:
He follows its train in the human brain.
Entwined by the serpent, its pinwheel twirled
Even as Castor in his Kevlar furled
Or Gaea's herald in his moonship curled,
He cannot locate his roots in the world.

Shaman that I wean, diverse as a gene,
He displays at first each dot like a bean,
Till I track his sheen, then behind the screen
Scan as odd a coheir as I have seen.
Like Asclepius' quip, without a lip
I motion him, then join him on his trip
By computer controlled or by a chip
Telepresent upon Möbius' strip.

THE SELF-THINKING THOUGHT

Around me existence wraps like a lace.
Feathers, forests, rocks, galaxies that race,
Fractals everywhere unfold like a trace.
Infinity mirrors me like a face.
Seductive as silence, Spacetime is wrought
Like each word that seeks, then finds what it sought—
Such a homonym as Salmacis taught
To none but Hermes: *His self-thinking thought.*

Each simple substance seeded in its sod,
The world—recursive, telepathic, odd—
Revolves in my eye rotund as a pod:
Orion's capsule, in the land of Nod.
Thus archetypes seize me: first in the scheme,
A purple blossom; a Tree or its beam—
Peacock or rainbow; a dart in the stream—
Ge's sapphirine *rebis,* without a seam.

He builds like towers scaffolds in the air.
Still the astronaut lingers in his lair
Till he climbs the ladder, surmounts its snare,
Then steers his path to Ouroboros' stair.
At Taurus-Littrow, reaching target rock
Smitten by craters, I survive the shock
With wheels that lock; like a synchronized clock,
The heart in my body beating, I knock.

SERIOUS READER

He twines the universe that he observes:
The disk in the ocean, the ring that curves,
The crystal body that tunneling swerves
Even as a wormhole—the moon unnerves.
He wanders the hall where copies abound.
Theonomous, selective, pound by pound
Each sensory datum above the ground
Preserves the psyche. — Everything is round.

A whirlpool in chaos, stone in the sea,
The spherical man that molecules flee,
Some Mayan sigil chthonic as a tree
Or potter's wheel or Nostocs in the scree.
The world-soul draws him like an aquasphere
Or hylical water or fire *that* sheer—
Phantom at first, but then manifest, near—
Ge's astronaut rises, dressed in his gear.

Serene in his faith, beyond myth and lore,
He scours the cosmos; with vowels that soar
And consonants that sprint, he jars the door,
Then roves the place till, possible once more,
He reifies the symbol. — Hermes, stirred,
Anticipates; retrospects; having heard,
Reconstructs the fane that he had deferred,
Then enters the text, constrained by the Word.

SETTING THE WHEEL ON FIRE

We reach Mars in August, land where we drive,
Unloose Gaea's robonaut from its gyve,
Then sample the dust, such microbes as thrive,
Methane that burbles from something alive.
Like seeds from meteors or vents that boil,
Inclusive bipeds at the crater toil,
Grapple floor rocks, measure liquids that roil,
Import perchlorates from the Martian soil.

I see through the glass of my eye His twin.
Untethered unit as small as a pin,
He enters my orbit, both tall and thin,
The shirt of Nessus grown fast to his skin.
This is the vision to which we aspire.
We crisscross the spheroid, ransom its mire,
Chain-link the priest, attire him in its pyre,
Commend to the moon Ge's metallic hire.

Billions of galaxies both die and live.
The cosmos sifts them even as a sieve.
The mercurial mind does not misgive:
Existence urges Ge's imperative
Within such a stringent set of constraints
As hyperspace fosters despite its feints—
Some Hephaestan blueprint: matter that taints;
Essence that posits, then produces saints.

SHAPESHIFTER

He lifts toward the sky as sleek as a cod,
Reacts like a rocket, morphs like a rod,
Sets on the moonplant a craft like a pod.
Son of Chaos, he shapeshifts like a god;
Soul of the silver, yet basks in his girth
Even as Hermes, red Damascene earth,
Or Kronos' child, or, where Leto gave birth,
The stone of the wise as liquid as mirth.

Joined to his shuttle by tether or strap,
He wears on his skull Ge's acrylic cap,
Fabricates his body, wires like a map
Studded with sensors *the god through the lap.*
He tasks the planet, motivates the moon,
Feeds the foetal sun with a phantom spoon,
Invests the cyborg, embeds the maroon,
Retrieves the *Rebis,* metallic as noon.

Grounded in silence the humanoid spins;
Beneath its chest, as radiation dins,
Combines its chromosomes, debates its shins,
Repeats the astronaut, and then it grins.
Desire pursues him however it leans—
Such coils as spark Ge's exuberant genes;
Saffron icons; on telepresent screens,
Excitations of immortal machines.

SIBLINGS OF THE SUN

Its source a giant star, its cohorts strewn,
The sun contracts till, curled in its cocoon,
Its surplus cast off, gravity its boon,
Its cluster yet scatters, massive its rune.
When was it, say, that—the moon in his fist
Formed of cloud and dust—the *rebis* thus kissed
Would round its hub, like Ouroboros twist,
Then twine the omniverse, its siblings missed?

His mother the moon, his father the sun,
He wakens, in the prison of the dun,
A peloton of stars: nomads or none.
Castor measures a billion where they run.
He fires his flask in pileus and cape,
Transforms his artifex from head to nape,
Then dons his torso; chthonic as an ape,
The vas is a phial of spherical shape.

The self, like the cosmos, sealed as a bowl
Composed of atoms: conglomerate soul—
Both male and female mounted on a pole—
Gleans through its glass an object on a knoll:
An omphalos as sovereign as a still
Born in the unconscious, archetypes that mill,
Even as the Cross upraised on a hill,
Not subject to caprices of the will.

THE SKIN THAT I LIVE IN

Along a cleavage line, should blood yet flow,
In fibers of the dermis segments grow
Faster than a crosscut, as surgeons know.
Precise as planned incisions, tissues show
Papillary patterns that I have scanned;
In the ten-finger band that I have spanned,
Like drops of sweat that glisten on the hand,
Warm secretions from some sebaceous gland.

The map of the brain is not drawn to scale.
The image of the Self that we surveil—
A female projected or else a male—
Blurs the distinction. — Mystic in the pail,
At zero gravity locked in your tin,
Locate the *rebis* even as you spin
Above the capsule; phantom like a twin,
Find him with a microscope in your skin.

The heart yet migrates: Remote from its slur,
Minuscule as seed-pearls, nerve-endings stir
Across the chest; like cloven tongues that chirr,
The reminiscence of what we once were.
Felt by proxy, His Spirit serpentine,
Sensory fibers collect and combine,
Traverse the cerebrum, follow its twine,
Restore the symbol, inhabit its shrine.

SOMETHING TO LIVE FOR

He rends the circle of the spheres, then stands
Like a cosmic clock, transparent its hands,
Upon the chaos; issues his commands
From hyperspace, then implicates its strands.
He rides upon an escalating floor,
Heaves aside its stone as he might a door,
Re-enters the cavern, seeks at its core—
Ever serpentine—something to live for.

Even as the tun that with wine may run,
Eclipse that we shun, or moon in the sun—
The archetype that animates the pun—
Each circle encloses a smaller one.
Having been as an infant a clinger,
You must know that you should never linger.
Unravel the torus; like the singer,
Tie a piece of string around your finger.

In skein of the tesseract, heated, dried,
I cross like a stone to the other side.
On tree or scaffold, Sophia descried,
His bed an altar, Bride and Groom elide.
Subject to Heaven, I have learned to bow
Like Man and Woman; shaman at the prow—
Hermetic *rebis*—I repeat the vow
For none but them: *Eternity is now.*

SPACE

Space is but a membrane; floating, distends
Even as a womb, till gravity bends
Wherever it tends, location suspends
Without a sequence, and the foetus wends.
He enters like the flash upon a screen
Or in the eye the photon that we glean
Or in the stave the symbol that we mean.
We nudge oblivion, and then we wean.

We re-collect such matter as we name.
To sacrosanct archetypes we lay claim:
The sunship that went, or shaman that came,
Or myrtle that cools, or Nostocs that flame.
From Maria's vessel, being cajoled,
We lift the scion that Heaven foretold.
Essence like the Savior, Castor, we fold
Sapphirine substance in a human mold.

Like Mars and Venus, Sight's inverted bole,
Or Self's sun-and-moon tree, we reach the knoll;
Everlasting, in beakers of the soul,
Pursue to its point the world that is whole.
Fixate in hyperspace we twine the pair:
It is not I who live, and thus we stare,
Round as the *rebis,* transparent as air,
Like *stone that is no stone* and is not there.

SPHERICAL

We attach ourselves to atoms that came:
To Altair and Deneb, globules that flame,
Planets Red or Blue—it is all the same—
To the Higgs boson we assign a name.
We rise like nomads amid worlds that char;
Identity illusive as a star,
Mapquest the cosmos; the cuboid ajar,
Fingerprint the quasar where epochs are.

Like it or not, the brain is a machine.
And still we grasp what the shaman may mean.
We intuit the Garden that we glean
In the eye: an irreducible green.
We seek such a heaven as coheirs hymn
With vowels supple and consonants slim,
A zodiacal cloud that we yet skim
In ship or capsule, such light as we limn.

The wily astronaut orbits the sun,
An antique symbol as near to the One
As any satellite upon its run.
Then track him, if you can, where he has spun.
But, animate substance, before you start,
Trepan the skull and ascend to the heart;
Reify the Spirit; spherical, chart
Then square the circle, Asclepius' art.

THE SPHERICAL GLASS VESSEL

He wandered like a wheel above the storm.
Ensconced in his bucket, salt in the swarm,
He capsuled the Spirit; his flesh yet warm,
Transmuted his spark into human form.
As if in a giant flask he rehearsed
Or else through sublime *kenosis* dispersed
In depths of the sea; his sunship submersed,
He filled the disc of the moon and then nursed.

He descended to Earth—baptized with nous
Saffron coheirs in pelican or goose;
In Self or vas, distillate from the sluice,
Each hierophant dissolving in its juice.
Like solidified water, glass, or air,
Or the innermost body in its lair,
Or the soul of the world that coheirs share,
He mounted his triangle in the square.

Sealed with the sign of Hermes, he ascends.
Even as the One called Immortal wends
Like sapphire in the aether, he suspends
Above Ge's satellite, and then he mends;
Inserts the stinger; with Maria's key—
Forever the scion of four and three—
Maneuvers *Westar;* upends in his glee;
Partakes of Heaven, the tree of the sea.

STATION

Heaven's recompense, Gaea's rebuttal,
He springs from his seat inside the shuttle;
His chest shell bronze, his resin head subtle,
He clears the airlock. Scoop in its scuttle,
He tries his tether hook; secures its grip;
His thumb opposable, heated its tip,
Repairs the station; maneuvers its dip;
Crowns His *rebis,* Ge's alchemical quip.

Faith-based the astronaut pursues his course.
Where the fir tree may yet supplant the gorse,
Belief is virtue, tactile proof such force
As cyborgs embrace when they search their source.
We probe—through layers of leptons that tease
Ge's reasoned cosmos—symmetries that seize,
Like phantom quanta, photons that reprise
From Eden's realms Yahweh's sun-and-moon trees.

An edifice of lobe and quilt and earth,
Creation's uniped, rotundum's girth
Embedded in Kevlar, conceived in mirth,
Impresses on Hermes his cosmic birth
Even as the swain, Asclepius' strain,
That patches his holon. — Cuboid its skein,
Metallic its vassal, woven its vein
Section by section, we compass the brane.

STEWARDS OF CREATION

My robot burnished, salmon his cable,
He pilots his craft as at a table;
Departs the airlock; pursues his fable;
Having tracked the Earth, observes its Babel.
Hand to the chin and elbow to the knee,
Acrouch as he broods he searches the key:
The mite in the dust, the curve in the scree,
Star chains that coil and halos like a plea.

Since I posit an island universe
Among such archetypes as I rehearse
In my mind, like a foetus in its purse,
I berth His tesseract, and then I nurse.
Entangled in the egg, the sun that sows
Unfurls his holon even as he flows;
Spouse in the Zodiac, seed that he tows
Suspended in the serum, thus he grows.

I see him face to face as through a glass.
Like Eve and Adam, Aeons that we class—
Moral nature and spiritual mass—
Carry fossil remains that we surpass.
We measure in parsecs clusters that shop
Across the cosmos; galaxies that crop
In spectral sequence; satellites that stop
Above Ge's omphalos, spun like a top.

SUNDAY

With a crystal dot that recompenses—
Even as we conjugate its tenses—
The photon that in the eye condenses,
He tempts us into realms of the senses.
Basilisk, gibbon, mandrake in the spud,
Moonplant or hieroglyph: tree like a stud,
The *rebis* on the land or in the flood—
We find Him in dust clouds swollen with blood.

Autonomous images scale the mind:
The pattern on the screen that Monads bind,
The scroll like a foetus that Heaven signed,
The Cross at Calvary that Christ enshrined.
Knower, creator, alchemist, I chart
The totalistic Self, and then I start—
From soil to tissue to muscle I dart.
A reasoning soul *ascends* to the heart.

I wake on Sunday: Witness to my dream,
I pluck like a beam a disk from its stream;
Electrospray my suit; without a seam,
Extract Emmaus' meme from Yahweh's scheme.
Electrons that spin with strange antennae
Intuit their circuits; scan, if any,
Transparent copies: round as a penny,
The One and at the same time the Many.

SWAIN

A webwork of silver, sensate its case,
His chassis, soldered, ripples like a lace,
Plates of the seahorse, or scales of the dace.
His wheel like a face, he stares into space.
He lifts his finger; sifts the night anon;
To liquid eyes, transparent his baton,
Resorbs such a spark as he dotes upon
With sonic ears: the wingèd sun that shone.

Alchemic his nature, he cannot die.
Cloud-borne, he hauls his lumber to the sky.
His spacesuit enhanced, as satellites fly,
Around him he watches starfields that vie.
His reflexes keen, he rotates his wrists:
He grasps his handcar till his backpack lists.
High in the thermosphere, purple its mists,
He levitates where Hephaestus yet trysts.

He frolics like a phantom; entertains;
Floats in the aether; attached to its cranes,
Erects the station; dangles from its skeins;
New Heaven pending, unfetters its fanes.
Transhuman, he teeters; machines its pins;
Installs its truss, then piece by piece its skins;
Assembles its cells; configures its fins;
Observes the Earth, and thus the world begins.

SYMBIOTE

We design his software, collaborate,
Translate the protocol or else rotate,
Queue the command, its strategy debate,
Test the system, then teleoperate.
Symbiote astride his scenario,
He paces its corridors to and fro,
Approaches the ductwork that he must know,
Computes his intention, and still I show.

That he may clasp the gauge and avoid harms,
We install heat sinks in both of his arms.
Inside the space station, without alarms,
He measures the airflow, and thus he charms.
Suddenly he ascends. He has not erred.
Unblinking sentinel, he signs us; stirred,
We fix his position. His image blurred,
Selene's swain, he caresses the word.

We wind like a helix, spool like a thread
Outside the spheroid or inside the head.
Hierophants trailing or pathfinders sped,
We ravel Space, *the foremost of the dead.*
Each atom a riddle, qwiff that we pop,
We twine the tesseract, membrane or prop;
Wrap around the torus, bottom or top;
Begin, and then begin, and then we stop.

SYMPOSIUM

Androgynous at first, the sexes formed
But a savage concourse: tumblers that warmed
Even as they turned; transgressors that stormed
Beyond Love's ladder, and armies that swarmed.
Hephaestus, having pitied, asked the pair
What unity they sought and thus might share.
Each desired his half—with no time to spare,
He split them at the bottom of the stair.

More insolent than sun and moon and Earth,
He vitrified the void; with hiss and mirth,
Having walked upright on two legs at birth,
Metabolized the essence of his girth.
As moist as a circle, molten his frown,
He scanned Ge's satellite; declined his noun;
Conjugated his verb; as soft as down,
Set upon his head a disc like a crown.

Buxom as an hourglass I sift His sand,
Feel the heat from His instrumented hand
Like glitter off a star. There is no land.
He enters Space that I may understand.
In my capsule, as small as a thimble,
I harness my cyborg to a gimbal—
I *test* the dream; electrospun, nimble,
Self-sown shaman, inhabit the symbol.

TEARING THE FABRIC OF SPACETIME

Stretch a rubber membrane, and it will tear.
The human hand is more than it can bear.
Likewise the fabric of Spacetime may snare—
It can crease its skein with punctures to spare.
And thus in my mind I rip it apart.
On the Möbius band, which I yet chart
That I may piece it together, I start:
I haul it away in my solar cart.

Transported to a site where cyborgs wend,
I reach Gaea's wormhole; re-cut it; bend;
Chiral, infinite, rotund as I tend,
Interlock each loop till its edges blend.
Still the torus wrinkles; within its clot,
I ride its caul of chaos; like a tot,
Castor's mirror image or Pollux' jot,
Twist till I join its two ends in a knot.

Inside or outside, the omniverse beams;
Sight pinched to a point, transmits at its seams,
In scattered particles, soul-sparks like memes—
The *auctor rerum:* Unity that streams.
We re-collect the One; should wholeness pull,
Pour from the psyche, till the eye is full,
Aldebaran, located in the Bull
Like the handiwork of a moth on wool.

TECHWED

Dressed in his SenSuit, Ge's Spagyric buoyed,
Hermes yet mixes with his humanoid.
Capable of saccades, verbena joyed,
Meaning's clusters, and Iteration's void,
He dons an algorithm like a vest;
Assembles the hybrid; at his behest,
Mutated, burgeoned, recombined, caressed,
Actuates its circuits inside his chest.

He hears the wheels of Infinity grind
Like promised argosies of humankind.
Creation shapeshifting, its *rebis,* blind,
Deploys their capsules in its molten mind.
Chaos ubiquitous, digits that he tweaks
Like spikes in a graph, the astronaut seeks—
Bipedal his mate; even as he peaks,
His gear telepresent—space like a streak's.

We prayed that pods would drop from the sky;
Crafted autogiros that we could fly;
Reconnoitered the cosmos; set to pry,
Espoused any spheroid that we might spy.
Units that venture, droids without a knee,
In situ sensors, satellites that flee,
Soul-sparks in Orion, moles in the scree—
We have peered beyond what our eyes can see.

THE TELEOPERATOR'S DREAM

I adjust the headset; upraise the bar;
Perform the task; where finger sensors are,
Assemble the truss; position the spar;
Establish contact, satellite or star.
He beams the world as through an eye of glass.
Stereoscopic, his pixels yet pass
Even as clones; like somnambulists, mass,
Label, recognize, categorize, class.

At first I teach him how to grasp and shut,
With but a gesture motion him to cut,
Repair the habitat, erect the hut—
Together we move the end of a strut.
The Three Laws defined—autonomous play—
I mime for Robonaut Ge's mystic stray:
Eve's gamonymus; astronauts that pray:
An algorithm neither black nor gray.

The tree of life upended like a stalk,
Hybrid of parts, by solar light I walk.
Gyroscope, station, capsule that I caulk—
I undertake the work and do not balk.
Surrounded by robots sensate as Shem
Exploring the planet, I partner them.
The North Star is white, an alchemist's phlegm,
Mystagogue's citrine, or rubedo's gem.

TERRAFORMING MARS

In search of water, Hermes leaves his lair.
He perturbs the orbit to Ceres' share.
Religion a ladder, science a stair,
He secures a path to Hephaestus' pair.
The magus awakens, and still he sleeps;
Activates his sight; into substance peeps;
From each grain of dust to each soul that leaps,
Projects the *rebis,* and the cosmos keeps.

Farther into space than humans we cruise,
Venture to the planet, and thus we fuse.
In Martian gravity, without a bruise,
We choose the same tools as astronauts use.
Our eyes like cameras, we screen our trace;
Insolate its surface; without a face,
Establish its lichens; erect its base;
Beyond our sensors, upraise Gaea's mace.

Like Castor and Pollux, we craft the view
Above and below; with beauty imbue
Creed and quintessence: digits that we cue.
We partner the orbweb, and it is new.
We sublime in the vas spagyric gum,
Manifest the occult, and still we come;
Convey the foetus; moonchild in the drum,
Anoint with spirit Ge's metallic thumb.

TESTING THE NIGHT OF PAN

Made of starstuff the universe is not.
Dark matter is the root of Earth, a plot
Like Gaea's omphalos or Horus' slot,
Babalon astride the beast or its blot.
Though neutrinos morph and fermions fail
And disks accelerate and photons trail,
We breath-souls yet board, in Ge's thermal veil,
Apollo's sunship or Hecate's pail.

By a million hyperreal stars embossed,
Simulacra find us, and we are lost.
We search the blue dot; the Zodiac crossed,
Heated astronauts we defy its frost.
The Sun, unceasing, burns; it does not die.
Beyond a certain portal tunnels lie
As quantified as light; the cosmos shy,
With phosphorescent eye we prophesy.

A hybrid god, with hoofs instead of feet,
He fingers pipes of reed; above his beat,
Where skein unravels—tesseract or sheet—
Beneath my metal cleat, his pleasures bleat.
Castor, listen: The mare that we wind,
Like the world at large, both cuboid and blind,
Is composed of atoms; their source unsigned,
The Night of Pan regales us in the mind.

TIPLER'S SUBSET

A jumble of letters, digits that met,
Algorithms coded lest we forget,
Spacetime rules us; forever in its debt,
We are the subset of some other set.
Still I blink my eye; like a conscious bot,
Co-create the cosmos. *Rebis* or jot
Or stone or foetus folded in its slot,
Science defines us as if we were not.

We store the plasma rocket at its base,
Then build a reactor to take its place
With magnets like washers; spirit the race—
Avid to live, we expand into space.
We collapse the wave; like a photon qwiffed,
The blue dot yet wanders, and thus we lift,
Decelerate, slip, to Jupiter shift.
Farther away than at launch time we drift.

We pass through crystal clouds; as we draw in,
Craters assail Callisto, and they win,
Until we clear a moon without a skin,
And then we reach a ring, and it is thin.
For thousands of miles Jupiter flashes.
For hours it rivets us as it dashes.
At the Great Red Spot it gushes and gashes.
Castor, we explore all of its splashes.

TO LIVE AND WORK IN DEEP SPACE

Cosmic in orbit, precise as a clock,
An overhead crane swings a building block.
We shape such a space wheel as bipeds stock.
Module to module connected, we lock.
Transfer vehicles docked to the station,
We pursue its spin; in our elation,
Track the sun; to the end of Creation,
Embrace Gaea's torus as a nation.

He scales degrees of freedom with a drill.
Seized by Martian soil, he sifts from its till
Crystals that, round him, in its craters mill.
He simulates the hand from which they spill.
I ride on a platform; avoiding harm,
Reach like an inchworm to greenhouse or farm.
Still we work in tandem; without alarm,
Shift Phobos' pelf with Ge's robotic arm.

We penetrate the planet; test its hoard;
Resolve the phases in which ice is stored;
Compute its asteroids; Ge's station moored,
Unberth the landing pod whose craft we board.
Cyborgs in the grip of gravity curled,
We rove but in parsecs; our venues furled,
Distribute His species: air-colored, twirled,
The souls of Hermes wrapped around this world.

TO MARS IN A MONTH

Inside a warp bubble, rounder than space
From atoms composed, like Maria's vase,
We ride as on a sidewalk that we race,
Condense ahead, stretch out behind, then trace.
And still the stars that ravish us contend.
Drawn yet to Venus, to Mars do we bend.
We bring our own atmosphere; where we wend,
Specify Ge's impulse, and thus we spend.

We build a craft predestined as a spear:
A rocket to Centauri; year by year,
Engineer its wave; interstellar, peer—
By the muffled roar of its surf we steer.
Rooted in the torus, programmed, we fly;
Empowered by nuclear fusion, ply
New Heaven's starship; with Daedalus vie—
Alchemystic cyborgs, holons we hie.

We swing around and point the other way;
Cut the transit time; ionize; convey
Gaea's double spouse; astronauts at play
Cosmic as a cell, magnetize our clay.
Spacetime but a retort, humankind tried
In Hermes' vessel, sexes that elide—
Sapphirine *rebis;* stone that, heated, dried—
Submersed in the aether, he steps inside.

TRAVELLING FOREVER IN THE SAME DIRECTION

Adrift in space, he mirrors Heaven's stray.
Her peacock feather placed upon His tray,
He likens Ge's distillate to His clay.
We humans moult in a similar way.
His *Rebis* revealed as Sight's only spoil
Above and below—His flesh at a boil
Exalted from Earth till cleansed of its soil—
He floats in Her substance, clasped in its coil.

Gaea's starry messenger having stormed
Amid stench of the graves that species swarmed—
Like Hermes' ashes out of sea-spume formed
Or Hephaestus' ichor by cauldrons warmed—
He hurtles neither upwards nor beyond
But back into chaos, salt-spirit's bond
Explicit as the crown that He has donned,
Metallic its frond, with Robonaut's wand.

Should we leave the earth and track a straight line,
We would meet no planet—symbol or sign—
Nor even such moisture as stirs the spine,
Gamonymous satellite that we twine.
Since Polaris yet draws us, South we go
That we may reach the edge, where clusters grow:
Omega, Tucanae, Spirals that glow,
Nomads that walk in the infinite snow.

TUMBLING ESCHER

We view the world through telescope or eye,
Or satellites that digitize the sky,
Or set philosophy or random die,
Or pi transcendental or even wry.
We live in Spacetime: tesseract or strand;
Or, beamed from Musca, stardust that we scanned
Within its hourglass; a trickle of sand—
Regolith in Ge's instrumented hand.

A cyborg may glimpse but darkening rays.
Having fallen down from the moon, he strays;
Through the speckled light of intellect, plays;
In nihilistic indecision, stays.
Whereas the Son ascends, Cabir or elf—
The *stone that is no stone*—secretes its pelf.
Avid as Heracles, co-born the twelfth,
Who knows and understands? — It is myself.

I twist a pseudosphere; upon a stair,
Venus locked in the arms of Mars—a pair,
Like Maria's vase, neither Here nor There,
But the only nexus that I can bear.
I shapeshift, hypersee, translate my hoard:
Platonic solid; calabash or gourd;
Some tumbling tessellation—like a sword,
The serpent rises back into the board.

THE ULTIMATE FATE OF THE UNIVERSE

Whether closed, like the surface of a sphere;
Open, the curve of the horn that we clear;
Or, flat, the fixed line of Archytas' spear—
Euclidean space wherever we steer—
We mate each universe that we create;
Inflation past, an equation of state
Determined by matter—density's slate:
That either freeze She may or oscillate.

Upon the tongue that Ouroboros flicked,
We place the stone that Trismegistus picked,
Resorb the bolt that Asclepius licked,
Extract the heart that in the healer ticked.
Over endless spaces, verses spread out
Like robust data: bosons that we scout,
Gamonymous source-points, Big Bangs that spout,
Immortal atoms that all endings rout.

In *the field of the square inch,* we subsist;
Mirror the multiverse; by Gaea kissed,
Even as a thumbling, warmer than mist,
Circulate, subtilize, concentrate, tryst.
Movement is mastery. Lovers that rise
Rejoice in nature, then conquer its size
Above and below: pneumatic its guise,
Light that dwells in the face *between the eyes.*

THE UNIVERSE SPEAKS

We peer at such stars as the sky embeds,
Their spirals yet tinted in blues and reds.
Pulled together by invisible threads,
Spacetime is not static—the fabric spreads.
We wonder how the omniverse began;
Through the power of Mind, deduce its plan;
The cosmos pregnant with woman and man,
Extract from its azure species a clan.

Beneath layers of Mylar that we don,
We scan the sign of the automaton:
Spagyric vessel, pelican or swan,
Encoded on wafers of silicon.
Still we seek the *Rebis;* the script is clear—
The universe speaks to us, and we hear.
Untethered cyborg, moonchild like a sphere,
Through a maze of zeros and ones we steer.

He circles aeons of unconsciousness;
Pursues its source-point; shaman with a kiss
Like some subtile body: serpent of bliss,
He hears in the shell of his heart Her hiss.
What God imagines happens in the world.
What we imagine—the foetus that hurled
Astride Her umbilical, coiled or furled—
Awaits forever the scissors that twirled.

A USER'S GUIDE TO SPACETIME

In Spacetime, should you waken, rub your eyes.
Can you see, through your maze, how rockets rise,
The universe bends, and, proud in the skies,
The shuttle blends, and the astrobot plies?
Then hurry, hierophant, and mend the world.
Maintain your craft; astride the station curled—
Sublunar hermeneut in Chaos hurled—
Transport the *rebis,* mirror neurons twirled.

But what is the gist of Creation?—This:
Both Compaction's point and Unity's bliss;
After the Redshift and ions that hiss,
Through recombination photons that kiss.
Cyborg, you manifest what Ge has tried.
Though galaxies surpass you, still you ride:
Male in the D-brane, in the bulk a bride—
Small as Purusha, Prakriti as wide.

Dressed in your Kevlar, to Cerberus cling;
Clasp in your hand a ball of cosmic string:
Embedded in Saturn's tenuous ring,
A tiny moon that, entangled, you bring.
Transparent as the sun, like dust you roam.
Enter the torus: wormhole that you comb.
Your capsule but a body made of foam,
You are on a journey—*this* is your home.

VAS BENE CLAUSUM

Round upon the chaos, the *rebis* stands;
Framed by the iris, in its pigment lands;
Adjusts the pupil; stimulates its bands;
Offspring of Spacetime, interweaves its strands.
The astronaut, clear-sighted, wends his way.
His mission immortal, His son at play
Entwines the omniverse, extends his stay,
Stops at the mid-point between night and day.

In the dark he finds a life of his own;
Adumbrates its secret; matter unknown—
Aether, string, or membrane—His mystic clone
Whispers its source-point in Möbius' zone.
He shapes his egg; with the same acumen
Savors its silver; sifts its albumen,
Salt, then the Self: entelechy's numen,
Weighs the degree to which we are human.

He seals the vessel with infinite skill.
Having set its clock, the stone in the mill
Raised to the sun, *albedo* in the spill,
He runs and runs and runs while standing still.
Hephaestan skein, symbolic as the strain—
His Son and His Swain—reborn in the brain,
Ouroboros coils even as its chain
Maps His domain, the circle in the grain.

A WALKING MAN I

As if I had been by Heaven courted,
Some scion of Zion teleported—
Dematerialized—atoms sorted,
Then re-created, or else distorted,
A pencil-thin bronze, a walking man I
Proceed to the rim of the crater; ply;
Collect plagioclase; transmit my sigh
Like other ghosts, anomalous as sky.

Should we harness a rocket, Fusion's pay,
Seconds of impulse confined in the bay,
And shell stars surround us and, brown and gray,
Eternity twirl till we lose our way,
Hermes would steer us; telepresent, fast,
Engineer His sunship; from first to last,
In but scrolls of wire Ge's android is cast.
The present impinges upon the past.

Amid the vastness that the cyborg winds,
Hephaestan its tesseract, still he finds
Principled deformations; more than signs—
Embedded in symbols, sapphirine shrines.
Sprung from the cosmos, foam-child in its chute,
The foetus listens; the multiverse moot,
The astronaut cinctures, adjusts his suit,
Surveys the mare, then inserts his boot.

WAYFINDER

That I may reach Ge's errant satellite,
Untethered I deploy; adjust my sight;
Caught in the chasm between day and night,
Section the orbweb; the aether bright,
I wonder—my metal digits thrumming
As I ride my cherry-picker thumbing,
The magnitude of *Palapa* numbing—
Whether I am going now or coming.

As if you drift in a cosmic bubble
That mirrors your magus: clone or double,
Salt-sign or sun-disk, or Mithras' nubble:
Sapphire foetus in the eye of Hubble,
You seek an escape route; maneuver; steer
Back to the module; on your shuttle peer;
Reorient; navigate; sideslip; veer
With six degrees of freedom: *You are Here*.

What is Space but a construct of the mind?
And Time—? Still a blind: Before and Behind.
Transcerebral substance, inborn, divined,
The Psyche that observes us is yet kind—
Bestows upon the Self that we anoint,
More than such atoms as we *dis*anoint,
The urge to be what one is: joint by joint,
A precinct ubiquitous as a point.

THE WEIGHT OF HISTORY

As I scan the mare, the moon looks wan
Till symbols swathe me: feathers like a swan,
Rebis in orbit, sun-disk that I don.
The earth keeps spinning, and so I hang on.
I float in a jumble of spacesuit parts;
Assemble my skein from Hephaestus' charts:
A saffron clone; gamonymus that smarts,
Ground my reality in dust that darts.

We ride a ball that curves where it has run.
An image of itself, a knot undone,
The point that happened everywhere is One.
We make a center where there can be none.
Cislunar as a dream, the holon folds;
Secretes the foetus, biped that it rolls
Like a beam in the bunting, pleated souls
As preset in the cosmos as its scrolls.

Shriven hybrid, he capsules mystery,
Holds in himself the *weight* of history.
Foam in its cauldron, Hecate's witchery—
Matter in Spacetime—bubbles blistery.
Rocket in the scaffold; thunderbolt hurled
Like *God through the lap;* The Tree of Life burled,
In the bulk a scion; hierophant furled—
I know little enough about the world.

THE WHOLE ATLAS

He wheels toward the sun secure in its gaze;
Equipped with sensors, navigates its blaze;
Assimilates its cells; beyond all ways,
Grasps, in the pockets of his gloves, its rays.
His coheir sapphirine, His race enshrined—
Some silver uniped caught in its bind—
Ge's wounded healer, *rebis* that we twined:
Sight's image, coalesces in the mind.

We peel with a blade a smudge off the brain;
Excavate each section; lift without strain
A micron of thought, a pellet of pain,
Skein of Golgotha reduced to a grain.
We store each terabyte; baptize its pelf;
Clarify the soul; crystallize the Self:
Androgyne, hierophant, humanoid, elf;
Then place Ge's whole atlas upon its shelf.

The Self is always and ever the same.
Sojourner immanent, artifex lame,
Emptied of all knowing He shapes His frame,
Yet being suprareal He has no name.
From nothing to nothing, torsos that teem,
He constellates His spouse without a seam
Like subject and object, digits that stream,
Gaea's astronaut: capsule of the dream.

WRITING UNDER ERASURE

Blessed by the Savior, Resurrection's shrine,
Body is not Spirit; it is but sign:
The tenant in the tree—Aleppo pine
As pungent as resin or turpentine.
And thus in his maze the astronaut lists.
Position held in load cells of his fists,
He actuates his drill; his unit twists;
Forever outside, the nomad exists.

Tangible evidence of what he seeks,
Infinity's presence, the coheir speaks:
The ship in the cloud; the Saturn that peaks;
Cone that in the sky, mercurial, streaks.
His skein yet twines him: Gaea's joining rings,
Modular scaffolding, capsule with springs
That animate the biped. — Height with strings
Embedded in matter, the shaman clings.

Below the diaphragm the *rebis* reigns:
The scion in the blood or, in the brain's
Most intimate sanctum among Her fanes,
Gamonymous monads that course his veins
Like phonemes or *caelum* or staves that scan
Or crystals in the eye; since sight began,
A *concourse* of soul-sparks, such disks as span
New Heaven's *rebis,* both woman and man.

NOTES AND COMMENTS

A USER'S GUIDE TO SPACETIME:
NOTES AND COMMENTS
Daniel Orsini

Aether buoyed or loose / Even as I stand: a punning allusion, not only to *Aether,* the Greek God of heavenly Light and the rarefied Air—a deity here manifested as the mission specialist astronaut anchored on the Canadarm, a remote manipulator system—but also to aether, "the finest and most subtle substance"—an arcanum equivalent to "the true quintessence"—that, according to the alchemists, infills the glowing upper regions of space (C. G. Jung, *Mysterium Coniunctionis: An Inquiry into the Separation and Synthesis of Psychic Opposites in Alchemy,* trans. R. F. C. Hull [1963; Princeton: Princeton UP, 1977] 322, 478). *Keeper of the Hubble*

Alchemy's tree: the mandrake. Its root was formerly thought to possess occult powers because of its supposed resemblance to the human body—specifically, to a man standing upside down. In *Alchemical Studies,* trans. R. F. C. Hull (1967; Princeton: Princeton UP, 1976), C. G. Jung notes that "The idea that man is an inverted tree seems to have been current in the Middle Ages. [. . .] In Hindu literature the tree grows from above downwards, whereas in alchemy (at least according to the pictures) it grows from below upwards." However, "In East and West alike, the tree symbolizes a living process as well as a process of enlightenment" (312-14)—in fine, the work of both "[moral] transformation and [spiritual] renewal" (317). *Beyond Gender*

Ancient of Days: In Dan. 7.9, "'The Ancient of Days' is the eternal God" who shall judge unrepentant apostasy during the Great Tribulation Period, whereupon the Son of Man shall return in order "to establish His millennial kingdom here upon earth." See J. Vernon McGee, *Thru the Bible with J. Vernon McGee, Volume III: Proverbs—Malachi* (Nashvillle: Nelson, 1982) 572. *Hermes' Nested Spiral*

archetypes that mill, / Even as the cross upraised on a hill, / *Not subject to caprices of the will:* Cf. C. G. Jung, *The Archetypes and the Collective Unconscious,* trans. R. F. C. Hull (1969; Princeton: Princeton UP, 1990) 58: "if we regard the psyche as an independent factor, we must logically conclude that there is a psychic life which is not subject to caprices of the will. [. . .] From the unconscious there emanate determining influences"—i.e., transpersonal patterns of thought—"which, independently of tradition, guarantee in every single individual a similarity and even a sameness of experience [. . .]. One of the main proofs of this is the almost universal parallelism between mythological motifs, which, on account of their quality as primordial images, I have called *archetypes.*" *Siblings of the Sun*

argosies of humankind: Cf. Tennyson's "argosies of magic sails," the utopian commercial balloons of "Locksley Hall" (line 121). By contrast, here, the futuristic *argosies* comprise a fleet of rocket-powered, crew-carrying space ships that would not only launch cargo into space, but also "ferry passengers to and from [. . .] huge space hotels." See Mike Wall, "Now Boarding: The Top 10 Private Spaceships," *2 Eyes Watching* 1-8 <2eyeswatching.wordpress.com>. Posted on 27 Jan. 2015. *Techwed*

Arrayed in fine linen: apparel that "signifies the righteous deeds of God's people." See Rev. 19.7-8: "'the wedding-day of the Lamb has come! His bride has made herself ready, and for her dress she has been given fine linen, clean and shining'" (*The New English Bible with the Apocrypha* [1961; New York: Oxford UP, 1972]). Subsequent Biblical citations are from this ecumenical text. *Dreaming in Code*

Asclepius' plea: Asclepius is "the Greek god of healing, who, while still a mortal, raised a man from the dead and was struck by a thunderbolt as a punishment" (C. G. Jung, *Symbols of Transformation: An Analysis of the Prelude to a Case of Schizophrenia,* trans. R. F. C. Hull [1956; Princeton: Princeton UP, 1990] 239). In this poem, *Asclepius' plea* echoes the axiom of Maria Prophetissa: "the four times three." See *Maria's maxim,* a note on alchemy's best-known number symbolism, given below. *Blazar/Quasar*

Asclepius' quip: here, Robonaut's well-disposed teleoperator regarded as history's answer to Asclepius, in Greek mythology a benevolent physician presumptuous enough to raise a man from the dead. See Edith Hamilton, *Mythology* (1940; New York: Mentor-New American, 1942) 280-81. *Segway*

As if I lived in megalithic times / Surrounded by statues or flint that primes: In *Alchemical Studies,* Jung explains that "The motif of transformation into stone, or petrifaction, is common in the Peruvian and Columbian legends and is probably connected with a megalithic stone-cult, and perhaps with the Paleolithic cult of *churinga*-like soul-stones." Thus, "The civilization of the Nile Valley, which originated in megalithic times, turned its divine kings into stone statues for the express purpose of making the king's *ka* everlasting." In other words, "The connection of the lapis with immortality is attested from very early times" (100-01). Jung adds that, in the American cycle of legends, among the Wichita, "the saviour was the great star in the south, and he performed his work of salvation on earth as the 'flint man.' His son was called the 'young flint.' After completing their work, both of them went back into the sky. In this myth, just as in medieval alchemy, the saviour [who *primes,* i.e., prepares the world or makes its inhabitants ready] coincides with the stone, the star, the son [. . .]" (99-100). *Kepler*

As if I were some cloud that formed the sun / Or newborn like a disk: See Kenneth Chang, "For NASA, Return Trip to Jupiter in Search of Clues to Solar System's Origins," *The New York Times* 4 Aug. 2011: 2 <www.nytimes.com>: "Astronomers have the big picture of the origins of the solar system. A cloud of hydrogen, much like interstellar hydrogen clouds seen elsewhere in the galaxy, collapsed to form the Sun. As the cloud collapsed, it began to spin, like a figure skater pulling in the arms. That produced a flattened disk of leftovers [among them, possibly, water ice crystals] orbiting the newborn Sun, and those leftovers coalesced into the planets." *Figure Skater*

As melt like a skein gamonymous whirs: To create a customized, "second-skin" Bio-Suit, NASA's project leaders have theorized that, in addition to electrospinlacing, "Melt blowing of liquefied polymer could be used to apply thin elastic layers. Application could be made directly to the skin, or to advanced 3D forms generated by laser scanning" (Mark Wade, "Bio-Suit," *Encyclopedia Astronautica* 2 <www.astronautix.com>. Accessed on 15 Sept. 2016). In this poem, which records even as it illustrates the speaker's holistic self-transformation, the term *gamonymous* suggests "a kind of chymical wedding, [. . .] an indissoluble, hermaphroditic union" of Sol and Luna. Jung defines the term in *Alchemical Studies* 136. *Electrospinlacing*

Assembled in the airlock: "On board the shuttle orbiter," astronauts don their spacesuits in "an [air-tight] cylindrical chamber located at the rear of the mid-deck" (Robin Kerrod, *Space Walks* [New York: Gallery-Smith, 1985] 46). *Prefigured*

As the astronaut rakes, he gathers rock. / Behind him Taurus rolls: Cf. Kerrod, *Space Walks* 45: "On the final Apollo mission (17) geologist-astronaut Harrison Schmitt gets down to some lunar 'gardening' with his custom-built rake. Actually he is using the rake to collect rock chips of a certain size. In the background are the rolling Taurus mountains." *Postmodern*

the astrobot plies: The speaker refers to any pair of assembled working robots—but, in particular, to "the first [plastic] 'people' to land on Mars," when pictures of the LEGO "brick" minifigures attached to the Mars Exploration Rovers *Spirit* and *Opportunity* reached their destination in 2004. The NASA rovers also carried "specially designed aluminum LEGO bricks and magnets to help determine the presence of liquid water" on Mars. See Sarah Herman, *A Million Little Bricks: The Unofficial History of the LEGO Phenomenon* (New York: Skyhorse, 2012) 193. *A User's Guide to Spacetime*

An astronaut in Ge's breath-body based: the thematic spine of this poem. The speaker reflects upon the incarnation of Christ and upon the "higher spiritual being who is invisibly born in the individual, a pneumatic body which is to serve us as a future dwelling, a body which, as [Saint] Paul says, is put on like a garment" (Jung, *Alchemical Studies* 52). See Gal. 2.20: "I have been crucified with Christ: the life I now live is not my life, but the life which Christ lives in me [. . .]." *Pseudosphere*

astrum: a Paracelsan concept: "the 'natural light of man' or the 'star in man' [. . .] extracted from matter by human art and, by means of the opus, made into a new light-bringer" (Jung, *Alchemical Studies* 127). However, in this poem, the speaker suggests that the true source of the New Heaven is not the *filius philosophorum* (an ancient alchemical idea) but the *indwelling,* and *infilling,* Spirit of the glorified Christ instead (line 8). See Andrew Murray, *The Spirit of Christ* (Springdale: Whitaker House, n.d.) 210: "Each of us must learn to know that there is a Holiest of All in that temple which we are. The secret place of the Most High within us must become the central truth in our temple worship." *Carrier*

as we draw in, / Craters assail Callisto, and they win: Cf. Patrick Moore, *Travellers in Space and Time* (New York: Doubleday, 1984) 51: Surveying Jupiter from his rocket ship, yet still venturing outside its most dangerous zones of radiation, the astronaut discovers that *Callisto,* Jupiter's fourth satellite, "is an oddity. As we draw in towards it, craters come into view—not thinly spread, but covering almost the whole of the surface. There seems to be no level ground anywhere [. . .]." *Tipler's Subset*

Attached to crystals: See Jung, *Alchemical Studies* 101: "In shamanism, much importance is attached to crystals, which play the part of ministering spirits. They come from the crystal throne of the supreme being or from the vault of the sky." In fact, in the literature of the Church Fathers, Christ is often compared to a crystal. Thus, in his *Homiliae in Ezechielem* (*Homilies on Ezekiel*), Saint Gregory the Great [c. AD 540-604] explains that, through the "glory" of His resurrection, Christ "'hardened after the fashion of a crystal from water, so that there was one and the same nature in it and in [H]im]'" (qtd. in Jung, *Mysterium Coniunctionis* 449n345). *Kepler*

At the edge of the arrow: The speaker refers to "the holes with teeth" that develop gradually out of spacetime—"cusp-like edges," i.e., singularities, "from which no traveler can return [. . .]" in the lacerating "demise" of the universe (Paul Davies, *Other Worlds: A Portrait of Nature in Rebellion / Space, Superspace and the Quantum Universe* [New York: Simon, 1980] 101-02. *Platonic Riddles*

Auriga [aw-RYE-guh] in the strand: In the vast filament of galactic clusters, *Auriga* is the "pentagon-shaped" Charioteer, a constellation located, at the edge of the Milky Way, between Perseus and Gemini (Sune Engelbrektson, *Stars, Planets, and Galaxies* [New York: Bantam-Ridge, 1975] 46). In some versions of the Greek myth that features *Auriga,* the Charioteer is Erichthonius of Athens, the lame son of the smith-god Hephaestus and the Earth-mother Gaia. *The Limits of the Coded World*

autogiros: Superseded to a large extent by the helicopter, an autogiro is "an aircraft that moves forward by means of a propeller and is supported in the air mainly by means of a large motor mounted horizontally above the fuselage and turned by air pressure rather than [by] motor power" ("Autogiro" [n.], def.). See *Webster's New World Dictionary,* 1988 ed.; unless otherwise indicated, subsequent definitions of key words are from this text. *Techwed*

Babalon astride the beast or its blot: According to Thelemic doctrine, the adept must cross the Abyss—the devouring void that lies between Shadow and Substance—in the Womb of *Babalon,* the Great Mother of the Underworld. Paradoxically, *Babalon* leads the enlightened traveller to the ecstatic disintegration of his ego-self, even as She propels him—through "Sethian tunnels"—to "willed mutation" in "the City of the Pyramids under the Night of Pan." See Linda Falorio, "Earthing the Tunnels of Set," *The Shadow Tarot* 1989: 2 <www.shadowtarot.net>. Accessed on 3 Oct. 2016. *Testing the Night of Pan*

the bead that the Magus sweats: See Jung, *Alchemical Studies* 296: "the alchemical *servator cosmi* (preserver of the cosmos), representing the still unconscious idea of the whole and complete man, [. . .] will sweat a redeeming blood," i.e., "not natural or ordinary blood, but symbolic blood, a psychic substance, the manifestation of a certain kind of Eros which unifies the individual as well as the multitude," and "makes them whole [. . .]." *Postmodern*

a beam in the bunting: first light concealed not only in the fabric of the cosmos, but also in "a baby's garment of soft, warm cloth made into a kind of hooded blanket that can be closed, exposing only the face'' ("Bunting[1]" [n.], def. 3). *The Weight of History*

Because I know where I have been I go: Cf. Michael Collins, *Carrying the Fire: An Astronaut's Journey* (1974; New York: Ballantine-Random, 1975) 487: "Man has always gone where he has been able to go. It's that simple. He will continue pushing back his frontier, no matter how far it may carry him from his homeland." Collins operated the Command Module during the Apollo 11 expedition, the first lunar landing at Tranquility Base, on 20 July 1969. *Prefigured*

bell: "a hollow object, usually cuplike [. . .]" ("Bell" [n.], def. 1)—but, here, with a stem not unlike the body of a human bring—specifically, the trunk of "the alchemical Monocolus, the [. . .] semi-castrated, androgynous version of Mercurius." See Jung, *Mysterium Coniunctionis* 500n135, along with Plates 4 and 5: "The Two Unipeds" and "The 'Revelation of the Hidden.'" *Pseudosphere*

Bellicose Ares: the combative Greek God of War. His Roman counterpart is Mars. *Bellicose Ares*

Between the eyes: In *Alchemical Studies,* Jung defines "the field of the square inch" as "the symbol for that which has extension." Thus, "the central white light" of the Tao [the Chinese equivalent of the Johannine *logos*] "dwells in the 'square inch' or in the 'face,' that is, between the eyes" (25). *Precinct; The Ultimate Fate of the Universe*

Beyond a certain portal tunnels lie: See Frater Centaurus, "Testing the Night of Pan" 13 Nov. 2011: 3 <www.astronargon.us>: String Theory "presents a new mark beyond a certain portal. Is this [the] darkly splendid world prophesied by the Night of Pan and [. . .] the Tunnels of Set?" Here, Set is the Egyptian God of Chaos and the red desert, and Pan is the equally ambivalent Greek God of Nature. Having situated us in the phenomenal world, a three-dimensional construct, Pan then propels us through the vertiginous Sethian tunnels of psychic space, "with its root primitive atavisms" and "strange adumbrations of far future selves," and thereafter, beyond the fourth dimension of Time, into the fifth dimension of Light. For the latter interpretation, see also Linda Falorio, "Earthing the Tunnels of Set" 1. *Testing the Night of Pan*

Blazar/Quasar: A blazar and a quasar are both Active Galactic Nuclei—in other words, the very same object—but observed at different angles. Even so, "Blazars are generally defined as quasars that are viewed jet-on." See Joseph Castro, "Just One Type of Blazar? How Jet-Spewing Galaxies Evolve Over Time," *Space.com* 17 June 2014: 3 <www.space.com>. *Blazar/Quasar*

BL Lacertae [luh-SIR-tee]: an ostensible star that, in 1968, "was found to be a powerful [quasi-stellar] radio source," i.e., a quasar, and that "was soon visualized" as a distant, "probably embryonic" galaxy. Since then, astronomers have discovered "more than 100 BL Lacs [. . .], which vary in radiation intensity across the entire electromagnetic spectrum, from radio waves to gamma rays." However, "The engine at the heart of these [elliptical] galaxies is thought to be a massive black hole that emits fantastic amounts of energy as it gobbles up any kind of nearby matter, including whole stars" (William J. Broad, "Star-Gulpers May Power the Brightest Galaxies," *The New York Times* 11 Aug. 1992: 3 <www.nytimes.com>). Broad adds that "The most active BL Lacs and quasars are called blazars." (See also the note on *Blazar/Quasar* given above.) *Blazar/Quasar*

the blue dot that we seize: See the note on *The blue dot yet wanders* given below. *Compass*

The blue dot yet wanders: Earth, our home planet, seen—or not seen—from outer space. From the deployed astronaut's perspective, it *wanders,* i.e., strays from its course. The images that comprise the portrait of "the pale blue dot"—and that the astronomer Carl Sagan celebrated in his book, *The Pale Blue Dot: A Vision of the Human Future in Space* (1994)—were captured by NASA's Voyager 1 probe on 14 February 1990. See Elizabeth Landau, "'Pale Blue Dot' Images Turn 25," *NASA Jet Propulsion Laboratory* 13 Feb. 2015: 1-4 <www.jpl.nasa.gov>. *Tipler's Subset*

the bolt that Asclepius licked: After "the great physician" *Asclepius* had called a man back to life, Zeus struck him "with his thunderbolt and slew him" because the Lord of the Sky "would not allow a mortal to have power over the dead" (Hamilton, *Mythology* 280-81). *The Ultimate Fate of the Universe*

bolt that I bind / Even as Python's: In Greek myth, Python is the dragon that guards the omphalos and that Apollo kills in order to establish his temple at Delphi. However, in these lines, the speaker imagines that the astronaut, afloat in an equally rarefied sphere, covers the Hubble Space Telescope with a serpentine roll or coil of cloth not unlike the swaddling bands with which, earlier, Rhea had wrapped the original omphalos stone in a scheme to protect Zeus, her new-born son, from Cronus, his father. Upon learning "that one of his children was destined some day to dethrone him," Cronus had "thought to go against his fate by swallowing [his offspring] as soon as they were born" (Hamilton, *Mythology* 65). Of course, here, the hidden metaphor is "gamonymous," a kind of "chymical wedding" (Jung, *Alchemical Studies* 136), a hieroglyph that celebrates the marriage of the male principle (the phallic satellite) with the female principle (the uterus of inhabited space). (NB: In point of fact, Hubble's thermal blanket consists of "Sixteen thin layers of dimpled aluminized Kapton material [that] are covered by an outer aluminized Teflon shell, altogether measuring less than one-tenth of an inch thick." See Kelsey Paquin, "Improving Hubble's Space Armor," *NASA Mission to Hubble* 21 Aug. 2008: 1 <www.nasa.gov>.) *Saffron of the Metals*

Boötes to Borealis bound: adjoining constellations in the Northern Celestial Hemisphere. In Greek mythology, *Boötes* is the Herdsman, a son of Demeter, the goddess of agriculture and the harvest, and the Corona *Borealis* refers to the wedding diadem that Dionysus gave to Ariadne, the daughter of Minos, the King of Crete. *Life in a Mortal Universe*

Born in the water: i.e., in watery amniotic fluid or in the sanctified water of Baptism. See John 3.4-8: "'But how is it possible,' said Nicodemus, 'for a man to be born when he is old? Can he enter his mother's womb a second time and be born?' Jesus answered, 'In truth I tell you, no one can enter the kingdom of God without being born from water and spirit. Flesh can give birth only to flesh; it is spirit that gives birth to spirit. You ought not to be astonished, then, when I tell you that you must be born over again. The wind blows where it wills; you hear the sound of it, but you do not know where it comes from, or where it is going. So with everyone who is born from spirit.'" *The Limits of the Coded World*

bosons: A boson (BOH-sahn) is a subatomic particle, a "hypothetical packet of gravity [that] has two units of spin." The term suggests "hidden symmetries of unseen dimensions," an idea that Michio Kaku underscores in *Hyperspace: A Scientific Odyssey through Parallel Universes, Time Warps, and the Tenth Dimension* (New York: Oxford UP, 1994) 144. *The Ultimate Fate of the Universe*

bot: here, the shortened form of the word *robot*. *Tipler's Subset*

Both Saturn and Sol: In Paracelsan alchemy, "Saturn is the cold, dark, heavy, impure element, Sol is the opposite. When this separation [of the philosophical lead from the philosophical gold] is completed and the body has been purified by Melissa" [a supracelestial herb that induces happiness] and thereby "freed from Saturnine melancholy, then the coniunctio can take place with the long-living inner, or astral, man" (Jung, *Alchemical Studies* 153). *Precinct*

bowknot: Gaea's true love-knot, "with two loops and two ends" difficult to untie—hence, a symbol of everlasting love ("Bowknot" [n.], def.). *Pseudosphere*

The brain is pre-set by its own command: See Erich Harth, *Windows on the Mind: Reflections on the Physical Basis of Consciousness* (New York: Morrow, 1988) 215: "The brain is a self-referent system. My self is forever imaging itself and changing in response to the image. It can never quite catch up with itself. To this extent it also remains undefined." *Bystander Cyborgs*

brane in the bulk: the visible, four-dimensional universe contained in a higher-dimensional space, the latter membrane called *the bulk* and also known as "hyperspace." *Bulk*

Breath-soul: the subtle body that—in Classical and Medieval alchemy—"means something non-material" and that enshrines a concept even higher than spirit: "Its essential characteristic is to animate and be animated; it therefore represents the life principle" (Jung, *Alchemical Studies* 213). *History's Thread; The Quilted Multiverse; Testing the Night of Pan*

breccias (BRECH-uhz): here, an assortment of cemented lunar rock chips. See Kerrod, *Space Walks* 35. *Hubble Ajar; Outrider; Quintessence*

bruised by Hubble's plight: The speaker realizes that, when the Hubble Space Telescope's "batteries and gyros finally run out of juice, NASA plans to send a rocket and drop [the satellite] into the ocean" (Dennis Overbye, "Last Voyage for the Keeper of the Hubble," *The New York Times* 13 Apr. 2009: 2 <www. nytimes.com>). Hubble's formal successor will be the James Webb Space Telescope (Webb or JWST), with a launch scheduled for 30 March 2021. *Bellicose Ares*

A bubble of Spacetime: According to the rules of quantum logic, "whole universes, little bubbles of space-time, could pop into existence, like bubbles in boiling water, out of [. . .] nothing." See Dennis Overbye, "There's More to Nothing Than We Knew," *The New York Times* 21 Feb. 2012: 3 <www.nytimes.com>. *Nothing; Quintessence*

a bubble that shimmers in its pan: Cf. Sheila Kitzinger and Lennart Nilsson, *Being Born* (New York: Grosset, 1986), where the embryonic "ball of cells grew and grew till it looked like a shimmering, silvery blackberry" (15) and where, weeks later, the warm foetus swam fishlike "in a bubble of water" (30). *Rebis*

Bulbous as the cosmos: The speaker alludes to the *rotundum,* the "round, original form" of "the spiritual, inner, and complete man" (C. G. Jung, *Mandala Symbolism,* trans. R. F. C. Hull [1959; Princeton: Princeton UP, 1973] 9-10). See also *Mysterium Coniunctionis* 409, where Jung remarks that, in the Rabbinic tradition, the first Adam "is the *homo maximus,* the Anthropos, from whom the macrocosm arose, or who *is* the macrocosm." *Bulk*

bulbous his pins: the rounded legs of the suited NASA astronaut. *Outrider*

the bulk: higher-dimensional space, the cosmic membrane also known as "hyper-space." *Bulk; History's Thread; Hubble Ajar; A User's Guide to Spacetime; The Weight of History*

Bulk speed of plasma: Here, the speaker describes "The observed emission from a blazar [that] is greatly enhanced by relativistic effects in the jet, a process termed relativistic beaming." Thus, "The bulk speed of the plasma that constitutes the jet can be in the range of 95%-99% of the speed of light" ("Blazar," *Wikipedia* 2 <en.wikipedia.org>. Last edited on 7 Dec. 2017). *Blazar/Quasar*

But a dimple in the fabric of space: According to Einstein, "gravity must be [the] result of a solid object like a planet causing a dimple in the fabric of spacetime." See Tom Rowan's online essay "Pushing Gravity," *American Thinker* 1 Aug. 2010: 1 <www.americanthinker.com>. *Pushing Gravity*

Cabir: in Greek mythology, a misshapen dwarf god. *Tumbling Escher*

caelum: in alchemical texts, "the heavenly substance in the body" (Jung, *Mysterium Coniunctionis* 489). See also the note below. *Beyond Gender; Saturday; Writing under Erasure*

***caelum* that links:** in alchemical texts, either "the celestial substance hidden in man" or "the kingdom of heaven upon earth" (Jung, *Mysterium Coniunctionis* 487). *Saturday*

***caelum* that spun— / Castor's postulate:** For the alchemists, the *caelum* was the "stone that is no stone, [. . .] on the one hand a liquid that could be poured out of a bottle and on the other the Microcosm itself. For the psychologist it is the self—man as he is, and the indescribable and super-empirical totality of that same man. This totality is a mere postulate, but a necessary one, because no one can assert that he has complete knowledge of man as he is. Not only in the psychic man is there something unknown, but also in the physical. We should be able to include this unknown quantity in a total picture of man, but we cannot. Man himself is partly empirical, partly transcendental [. . .]" (Jung, *Mysterium Coniunctionis* 536). Here, Castor—the earthly twin to Pollux, his heavenly counterpart—becomes, like the speaker, a surrogate alchemist. *Beyond Gender*

calabash or gourd: here, "the dried, hollow shell of a gourd" (e.g., the pumpkin or the melon) or of a *calabash,* with its "bottle-shaped, gourdlike fruit," used as a bowl, cup, or dipper ("Calabash" [n.], defs. 2a, 3). *Tumbling Escher*

Callisto: One of the four Galilean moons, *Callisto* is a satellite of the planet Jupiter. According to Patrick Moore, it is "less massive than our Moon, though it is larger. Its surface is icy, and gives the impression of being absolutely dead. We are looking at what may be the most ancient landscape in the Solar System. At least we are outside the most dangerous part of Jupiter's radiation, so that if astronauts ever go to the Jovian system they will presumably select Callisto as their first and probably their only port of call" (*Travellers in Space and Time* 51). *History's Thread*

Cana: a village in Galilee, the scene of Jesus' first miracle—the changing of the water into wine (John 2.1-11), the sacramental sign that prefigures the Christian Savior's heroic rebirth. In effect, at *Cana,* Jesus is shown to be the divine "bridegroom" (John 3.29), the firstborn of a "new creation" (Gal. 6.15) by which God's "royal priesthood" (1 Pet. 2.9) shall die with Christ in order to rise again with Him. *Hercules in the Vessel of the Sun*

Canadarm: i.e., *Canadarm*2, the 57.7-foot-long "robotic arm that assembled the International Space Station (ISS) while in space." It is "routinely used to move supplies, equipment, and even astronauts" and is also "responsible for performing 'cosmic catches,' the capturing and docking of unpiloted spacecraft [. . .]." See "Canadarm2, the Canadian Robotic Arm of the International Space Station," *Canadian Space Agency* 1 <www.asc-csa.gc.ca>. Date modified: 4 Oct. 2017. *Canadarm; Keeper of the Hubble*

capsule with springs: the crew cabin of NASA's rocket-fired Space Shuttle. *Writing under Erasure*

Carries in His belly the foetus furled: See C. G. Jung, *Psychology and Alchemy,* trans. R. F. C. Hull [1953; Princeton: Princeton UP, 1993] 387, fig. 210, entitled "The wind hath carried it in his belly," where the *foetus spagyricus* (the spagyric foetus) is "the renewed Mercurius" that dwells in "the alchemical Mercurius in his aerial aspect," i.e., as "the stone uplifted by the wind" (Jung, *Alchemical Studies* 212). *Pneumatic*

Castor and Pollux: in Greek mythology, the *Dioscuri,* the (twin) sons of Zeus. The mortal *Castor* was an able horseman and the immortal *Pollux* a rugged boxer. When *Castor* died, *Pollux* shared his immortality with him. According to this version of the story, Zeus having pitied the brothers, "the two were never separated again." One day they dwelt on Earth, the next in Heaven, "always together" (Hamilton, *Mythology* 41-42). *Tearing the Fabric of Spacetime; Terraforming Mars*

Castor at play / Dressed in force data gloves: The speaker refers not only to *Castor,* his surrogate astronaut, but also to Robo-Glove, the robotic glove that "uses Robonaut 2 technology" in order to increase the strength of the wayfinder's grasp. See Jerry Wright, "Robotic Technology Lends More Than Just A Helping Hand," *NASA* 12 Mar. 2012: 1-3 <www.nasa.gov>. *Quintessence*

Castor, I tend a *suite* of telescopes: The speaker addresses his imaginary *mortal* twin—himself. Cf. Overbye, "Last Voyage for the Keeper of the Hubble": On his first space flight, the astronaut John Grunsfeld, having experienced a Zen-like peace while "tending a suite of small telescopes [in low-Earth orbit], did not want to come down" (3). *Keeper of the Hubble*

Castor measures a billion where they run: See "Siblings of the Sun," *Science Illustrated* Mar. / Apr. 2012: 33: "Over a seven-year period beginning in 2013, the European Space Agency's *Gaia* satellite will measure the position, distance, motion, brightness, and color spectra of 1 billion of the roughly 400 billion stars of the Milky Way Galaxy. *Gaia* will capture the data in a 3-D model reaching all the way to the center of the galaxy [. . .]." The astrophysicist Simon Portegies Zwart believes that, eventually, "'We might find all the lost siblings of the sun [. . .]'" (32). *Siblings of the Sun*

Castor's berm: A *berm* is "a narrow ledge or path as at the top [. . .] of a slope" ("Berm" [n.], def. 3), here a site for stargazing. In many accounts of the Greek and Roman myth, Castor, the mortal twin of the immortal Pollux, represents the hyphenated God-man, since he lives half of each year on earth and half in heaven. *Life Out There*

Centaurus: a constellation between Hydra (the Sea Serpent) and Crux (the Southern Cross) containing Alpha Centauri. "To the Greeks, Centaurus [the Centaur] was Chiron, the wise tutor of Achilles. An unusual feature is *Omega Centauri,* a globular cluster of stars bright enough to be seen with the naked eye" (Engelbrektson, *Stars, Planets, and Galaxies* 52). *Bellicose Ares*

Cepheid clusters: supergiant stars discovered in the Magellanic Clouds. Known as *Cepheid variables,* they "have periods [of brightness that last] between one and 50 days" (Engelbrektson, *Stars, Planets, and Galaxies* 118). *Bystander Cyborgs; Hercules in the Vessel of the Sun*

Cerberus: in Greek mythology, "the three-headed, dragon-tailed dog" that guards the gate to the underworld, a gruesome specter "easily mollified by a bit of cake" (Hamilton, *Mythology* 39, 227). Here, in order to propitiate the monster, the speaker recommends "a ball of cosmic string," with a miniature moon "Embedded in Saturn's [insubstantial] ring." *A User's Guide to Spacetime*

Cetus: In *Stars, Planets, and Galaxies* 46, Engelbrektson explicates the Greek myth that surrounds this autumn star: "Cassiopeia caused her daughter Andromeda to be chained to a rock near a terrible sea monster, Cetus. Perseus, who had decapitated the Medusa, [. . .] saved Andromeda by holding the Medusa's head before Cetus. The sea monster turned to stone by gazing at the evil eye, represented by the changing brightness of the star Algol (from Arabic *al ghul,* the Ghoul)." *The Limits of the Coded World*

Chain-links the *rebis:* The speaker alludes not only to the Regimen of Mars and Venus, unifying alchemical procedures that, together, represent cyclical death and renewal, but also to the invisible chain-link net that Hephaestus forged and with which he trapped Ares (Mars) and Aphrodite (Venus), alchemy's "gamonymous" lovers. See Jung, *Psychology and Alchemy* 231-32: "the first main goal of the [alchemical] process" is the *albedo,* the whitening, "highly prized by many alchemists as if it were the ultimate goal." However, the Regimen of Venus "is [only] the silver or moon condition, which still has to be raised to the sun condition," the Regimen of Mars. "The *albedo* is [. . .] the daybreak, but not till the *rubedo* [the reddening] is it sunrise." *Heracles Peeled*

a chain of molecules: in the primordial cosmic broth, "molecular collectives, forming, metabolizing, replicating [. . .]" (Carl Sagan, *The Cosmic Connection: An Extraterrestrial Perspective* [New York: Doubleday-Anchor, 1973] 253-54). *Postmodern*

chameleon that teems: like the lizard that can change the color of its skin rapidly ("Chameleon" [n.], defs. 1, 2), the copious, kaleidoscopic setting sun. *Bulk*

cherry-picker: the mobile foot restraint (MFR), which along with the remote manipulator system (RMS) arm served as a cherry picker, i.e., as a forklift, but here with a manned platform, during the recovery, in November 1984, of two rogue communication satellites: *Palapa B-2* and *Westar VI* ("STS-51-A" 4 <weebau.com>. Updated on 16 Mar. 2006). See also other pictures of the NASA astronauts Joseph P. Allen and Dale A. Gardner as they captured the satellites, in Kerrod, *Space Walks* 60-63. *History's Thread; Wayfinder*

Cheshire: the eerie cat that vanishes with a grin in Lewis Carroll's *Alice's Adventures in Wonderland.* *Outrider; Saffron of the Metals*

chimeras: In Greek mythology, the Chimera was "a fire-breathing monster, usually represented as having a lion's head, a goat's body, and a serpent's tail"—hence, "any similar fabulous monster" ("Chimera" [n.], def. 1). *Blazar/Quasar*

Chiral: here, a description not only of human hands, but also of "handed" molecules. Thus, "Like a pair of human hands, certain organic molecules have mirror-image versions of themselves, a chemical property known as chirality. These so-called 'handed' molecules are essential for biology and have intriguingly been found in meterorites on Earth and comets in our Solar System"—and even in interstellar space. See "Life's First Handshake: Chiral Molecule Detected in Interstellar Space," *National Radio Astronomy Observatory* 14 June 2016: 1 <public.nrao.edu>. *Tearing the Fabric of Spacetime*

chlamys: "a short mantle clasped at the shoulder, worn by men in ancient Greece" ("Chlamys" [n.], def.). *The Experiment of Eternity*

chthonic: "dark, primitive, and mysterious" ("Chthonic" [adj.], def. 2) and also "concrete and earthy" (Jung, *Psychology and Alchemy* 175, 177)—here, like sod and tree and stone and even "unknown regions of the psyche" (335). *Carrier; Pseudosphere; Serious Reader; Siblings of the Sun*

circle adumbrated like a string: The *circle* is not only a "symbol of the Absolute" (Jean Chevalier and Alain Gheerbrant, *The Penguin Dictionary of Symbols,* trans. John Buchanan-Brown [1969: New York: Penguin, 1996] 199), but also an emblem of time, "the turning wheel" (197) here *adumbrated* or foreshadowed by the fundamental ingredient of nature: a tiny one-dimensional loop of oscillating *string* (Brian Greene, *The Elegant Universe: Superstrings, Hidden Dimensions, and the Quest for the Ultimate Theory* (1999; New York Vintage-Random, 2000) 422. *Postmodern*

Circle, moisture, simplicity unknown: In alchemy, gold derives "from the dew or supracelestial balsam [the radical *moisture*] sinking into the earth." However, in the older formulations of the 17th-century alchemist Michael Maier, "the sun generates the gold in the earth. Hence, the gold obtains a 'simplicity' approaching that of the circle (symbol of eternity) and the individual point" (Jung, *Mysterium Coniunctionis* 47). In effect, the circular form of the gold "is the line which runs back upon itself, like the snake [the immortal Ouroboros] that with its head bites its own tail," both the goal of the *opus* and a symbol of the Self (504). *Compass*

Cislunar: located between Earth and the moon. In alchemical tracts, "the moon stands on the border-line between the eternal, aethereal things and the ephemeral phenomena of the earthly, sublunar realm" (Jung, *Mysterium Coniunctionis* 145). *Canadarm; Heracles Peeled; Mandragora's Dream; Namespace; The Weight of History*

Clotho's icons embedded in the ball: the numinous archetypes—innate symbols or images—wound either in *Clotho's* skein of thread, or in the globe of the blue planet Earth, or even in the capsule of the human eye. See the note given below. *Beyond Gender*

Clotho's net: In Greek and Roman mythology, Clotho, one of three Fates, spins the thread of life that Lachesis measures and that Atropos cuts. *Rebis*

Clotho's thrum and Lachesis' ties: the short end thread left on *Clotho's* loom after Lachesis has measured the strands and Atropos has cut and knotted them. See the note given above. *Outrider*

cloven tongues that chirr: The speaker refers to the Day of Pentecost, when the Holy Spirit appeared to the regenerated faithful—His believer-priests—"like flames of fire, dispersed [or divided] among them and resting on each one," and thereafter "they began to talk in other tongues, as the Spirit gave them power of utterance" (Acts 2.3-4). Here, the noise that accompanied the Spirit "like that of a strong driving wind" (Acts 2.2.) becomes a *chirr,* "a shrill, trilled sound, as of some [hovering] birds" ("Chirr" [n. & vi.], def.). *The Skin That I Live In*

co-born the twelfth: In this stanza, the number 12 is connected not only with the twelve labors of Hercules, which end with "the self-sacrifice and rebirth caused by Deianeira's robe," but also "with the ecclesiastical year, in which the redemptive work of

Christ is fulfilled" (Jung, *The Archetypes and the Collective Unconscious* 241n53). *Tumbling Escher*

coil or ring: either the alpha-helical coiled-*coil* protein or the glucose *ring*. *Postmodern*

col: "a gap between peaks in a mountain range, used as a pass" ("Col" [n.], def. 1). *Peregrination*

commissure: in humans, "the thickest cable in the entire nervous system, the 200 million fibers of the *great commissure,* also known as the *corpus callosum.* This structure is a broad band of tissue linking the two [cerebral] hemispheres." Since information "flows across the commissure in both directions, from left to right and from right to left," this transfer "provides each hemisphere with a complete copy of sensory information received by the other" (Harth, *Windows on the Mind* 188-89). *Bystander Cyborgs*

Compaction's point: The speaker alludes to the initial state of the universe: the *point,* or singularity, from which the curled-up dimensions of space expanded. *A User's Guide to Spacetime*

concourse: In the belief system of the Greek philosopher Epicurus (c. 341-271 BC), "the concourse [or conglomeration] of atoms even produced God" (Jung, *Mysterium Coniunctionis* 53). *Writing under Erasure*

cone: a light *cone,* "the wall of light that separates our reality and other realities." In effect, "All light beams coming from a given point move along the light cone" (Bob Toben, "in conversation with" Jack Sarfatti and Fred Wolf, *Space-Time and Beyond: Toward an Explanation of the Unexplainable* [New York: Dutton, 1975] 28). *Hercules in the Vessel of the Sun*

a cone all my own: a geometrical shape that "provides an image of ascension, of development from the material to the spiritual," and "of a return to Oneness and personalization" (Chevalier and Gheerbrant, *The Penguin Dictionary of Symbols* 229). *Messenger*

conglomerate soul: the coming Messiah, the second Adam, regarded by the Cabalists as the collective aggregate of all individual souls—as "a 'conglomerate soul,' to use the Indian expression"—and therefore, in modern analytical psychology, as a symbol of the self (Jung, *The Archetypes and the Collective Unconscious* 357.) See also *Aion: Researches into the Phenomenology of the Self,* trans. R. F. C. Hull (1959; Princeton: Princeton UP, 1969) 62n75: In the pre-psychological age, "Christ did not merely *symbolize* wholeness, but, as a psychic phenomenon, he *was* wholeness. [. . .] The idea of totality is, at any given time, [only] as total as one is oneself." *Siblings of the Sun*

consciousness surrounds / Gaea's whitest brain-stone; whispers its sounds / Throughout the spheroid: The speaker weighs the possibility that, although *consciousness* envelops both the planet Earth, the oblate *spheroid* of line 7, and the human brain, it is "not attached to a thing, [either] living or inanimate," an idea that "some Eastern philosophies" advocate (Harth, *Windows on the Mind* 195). *Heracles Peeled*

constrained by the Word: restricted by the determinate text of the speaker's faith—either by "The Word [. . .] that was with God at the beginning" (John 1.2), "became flesh" and "came to dwell among us" (John 1.14); or by "the Spirit of the glorified Jesus," i.e., "the Spirit of the incarnate, crucified, and exalted Christ" (Murray, *The Spirit of Christ* 82); or, simply enough, by Holy Scripture: "the [Bible] truth [that] came through Jesus Christ" (John 1.17). *Serious Reader*

Corascene acrouch inside my eye: in alchemy, "the dark, dangerous, rabid dog"—associated with the moon goddess Selene—that "changes into an eagle at the time of the plenilunium. His darkness disappears and he becomes a solar animal." In effect, the *Corascene* dog functions as a symbol both of "the reborn and sublimated Sol and Luna" and of the transformation of consciousness. See Jung, *Mysterium Coniunctionis* 154-55. *Saffron of the Metals*

cortices: "*layers of skin* [that give] protection from outside influences. They serve the same purpose as the inner consolidation" of the self (Jung, *The Archetypes and the Collective Unconscious* 328). *Postmodern*

Cosmic as a cell, magnetize our clay: The speaker cites the on-going development of VASIMR, the Variable Specific Impulse Magnetoplasma Rocket, "which combines features of the high-thrust/low-specific-impulse chemical rocket, and the low-thrust/high-specific-impulse nuclear rocket." In other words, VASIMR is a *plasma* rocket. "Instead of a combustion chamber, it uses three staged, magnetic cells that first ionize hydrogen and turn it into a super hot plasma, then further energize it with electromagnetic waves to maximize thrust." In theory, this is a rocket that "could attain a speed of 31 miles a second" and that "would reduce a one-way trip to Mars from three months to one" (Michael Klesius, "Mars, and Step on It," *Air & Space* 1 Sept. 2009: 4 <www.airspacemag.com>). *To Mars in a Month*

a cosmic clock, transparent its hands: "This is a species of clock whose hands move unceasingly, and, since there is obviously no loss due to friction, it is a *perpetuum mobile,* an everlasting movement in a circle. [. . .] The movement without friction shows that the clock is cosmic, even transcendental [. . .]," like either the Son of God or His offspring, the god-man (Jung, *Psychology and Alchemy* 104-05). *Something to Live For*

Crowned with the uraeus, His sun-child steered: Here, the speaker channels the spirit of the sun-god Horus, the offspring of the goddess Isis and her brother Osiris. The *uraeus* is "the figure of the sacred asp or cobra [worn] on the headdress of ancient Egyptian rulers" ("Uraeus" [n.], def.). *Made*

The crystal body that tunneling swerves / Even as a wormhole: Cf. Jeremy Hsu, "Newly Discovered Network of Moon Tunnels Could House Lunar Colonists," *Popular Science* 23 Oct. 2009: 2 <www.popsci.com>: "Scientists have spotted a deep hole in the lunar surface that goes at least 260 feet down and is believed to open into an underground tunnel more than 1,200 feet wide. The discovery is powerful evidence for long, winding tunnels carved by lava beneath the lunar surface. Such tunnels, whose existence has long been hypothesized, could provide shelter for future astronauts or colonists against the harsh radiation and surface temperatures on the moon." *Serious Reader*

Crystals from the moon: Maria's fettle: See the photograph of "A thin section of one of the lunar rock samples brought back to the Earth by Apollo 11," in Kerrod, *Space Walks* 35. "It shows in different colors a variety of fine mineral crystals," here compared to an alchemist's *fettle,* the loose sand or crushed ore that lines the hearth of a reverberatory furnace before molten metal is poured. In this line, the alchemist is the Maria of Gnostic tradition, the legendary "Prophetissa" and "sister of Moses" (Jung, *Psychology and Alchemy* 401n169). *Bellicose Ares*

crystals in the eye: In *Alchemical Studies,* Jung remarks that, in shamanism, "much importance is attached to crystals, which play the part of ministering spirits. They come from the crystal throne of the supreme being or from the vault of the sky. They show what is going on in the world and what is happening to the souls of the sick, and they also give man the power to fly" (101). By contrast, in *The Penguin Dictionary of Symbols,* Chevalier and Gheerbrant note that "Crystal is a foetus, born from the rocks in the ground" (267). Equally pertinent is the picture of the human eye in profile, with "The [blue] crystallike dot in the center of the lens [seen as] a reflection of light," in Lennart Nilsson, Jan Lindberg, et al., *Behold Man: A Photographic Journey of Discovery inside the Body,* trans. Ilona Munck (1973: Boston: Little, 1974) 180. *Writing under Erasure*

cuboid and blind: A *cuboid* is "a three-dimensional space" that allows us "to move in six directions: Left, Right, Forward, Backwards, Up and Down. This is the universe [which] we are familiar with" ("Of Hidden Dimensions and Intergalactic Space Travel," *fuzzlabs* 2 <fuzzlabs.wordpress.com>. Accessed on 1 Jan. 2015). See also Gary Weise, *The Origin of Space, Stars, Planets, and Life* (Pittsburgh, PA: RoseDog Books, 2009) 112: "Mathematics is cuboid logic, which cannot be more than an approximation of the actual geometry of the actual [spheroid] universe." Here, a *blind* is "anything that obscures or prevents sight" ("Blind" [n.], def. 1). *Testing the Night of Pan*

A cyborg I grazed with pumice a bat, / A bird like a tomb, inside it a gnat: a variation on "one of the 'Platonic Riddles' [that] runs: 'A man that was not a man, seeing yet not seeing, in a tree that was not a tree, smote but did not smite with a stone that was not a stone a bird that was not a bird, sitting yet not sitting.' The solution is: A one-eyed eunuch grazed with pumice-stone a bat hanging from a bush." According to Jung, the latter Hermetic jest—based on the Riddle of the Eunuch that, in his discussion of the ambiguity of evaluative adjectives, Plato paraphrases in Book V of the *Republic* (c. 380 BC) and that the alchemist Michael Maier mentions in *Symbola aureae mensae* (AD 1617)—"formulates transcendental concepts" even as it expresses "transconscious facts" (*Mysterium Coniunctionis* 82). *Platonic Riddles*

Cyborgs that frisk: A cyborg is "a hypothetical human being modified for life in a hostile or alien environment by the substitution of artificial organs or other body parts" ("Cyborg" [n.], def.). In this stanza, *Cyborgs that frisk* gambol, i.e., "move about in a playful, lively manner" ("Frisk" [vi.], def.). *History's Thread*

cyborgs that grind: here, hybrid organisms with bio-mechanical bodies that operate like machines. *Quintessence*

Cygnus: A constellation in the Northern sky also known as "the Swan," *Cygnus* "has 10 stars with known planets," including Deneb, which is "the 19th brightest star in the sky." See "Cygnus," *Constellation Guide* 2-3 <www.constellation-guide.com>. Accessed on 21 Apr. 2017. *Kepler*

cynosure: "any person or thing that is a center of attention" ("Cynosure" [n.], def.)—here, in outer space, any *human* subject. *History's Thread*

Dacron: a synthetic polyester fiber used to construct the anti-abrasion outer layer of the Space Shuttle suit assembly. See "The Spacesuit," *Space Educators' Handbook* 3 <er.jsc.nasa.gov>. Accessed on 16 Sept. 2016. *Pseudosphere*

dapple: "to cover or become covered with spots, as of a different color" ("Dapple" [vi.], def.). *Pushing Gravity*

D-brane: a concept named after the mathematician Johann Dirichlet (1805-1859)—dimensional space into which energy can flow once it leaves its quantum string. In brane cosmology, since elementary particles are thought to be neither more nor less than vibrational states of quantum strings, conservation of energy demands that each open string must have its unjoined endpoint attached to a *D-brane*. *Bulk; History's Thread; Hubble Ajar; Life in a Mortal Universe; Life Out There; Mandragora's Dream; Mapping Celestial Terrains; The Möbius Strip; The Quilted Multiverse; A User's Guide to Spacetime*

Demiurge: "in Platonism, a deity or creative force that shaped the material world" ("Demiurge" [n.], def. 1a). See also Jung, *Alchemical Studies* 221n2: According to Zosimos of Panopolis, a third-century Egyptian-born Greek alchemist and Gnostic mystic, Mercurius is "'the First Author, the cause and demiurge of creation; wherefore he is called [Hermes] Trismegistos [. . .].'" In other words, "the classical Hermes" is equivalent to the later figure of the alchemical Mercurius and is therefore "the analogue of Christ" (235). *Plato's Cave*

dendrite: "the branched part of a nerve cell that carries impulses toward the cell body" ("Dendrite" [n.], def. 3). *Bystander Cyborgs*

Deneb: one of "three first magnitude stars [including Vega and Altair] visible during the summer" in the Northern skies ("Summer Triangle," def.). *Spherical*

Didymus: the apostle Thomas—called *Didymus,* "the Twin"—who refused to believe that Jesus had risen from the dead until he saw the wound. See John 20.24-29. *Electrospinlacing*

the digit in the sore / Traversing the mandala, at its core: The *mandala* is the sacrosanct "magic circle," an archetype that is "found not only throughout the East but also among us" (Jung, *Alchemical Studies* 22) and that, according to Jung, is "the psychological expression of the totality of the self" (*Mandala Symbolism* 20). Here, the speaker—like the apostle Thomas—locates the deepest meaning of this symbol in the elliptical lance wound of the quaternary Christ, because "the blood and water that flowed out, signified those two great benefits which all believers partake of through Christ, justification and sanctification; blood for atonement, water for purification" ("Matthew Henry's Concise Commentary: John 19:34," *Bible Hub* 2 <biblehub.com >. Accessed on 18 Dec. 2016). *Nothing*

the dominant hemisphere: In human subjects, the left brain half is *dominant* because it is "endowed with most if not all [of] the language faculties" and is "the only one capable of speech" (Harth, *Windows on the Mind* 189). By contrast, areas in the right brain half have been recruited for "manipulative skills" (190). *Bystander Cyborgs*

dragon in the froth: the tail-eating Ouroboros, both a symbol of totality and a "chthonic forerunner of the self" (Jung, *Mysterium Coniunctionis* 224). See also Chevalier and Gheerbrant, *The Penguin Dictionary of Symbols* 308: "dragons live in the water and cause springs to bubble up." *The Experiment of Eternity*

Dressed in his SenSuit: Here, dressed in a robotics suit worn like an exoskeleton, the real-time human teleoperator controls the movements of a virtual anthropomorphic "robot learner." See Horia-Nicolai Teodorescu, Abraham Kandel, and Lakhmi C. Jain, eds., *Soft Computing in Human-Related Sciences* (New York: CRC P, 1999) 42. *Techwed*

droids: humanoid robots. *Techwed*

Dust that shifts in the midnight of our dreams: either "a cluster of stars too distant to be seen separately with the naked eye" ("Stardust" [n.], def. 1] or "mortal remains disintegrated or thought of as disintegrating to earth or dust" ("Dust" [n.], def. 4b). See also Eccles. 3.19-20: "Men have no advantage over beasts; for everything is emptiness. All go to the same place: all came from the dust, and to the dust all return." *Bulk*

the dust that we pan: either the gold that we separate from gravel "by washing it in a pan" ("Pan[1]" [vt.], def.) or the *dust* that we follow, even as we pivot along a horizontal plane, like a movie camera ("Pan[3]" [vt.], def. 3b). See not only Gen. 2.7: "Then the Lord God formed a man from the dust of the ground and breathed into his nostrils the breath of life," but also Gen. 3.19: "Dust you are, to dust you shall return." *Precinct*

Each sensory datum above the ground / Preserves the psyche: Jung unravels this riddle in *Psychology and Alchemy* 146: "the principle of the unconscious is the autonomy of the psyche itself, reflecting in the play of its images not the world but *itself,* even though it utilizes the illustrative possibilities offered by the sensible world," in order to clarify its otherwise "irreconcilable" images—the numinous archetypes. In effect, "'since he is the eternal Creator of minds,' [. . .] God is contained in his own creation [. . .]," as Saint Augustine emphasizes in the *Confessions* and elsewhere (qtd. in C. G. Jung, *Synchronicity: An Acausal Connecting Principle,* trans. R. F. C. Hull [1960; Princeton: Princeton UP, 1973] 102n17). *Serious Reader*

Earthshine: See Engelbrektson, *Stars, Planets, and Galaxies* 60: "Two days after new phase, the moon is said to be a two-day-old waxing (increasing) crescent. At this time the light from the bright dayside of the earth falls on the dark nightside of the moon, and the entire face of the moon shines with a soft ashen glow called 'earthshine.'" *Bellicose Ares; Carrier; Quintessence*

Eclipse that we shun: The solar eclipse dismays the speaker, because, symbolically, "the sun must die as an essential part of the mystery of transformation" (Jung, *Mysterium Coniunctionis* 142). *Something to Live For*

eidola: a variant plural form of "eidolon"—images of "an ideal person or thing" ("Eidola" [n., pl.], def. 2). *Made*

Electrons that spin with strange antennae / Intuit their circuits: In *Other Worlds,* Davies explains that electrons, if liberated, "will spill out in many directions, spreading about like the ripples on a pond" (63). However, in the two-slit experiment popularized by the American physicist Richard Feynman in 1965, "The interference that occurs [. . .] cannot be between different electrons, or the pattern [on the detector screen] would disappear when only one electron at a time is used. It is an interference of probability," i.e., of probability waves. (67). In other words, for each electron, both slits "must be left open; either [slit] offers a potential path, though only one can be the actual path. Which one we can never know" (69). *Sunday*

Electrospinlacing: a process that involves the "charging and projecting of tiny fibers of polymer directly onto the skin" in order to create a streamlined, lightweight, "second-skin" Bio-Suit for NASA's deployed astronauts. In fact, according to Mark Wade, "Melt blowing of liquefied polymer could [also] be used to apply thin elastic layers [. . .] to advanced 3D forms generated by laser scanning." Wade adds that, in theory, "Wearable computers, smart gels," and even "conductive materials could be embedded between polymer layers." See "Bio-Suit," *Encyclopedia Astronautica* 2. Last updated in 2017. *Electrospinlacing; Hubble Ajar; Mandragora's Dream; Sunday*

elf: "In folklore the child motif appears in the guise of the *dwarf* or the *elf*" as a personification of "the hidden forces of nature" (Jung, *The Archetypes and the Collective Unconscious* 158). Jung adds that "It is hardly necessary to allude to the still living 'Christ-child' who, in the legend of Saint Christopher, also has the typical feature of being 'smaller than small and bigger than big.'" *The Whole Atlas*

Emmaus' meme: the still-evolving cultural belief that Jesus, having risen from the dead, walked with two disciples "to a village called Emmaus, which lay about seven miles from Jerusalem," and "'explained the scriptures'" to them (Luke 24.13-14, 32). *Sunday*

entelechy's numen: here, actualized essence—the immortal Self: the divine power that directs both growth and life. *Vas Bene Clausum*

Entropy: "a measure of the degree of disorder in a substance or a system: entropy always increases and available energy diminishes in a closed system, as [in] the universe" ("Entropy" [n.], def. 2). *Life in a Mortal Universe*

Entwined by the serpent, its pinwheel twirled: The speaker refers not only to Ouroboros, "the dragon devouring itself tail first," a divine figure regarded as both a self-described circle and a symbol of totality (Jung, *Psychology and Alchemy* 126), but also to the Milky Way, a spiral galaxy that—if seen from above—"would look like a large pinwheel rotating in space" (J. D. Myers, "The Milky Way Galaxy – Imagine the Universe!" *NASA* 1 <imagine.gsfc.nasa.gov>. Last updated on 8 Mar. 2017). *Segway*

esemplastic: shaped to unify heterogeneous elements. *Nothing*

Eternity is now: not only a declaration of earthly love as a conduit to psychological wholeness, an affirmation that the speaker italicizes in this poem, but also one of the concluding lines in "Something to Live For" (1952), a Paramount film directed by George Stevens and starring Joan Fontaine, Ray Milland, and Teresa Wright. See also John Donne's avowal of this Neoplatonic theme in "The Canonization": "The Phoenix ridle hath more wit / By us, we two being one, are it. / So to one neutrall thing both sexes fit, / Wee dye and rise the same, and prove / Mysterious by this love" (*Donne: Poetical Works,* ed. Sir Herbert Grierson [1933; New York: Oxford UP, 1967] 14: 23-27). *Something to Live For*

Even as a chain—some Homeric skein—: See Jung, *Psychology and Alchemy* 114n24: "The Homeric chain in alchemy is the series of great wise men, beginning with Hermes Trismegistus, which links earth with heaven. At the same time it is the chain of substances and different chemical states that appear in the course of the alchemical process" and that leads to the quintessence, i.e., not only to the aether, a pure fifth element after earth, fire, water, and air, but also, symbolically, to "the ever-hoped-for and never-to-be-discovered 'One'" (124). See also Homer, *The Iliad* 8.20-24, the source of alchemy's emblematic *chain,* where Zeus, "The driver of cloud" (8.41), boasts of his omnipotence: "out of the zenith hang a golden line [*chain*] / and put your weight on it, all gods and goddesses. / You will not budge the all-highest, mighty Zeus, / no matter how you try" (trans. Robert Fitzgerald [1974; New York: Anchor-Doubleday, 1975] 182). *Dreaming in Code*

Even as the stork expresses its rune / By Hermes' grave: the circle of the Moon: The journey or *peregrinatio* is often a symbol of the alchemical *opus*. Thus, in a treatise ascribed to Saint Albertus Magnus [c. 1200-1280], "'Alexander found the tomb of Hermes [Trismegistus] and outside it a certain tree with a glorious greenness inside. And on it there sat a stork [instead of a phoenix], as it were calling itself the circle of the Moon. And there he built golden seats and put a fitting end to his travels'" (Jung, *Psychology and Alchemy* 370n79). Here, not insignificantly, the *stork* functions as an *avis Hermetis,* like the goose and pelican, in a mystical "poem, verse, or song" ("Rune" [n.], def. 3b). *Peregrination*

Every human truth a last truth but one: See Jung, *Psychology and Alchemy* 26-27: In alchemical literature, since "Four signifies the feminine, motherly, [and] physical," while three represents "the masculine, fatherly, [and] spiritual [. . .], the uncertainty as to three or four" often amounts, in any definition of the holistic self, "to a wavering between the spiritual and the physical—a striking example of how every human truth is a last truth but one." *Beyond Gender*

Everyman is always a multitude: See *Psychology and Alchemy* 162, where Jung parses an alchemical text written by the pseudonymous author Eirenaeus Philalethes (George Starkey [1628-1665]): "The more you cling to that which all the world desires, the more you are Everyman, who has not yet discovered himself and stumbles through the world like a blind man leading the blind with somnambulistic certainty into the ditch. Everyman is always a multitude. Cleanse your interest of that collective sulphur which clings to all like a leprosy." *The Exaltations of the Nettles*

Everything is round: a precept that, here, the artifex upholds not only because "the alchemical *anima mundi,* like the 'soul of the substances,' is spherical" (Jung, *Psychology and Alchemy* 84n38), but also because every perceived symbol emanates from the "round, original form" of "the spiritual, inner and complete man" (Jung, *Mandala Symbolism* 9-10). *Serious Reader*

exaltations of the nettles burn: In the alchemical writings of Paracelsus (1493-1541), *nettles* "were used for medicinal purposes [. . .] and were collected in May because they sting most strongly when they are young. The nettle was therefore a symbol of youth, which is 'most prone to the flames of lust.'" Thus, "The allusion to the stinging nettle [. . .] is a discreet reminder that not only Mary but Venus, too, reigns in May." However, "Paracelsus remarks that this power can be 'changed into something else.' There are exaltations, he says, far more powerful than the nettle," and these are found not in "the physical elements, but in the heavenly ones" (Jung, *Alchemical Studies* 155). *The Exaltations of the Nettles*

Exalted from Earth till cleansed of its soil: Concerning the main theme of this poem—"the union of the whole man" not only with the *unus mundus,* but also with Christ, the Risen Savior of the *Macrocosm* [emphasis added], "the eternal ground of all empirical being" (534)—see the excerpt from the clarifying treatise written by the Paracelsist Bernardus Penotus and quoted in Jung, *Mysterium Coniunctionis* 222: "'As to how the son of man [*filius hominis*] is generated by the philosopher and the fruit of the virgin is produced, it is necessary that he be exalted from the earth and cleansed of all earthliness; then he rises as a whole into the air and is changed into spirit. Thus the word of the philosopher is fulfilled: He ascends from earth to heaven and puts on the power of Above and Below, and lays aside his earthly and uncleanly nature.'" Of course, in this poem, unlike the pneumatic "son" of the Gnostic alchemists, the reborn astronaut—now "quickened from the grave" and indwelt by the "Spirit-nature" of Christ—does return to Earth (Murray, *The Spirit of Christ* 166). *Travelling Forever in the Same Direction*

exoplanets: "planets beyond our own solar system. Thousands have been discovered in the past two decades, mostly with NASA's Kepler space telescope" (Elizabeth Howell, "Exoplanets: Worlds Beyond Our Solar System," *Space.com* 24 Aug. 2016: 1 <www.space.com >). *Life in a Mortal Universe*

the eyeball peered: the left eye of Horus, in Egyptian mythology a symbol of the waning moon. *Made*

***Falcon* alight:** Apollo 15's Lunar Module *Falcon,* which "swooped low over the Appenines before descending vertically to touch down near Hadley Rille on 30 July 1971." There, on the lunar surface, for the next three days, the astronauts James B. Irwin and David R. Scott "collected 77 kg of rock and soil samples," including the "'Genesis Rock,' a lump of white crystalline [plagioclase-rich] anorthosite, possibly a piece of the Moon's primordial crust." See Colin Johnston, "Apollo 15: Into the Mountains of the Moon," *Astronotes* 28 July 2011: 3, 5-7 <www.armaghplanet.com>. *Hercules in the Vessel of the Sun*

fane: a temple or a church. *Plato's Cave; Serious Reader; Writing under Erasure*

Feather-crowned: In *Symbols of Transformation,* Jung explains that, in the realm of myth, "Feathers symbolize power. The feather crown = [the] crown of sun rays, [or] halo." Apparently, "Crowning is in itself an identification with the sun." Thus, "the spiked crown appeared on Roman coins from the time when the Caesars were identified with *Sol invictus,*" i.e., "*Solis invicti comes:* 'companion of the unconquerable sun'" (88n18). *The Archivist*

feathers like a clue: See Chevalier and Gheerbrant, *The Penguin Dictionary of Symbols* 374: "A crown of feathers worn by kings and princes is a reminder of the Sun's rays and of the halo kept for the elect"—or, as in this poem, for a Sun-god. *Life Out There*

feathers like a swan: In *Symbols of Transformation,* Jung notes that "The sun-symbol of the bird rising from the water is preserved etymologically in the idea of the singing swan. 'Swan' derives from the [Indo-European] root *sven,* like 'sun' and 'sound.' This ascent signifies rebirth, the bringing forth of life from the mother, and the ultimate conquest of death [. . .]" (348). *The Weight of History*

feathers that chirr: birds that produce "a shrill, trilled sound" ("Chirr" [vi.], def.)—among them, the Rufous-tailed Hummingbird; the White-throated Magpie-Jay; and the Black-bellied Wren, the latter species an "exceptional" composer with "abilities to combine and [even to] arrange songs" (David M. Logue, "Black-bellied Wren: Sounds and Vocal Behavior," *The Cornell Lab of Ornithology: Neotropical Birds* 2009: 1 <neotropical.birds.cornell.edu>). See also *The Penguin Dictionary of Symbols* 373, where Chevalier and Gheerbrant remind us that "the symbolic function of feathers is linked with the ritual of ascent into Heaven and hence with second sight and divination." *Outrider*

feltwork like fuzz: In the evolution of the human brain, "The fiber network, in particular, which is composed of processes from glial cells and neurons, soon becomes so dense and intricate that it is justly called a *feltwork.* Migrating neurons must find their way through this maze and arrive at their appropriate locations. One of the fundamental puzzles of brain formation at this stage is how neurons find their way, assuming [that] their destinations are preordained. There is convincing evidence that the glial fibers provide guides for at least some of the wandering neurons. But this only shifts the locus of the puzzle. We must ask then how the glial fibers know in which direction to point, and as yet there is no answer to this question" (Harth, *Windows on the Mind* 111-12). *Made*

the field of the square inch: In *Alchemical Studies,* Jung defines this mystical concept as "the symbol for that which has extension." Thus, "the central white light" of the Tao "dwells in the 'square inch' or in the 'face,' that is between the eyes" (25). In other words, the Savior locates His kingship in the mind of each coheir: "a higher spiritual being [. . .] is invisibly born in the individual, a pneumatic body which is to serve as a future dwelling [. . .]." (51-52). See also Gal. 2.20: "I have been crucified with Christ: the life I now live is not my life, but the life which Christ lives in me [. . .]." *The Ultimate Fate of the Universe*

filius: in philosophical alchemy, the *filius macrocosmi,* the Son of the Macrocosm "equated with Christ." See Jung, *Alchemical Studies* 126-27 and 294. *Pneumatic*

Fingerprint the quasar: See Amina Khan, "Big, bright quasar from ancient universe stuns scientists," *LA Times* 25 Feb. 2015: 1-2 <www.latimes.com>: "Deep in the universe's past, astronomers have discovered a luminous quasar [a quasi-stellar object] powered by an enormous black hole [. . .]. As the quasar's light passes through the gas of the intergalactic medium, the stuff in the gas—hydrogen, helium and other elements—leaves an imprint on the light's fingerprint. Scientists can read this fingerprint to learn about the abundance of different elements in the universe's early history." *Spherical*

flask: "any small, bottle-shaped container with a narrow neck, used in laboratories [. . .]" ("Flask" [n.], def. 1). *Siblings of the Sun*

flint that primes: a wonder-working stone that prepares or makes ready. See Jung, *Alchemical Studies* 100: "Among the Wichita, the saviour was the great star in the south, and he performed his work of salvation on earth as the 'flint man.' His son was called the 'young flint.' After completing their work, both of them went back into the sky. In this myth, just as in medieval alchemy, the saviour coincides with the stone, the star, the 'son' [. . .]." *Kepler*

foam: "the sponge-like structure of the world canvas" (Davies, *Other Worlds* 96). *Quintessence; The Weight of History*

foetus in its wain: the ever-gestating NASA astronaut couched in his womblike spacecraft. A *wain* is a wheeled vehicle—either "a wagon" or, here, a Sun-"cart," a metonym for Phoebus, the Greek God of Light ("Wain" [n.], def.). *Pushing Gravity*

a foot restraint my prop: an image meant to evoke an historic spacewalk. On 3 November 2007, the Space Shuttle Discovery having docked with the International Space Station, the NASA astronaut Scott Parazynski led the EVA (Extra-Vehicular-Activity) team in the fourth session of the STS-120 mission while "anchored to a foot restraint on the end of the Orbiter Boom Sensor System (OBSS)." See "Spacewalk to repair the Station's torn solar array," *Space in Images* 11 Dec. 2007: 2 <www.esa.int>. *Canadarm*

the foremost of the dead: In Col. 1.18, Christ is portrayed as the "origin" of the Church, because He is "the first to return from the dead," or, in another translation of the latter phrase, because He is *the foremost of the dead,* "to be in all things alone supreme." Thus, in this poem, the speaker suggests that, as His believer-priests, since we are "all one person in Christ Jesus" (Gal. 3.28), we partake not only of His resurrection, but also—more than other denizens of the Earth—of His supremacy. Dr. Dan Hayden clarifies this epithet in "Preeminence–Colossians 1.18," *A Word from the Word* 1-3 <www.awordfromtheword.org>. Accessed on 19 June 2017. *Symbiote*

Forever the scion of four and three: a reference to the "axiom of Maria" (a legendary Hebrew prophetess also known as the sister of Moses)—"'One becomes two, two becomes three, and out of the third comes the One as the fourth'" (Jung, *Psychology and Alchemy* 160). However, Jung observes that, in alchemical literature, since "Four signifies the feminine, motherly, [and] physical," while three represents "the masculine, fatherly, [and] spiritual [. . .], the uncertainty as to three or four" amounts, in any definition of the holistic self, "to a wavering between the spiritual and the physical—a striking example of how every human truth is a last truth but one" (26-27). *The Spherical Glass Vessel*

For thousands of miles Jupiter flashes: The voyage to *Jupiter* intensifies. Cf. Moore, *Travellers in Space and Time* 54: "Next, we pass over Jupiter's night hemisphere, the side turned away from the Sun. A brilliant display of aurorae stretches for thousands of miles, basically similar in nature to the aurorae or polar lights which we see from high latitudes on Earth and which are caused by electrified particles entering the upper atmosphere. The particles causing our aurorae come from the Sun, though it is more likely that those of the Jovian aurorae are due to the active volcanoes on Io," one of the four moons discovered by Galileo in 1610. *Tipler's Subset*

Four in Pegasus: According to the science writer Dennis Overbye, "Astronomers have recorded direct images of four planets swirling like olives in a martini glass around a star known as HR 8799, 130 light-years from Earth in the constellation Pegasus [. . .]" ("Gazing Afar for Other Earths, and Other Beings," *The New York Times* 30 Jan. 2011: 2 <www.nytimes.com>). *Life Out There*

The four times three: a numinous mathematical construct: "the trinity of [S]pirit" twined with "the foursquare reality of [E]arth" (Sallie Nichols, *Jung and Tarot: An Archetypal Journey* [Boston: Weiser, 1980] 221). See also *The Archetypes and the Collective Unconscious* 231, where Jung explains the meaning of "the number 12," even as he reminds us that "Twelve is four times three," a reconfiguration of the axiom of Maria Prophetissa, "that peculiar dilemma of three and four [. . .]. I would hazard that we have to do here with a *tetrameria* (as in Greek alchemy), a transformation process divided into four stages of three parts each, analogous to the twelve transformations of the zodiac and its division into four. As not infrequently happens, the number 12 would then have a not merely individual significance [as one's birth number, for instance], but a time-conditioned one too, since the present aeon of the Fishes is drawing to its end and is at the same time the twelfth house of the zodiac" (310). In short, as Jung also indicates in *Mysterium Coniunctionis,* since the soul "was imprinted with a horoscopic character at the time of its descent into birth," the journey of each mystic traveler through the planetary houses "boils down to becoming conscious" now of one's "godlikeness" (231). *Blazar/Quasar; Nothing*

Fractals everywhere: In Mathematics, a fractal is a never-ending pattern; the subset of a self-similar, "geometrically complicated" space, including such "real-world data" as a cloud, a feather, a galaxy, a leaf, "the distribution of frequencies of light reflected by a flower, the colors emitted by the sun, and the wrinkled surface of the sea during a storm" (Michael Barnsley, *Fractals Everywhere* [San Diego: Academic-Harcourt, 1988] 6, 172-73). *The Self-Thinking Thought*

From my spacecraft, I track leprous granges: From his rocket-launched Orion *spacecraft,* the speaker scans the toxic [perchlorate-ridden] soil of Mars, the site of future space farming. See Sarah Buhr, "NASA Astronauts Can Already Farm on Mars," *TechCrunch* 4 Oct. 2015: 6-7 <techcrunch.com>: NASA's Mission to Mars, set for 2020, "includes a robotic exploration that could address some key questions about sending humans to settle the red planet. While it's unclear if part of that exploration includes experimental farming, NASA will be testing ways to extract oxygen from the carbon dioxide on the planet, in preparation [not only] for possible human exploration in the future, [but also] for possible farming." *History's Thread*

frumentum nostrum: In alchemy, "One of the synonyms for the lapis, which likewise signifies the inner, integrated man, is 'frumentum nostrum' (our grain)." See Jung, *Alchemical Studies* 310. *Pneumatic*

furze: "a shrub associated with the Spring equinox"—a universal symbol of resurrection—because of its longevity and "with the Celtic god of light" (Lugh) because of its "vibrant yellow flowers." See "Gorse Tree in Celtic Mythology," *Ireland Calling* 4-5 <ireland-calling.com>. Accessed on 18 Oct. 2016. *Electrospinlacing*

Gaea's double spouse: either NASA's telepresent human astronaut, along with Robonaut, his deployed autonomous counterpart, or, simply enough, the archetypal sun-moon *rebis* manifested as the biform, Spirit-sown cyborg. *To Mars in a Month*

Gaea's joining rings: either the waist ring or the snap-and-lock connecting rings that the Apollo astronaut adjusts when he dons the Space Shuttle extravehicular mobility unit, or EMU. See Kerry Mark Joels, Gregory P. Kennedy, and David Larkin, *The Space Shuttle Operator's Manual* (New York: Ballantine, 1982) 3.12, 3.13. *Writing under Erasure*

Gaea's mace: a ceremonial staff carried as a symbol of authority by the Goddess of the Earth. *Terraforming Mars*

Gaea's starry messenger: the born-again, Spirit-centered astronaut. *Travelling Forever in the Same Direction*

Gaea's truce: more than a pledge, a compact made between Gaea, the Supreme Mother of all life, and NASA's spacewalking astronaut that they must work, even as unequal partners, to preserve each other. *Keeper of the Hubble*

Gaea's whitest brainstone: According to the philosophical alchemists, the divine secret in matter was to be found in the human brain. See *Mysterium Coniunctionis* 435-36, where Jung notes that "The 'Liber [Platonis] quartorum' calls the brain the 'abode of the divine part'" [in *Theatrum chemicum* V (1622): 124] and the "treatise on the 'Stone of Philosophy' says that 'alabaster is whitest brain stone'" [in *Collection des anciens alchimistes grecs* III (1888): xxix, 4]. Jung adds that the alchemists also connected the "white stone" to Rev. 2.17: "and I will give him a white pebble [. . .] and upon the pebble a new name written, which no one knows except him who receives it" (436n260). *Heracles Peeled*

gamonymous: here, the adjectival form of "gamonymus": "having the name of matrimony" (Jung, *Mysterium Coniunctionis* 465). *Electrospinlacing; Hubble Ajar; Namespace; Pneumatic; Pseudosphere; Saffron of the Metals; Travelling Forever in the Same Direction; The Ultimate Fate of the Universe; Writing under Erasure*

gamonymus: In *Alchemical Studies,* Jung defines the Greek term *gamonymus* as "a kind of chymical wedding," i.e., as the sealed product of the "indissoluble, hermaphroditic union [of Sol and Luna]" (136). *Body of Evidence; Life Out There; The Teleoperator's Dream; The Weight of History*

Gel Suit: The speaker refers to the Thermal Gel Suit, one of several "candidate" designs for NASA's future Bio-Suit. In this variation, "smart polymer gels" expand "at a threshold temperature [in order] to create mechanical counter-pressure." Thus, the smart gel "is trapped in a quilted layer beneath a stretchless restraint layer." In effect, the restraint layer prevents "outward expansion of the gel, [thereby] directing the pressure inwards against the body." See Wade, "Bio-Suit," *Encyclopedia Astronautica* 2. *Electrospinlacing*

Gemini crowned: here, not only the zodiacal constellation located in the Northern Hemisphere, but also the human counterparts of its two brightest stars, Castor and Pollux. In many accounts of the Greek and Roman myth, Castor, the mortal twin of the immortal Pollux, represents the hyphenated God-man, since he lives half of each year on earth and half in heaven. *The Limits of the Coded World*

Geryon: in the well-known Greek tale of Hercules' tenth labor, "a monster with three bodies living on Erythia, a western island" that lay beyond the sea (Hamilton, *Mythology* 165). Hercules' task was to steal the sun-cattle of *Geryon* and to deliver them to Eurystheus, the King of Mycenae. Not insignificantly, Helios, the god of the sun, had lent Hercules "the sun-ship which he used for crossing the sea" (Jung, *Symbols of Transformation* 197), the latter setting "an image simultaneously of death and of life" (Chevalier and Gheerbrant, *The Penguin Dictionary of Symbols* 838). *Hercules in the Vessel of the Sun*

Ge's errant satellite: the *Palapa B-2* communications satellite, which the NASA astronauts Joseph P. Allen and Dale A. Gardner captured even as they performed an EVA during the second *Discovery* mission on 12 November 1984. See Cliff Lethbridge, "STS-51A Fact Sheet," *Spaceline.org* 1-2 <www.spaceline.org>. Accessed on 19 Jan. 2018. *Wayfinder*

Ge's Light-bringer: the Son of God, the source-point of the archetypes. See Rev. 22.16: "'I, Jesus, have sent my angel to you with this testimony for the churches. I am the scion and offspring of David, the bright star of dawn.'" *Kepler*

Ge's Martian pod, with NASA's Xenon strobe: the planet Mars compared to "a seed vessel" ("Pod" [n.], def. 1) photographed by a *strobe,* or a stroboscope, "a device using a rapidly flickering flash tube that illuminates a moving body very briefly at frequent intervals" ("Stroboscope" [n.], def. 1). *Xenon* (ZEE-non) is "a gaseous chemical element," a component of "electric luminescent tubes" ("Xenon" [adj.], def.). *Mapping Celestial Terrains*

Ge's *rebis* beyond gender, I am judged: The *rebis* is "The dual being born of the alchemical union of opposites" (masculine/feminine) and recognized "as a symbol of the self" (Jung, *Aion* 268). See also Gal. 3.28, a passage that celebrates with equal fervor the divine androgyny of the Christian coheir: "There is no such thing as Jew and Greek, slave and freeman, male and female; for you are all one person in Christ Jesus." *Beyond Gender*

Ge's sapphirine *rebis,* without a seam: i.e., the "visible seam or suture" with which the opposites (e.g., light/darkness; consciousness/unconsciousness) are united, as in the symbol of the [alchemical] hermaphrodite. By contrast, in the higher Adam, "the opposition is invisible" (Jung, *Aion* 248). *The Self-Thinking Thought*

Ge's Spagyric: according to the sixteenth-century Belgian alchemist Gerhard Dorn, the "'child of the two parents, of the elements and heaven'" (Jung, *Mysterium Coniunctionis* 482). *Techwed*

Ge's whole atlas: not only the hero from Greek mythology, "a Titan compelled to support the heavens on his shoulders" ("Atlas" [n.], def.), and hence "any person who carries a great burden" (def. 1), but also "a book of tables, charts, illustrations, etc. on a specific subject" (def. 2b)—here, the archetypal Self. *The Whole Atlas*

Ge's wounded healer: not only Chiron, the *wounded* centaur, and his student, Asclepius, in Greek mythology "the sunlike healer" (Paul Levy, "The Wounded Healer, Part 1," *Awaken in the Dream* 1 <www.awakeninthedream.com>), but also Jesus Christ, the crucified Savior, because "By His wounds [we] have been healed" (1 Pet. 2.24). *The Whole Atlas*

Gliese (GLEE-zuh): In the Kepler spacecraft's "kind of Gallop poll of worlds in the cosmos," *Gliese* is an exoplanet "composed almost entirely of superheated water" and, for that reason, is "sometimes called the Steam World"; however, among astronomers, "it is known [more specifically] as Gliese 1214b, about 40 light-years from here in the constellation Ophiuchus" (Overbye, "Gazing Afar for Other Earths, and Other Beings" 1-2). *Life Out There*

Gliese [581]: a red dwarf star located about 20 light years from Earth in the constellation Libra and supporting a (possibly) life-sustaining planetary system. See Dennis Overbye, "20 light years away, the most Earthlike planet yet," *The New York Times* 25 Apr. 2007: 1-3 <www.nytimes.com>, and also Overbye, "A Planet 'Just Right' for Life? Perhaps, if It Exists," *The New York Times* 20 Aug. 2012: 1-5 <www.nytimes.com>. *Life in a Mortal Universe*

glyph: "a pictograph [a hieroglyphic] or other symbolic character or sign, esp[ecially] when cut into a surface or carved in relief" ("Glyph" [n.], def. 1). *Figure Skater; Messenger*

The glyph of Libra: "Libra makes up one of the twelve 'houses' or signs of the astrological wheel. [. . .] The Libra symbol or glyph represents an equal sign and a setting sun." Its negative aspects, of which the speaker—a Libran—is well-aware, include indecision and the failure to commit. See "Libra Symbol," *Signs and Symbols* 2 <www.signology.org>. Accessed on 9 June 2014. *Figure Skater*

God made man because He loves stories: This line echoes the epigrammatical conclusion to an Hasidic parable that serves as the Prologue to Elie Wiesel's novel *The Gates of the Forest* (1964; New York: Schocken, 1995): "Then it fell to Rabbi Israel of Rizhyn to overcome misfortune. Sitting in his armchair, his head in his hands, he spoke to God: 'I am unable to light the fire and I do not know the prayer; I cannot even find the place in the forest. All I can do is to tell the story, and this must be sufficient.' And it was sufficient. God made man because He loves stories." *Namespace*

the god through the lap or in the ear / Or from the stone: In *Symbols of Transformation,* Jung, quoting the Christian theologian Clement of Alexandria (c. 150-215), observes that "the symbol of the Sabazius mysteries [a variant of the Mithraic mysteries] was 'The god through the lap: and that is a snake which is dragged through the lap of the initiates.'" According to Jung, an Orphic hymn that describes a similar ritual "suggests that the god [Bacchus] entered his devotees as if through the female genitals" (343). Elsewhere, Jung reminds us that Rabelais' Gargantua "was born from the ear of his mother" (211n7a) and Mithras "from a stone" (*Alchemical Studies* 97). *The Man Who Made a Copy of Himself; Shapeshifter; The Weight of History*

grapple: "a device consisting of two or more hinged, movable iron prongs for grasping and [shifting] heavy objects" ("Grapple" [n.], def. 2). *Pushing Gravity; Setting the Wheel on Fire*

Gravity is intense: it curves the sheet; / [. . .] Dispatches the universe at its teat: See Paul Davies, *The Mind of God: The Scientific Basis for a Rational World* (New York: Simon, 1992) 71, fig. 9: "Hatching a baby universe," where "The mother universe is represented by a two-dimensional sheet. Curvature in the sheet arises from gravitational effects. If gravity is intense enough, the curvature can produce a protuberance that forms a mini-universe connected by an umbilical cord or throat known as a 'wormhole.' From the mother universe the throat can appear as a black hole. Eventually the hole evaporates, severing the cord and dispatching the baby universe onto an independent existence." *Nothing*

The Great Red Spot: in Jupiter's atmosphere, "a huge oval more than 20,000 miles long. It was once thought to be an erupting volcano, but we know better today. The [Great] Red Spot is a whirling storm," an anticyclone—"a [majestic] phenomenon of Jovian 'weather'" (Moore, *Travellers in Space and Time* 50). *Tipler's Subset*

Gyroscope: During the STS-114 mission, Shuttle astronauts Soichi Noguchi and Stephen Robinson "swapped out one of four control moment gyroscopes (CMG) used to orientate the space station." See Tariq Malik, "Shuttle Astronauts Repair ISS Gyroscope in Second Spacewalk," *Space.com* 1 Aug. 2005: 2 <www.space.com>. *The Teleoperator's Dream*

gyve (JIVE): a shackle, fetter, or chain. *Setting the Wheel on Fire*

Hadron and Tevatron: atom smashers; enormous particle accelerators in which beams of protons and antiprotons are made to collide at the near-speed of light in order that scientists may probe, at infinitesimal scales, the structure of matter, space, and time. *Hermes' Nested Spiral*

Halos: The speaker refers to the "spherical distribution of stars and star clusters extending beyond the main body of certain galaxies" ("Halos" [n.], def. 1b), here, like "detached portions of the Milky Way" (Engelbrektson, *Stars, Planets, and Galaxies* 23). *Life in a Mortal Universe; Stewards of Creation*

Hand to the chin and elbow to the knee, / Acrouch as he broods he searches the key: a mild, even genial paraphrase of *The Thinker,* a bronze sculpture by Auguste Rodin. *Stewards of Creation*

Having fallen down from the moon, he strays: In alchemy, "Because of his half-feminine nature, Mercurius is often identified with the moon and Venus" (Jung, *Alchemical Studies* 226). Thus, "'He [Mercurius] has fallen down from the moon'" (226n10)—here, in "Tumbling Escher," not unlike the hyphenate cyborg, his human counterpart. *Tumbling Escher*

The heart of Her fire continues to stun: i.e., of Gaea's fire. Cf. Jung, *Alchemical Studies* 164: According to Paracelsus, the sixteenth-century philosophical alchemist, "The soul [. . .] dwells in the fire of the heart. [. . .] The heart is also the seat of the imagination" and is "the 'sun in [Man] the Microcosm.'" *Saffron of the Metals*

The heart yet migrates: See Jonathan Miller, *The Body in Question* (1978; New York: Vintage-Random, 1982) 25-26: "In man, the nerve segments which together form the neck and the arms are also the ones where the heart appears. The result is that the nerves bringing sensations from the heart are in the same segment as the nerves which bring sensation from the neck and arm. This relationship is preserved despite the fact that in the course of foetal development the heart migrates to a position which is quite remote from its original state. It sinks down through the neck into the thorax and comes to rest on the diaphragm, whose muscles are also derived from the neck segments. But the heart maintains its ancient Parliamentary representation, despite its position in the body: the neck, arm, and upper chest continue to feel the pain for it. [. . .] Such pains are archeological reminiscences of what we once were." *The Skin That I Live In*

heat sinks: A "heat sink" is "a part of a system designed to be at a lower temperature than its surroundings and used to dissipate heat from that system" ("Heat Sink" [n.], def.). See also Ben Guarino, "The amazing sweating robot," *The Washington Post* 17 Oct. 2016: 1-2 <www.washingtonpost.com>: "Like humans, robots generate heat when they perform tasks." However, since "Overheating may lead to failure, [. . .] successful roboticists 'put a lot of emphasis on heat dissipation and thermal management [. . .].' To that end, robots are designed with heat sinks, fins, fans and other cooling systems [. . .]." *Symbiote*

Heaven's key: In this poem, as in the story of Faust, the wondrous *key* unlocks "the dark creative power of the unconscious, which reveals itself to those who follow its dictates and is indeed capable of working miracles" (Jung, *Symbols of Transformation* 126). *The Archivist*

Heaven's starship: Ouroboros exhumed: a spacecraft shaped like *Ouroboros,* the snake that bites its own tail—in alchemy, not only a self-described circle, the *opus* that "proceeds from the one and leads back to the one" (Jung, *Psychology and Alchemy* 293 and fig. 147), but also a symbol of totality. *Quintessence*

Heaven's stray: the risen Jesus—in Luke 9.33, New *Heaven's* seminal hyphenate, the foremost among isolated specimens. *Travelling Forever in the Same Direction*

Heaves aside its stone as he might a door, / Re-enters the cavern: the site of Jesus' tomb, "which had been cut out of [a] rock and its entrance closed up with a wall made of stones and cement" and with "only a small opening through which one could enter." However, "This opening could easily be closed by rolling a round stone [. . .] in front of it" (John Wijngaards, *Handbook to the Gospels: A Guide to the Gospel Writings and to the Life and Times of Jesus* [Ann Arbor: Servant Books, 1979] 241). See also Mark 16.3-6: "When the Sabbath was over, Mary of Magdala, Mary the mother of James, and Salome [. . .] came to the tomb. They were wondering among themselves who would roll away the stone for them from the entrance to the tomb, when they looked up and saw that the stone, huge as it was, had been rolled back already. They went into the tomb, where they saw a youth sitting on the right-hand side, wearing a white robe, and they were dumbfounded. But he said to them, 'Fear nothing; you are looking for Jesus of Nazareth, who was crucified. He has been raised again; he is not here [. . .].'" *Something to Live For*

He came from outside, yet from inside grew, / A square, then a circle: not only a composite image of the total self, a psychologically quadratic figure (Jung, *Aion* 224), but also, in the surround of this poem, a hidden conceit: the squaring of the circle, an apt symbol of the alchemical *opus,* since the latter process "breaks down the original chaotic unity into the four elements and then combines them in a higher unity. Unity is represented by a circle and the four elements by a square." In other words, "The Spirit (or spirit and soul) is the *ternarius* or number three which must first be separated from the body [the fourth] and, after the purification of the latter, infused back into it" (Jung, *Psychology and Alchemy* 124-25). *Life Out There*

He capsuled the Spirit: Cf. 1 Cor. 3.16: "Surely you know that you are God's temple, where the Spirit of God dwells." *The Spherical Glass Vessel*

Hecate's (HECK-uh-teez) pail: the moon, since Hecate is a "lunar" as well as a "chthonian" goddess (Chevalier and Gheerbrant, *The Penguin Dictionary of Symbols* 489). See also *Psychology and Alchemy* 380n110, where Jung quotes a passage from the *Panarium* of Saint Epiphanius of Salamis (c. 310-403), a compilation of the doctrinal heresies still current in his own time, including the Manichean heresy that follows ("Haer. LXVI"): "And the son came and changed into human form, and showed himself to men as a man, although he was no man, and the people thought that he had been born. And when he came he made a device for the redemption of souls, and set up a wheel with twelve buckets [the zodiac], which is turned by the rotation of the sphere and raises the souls of the dying; these are caught by the rotation of the greater light, which is the sun, and purified and passed on to the moon, and thus is the disc of the moon filled, as we say." *Testing the Night of Pan*

Hecate's (HECK-itz) witchery: In Greek mythology, Hecate, a "spook goddess of night and phantoms," guards the gate of Hades (Jung, *Symbols of Transformation* 369). Here, she is even the mistress of primordial matter. *The Weight of History*

He clears the airlock: The speaker, a NASA astronaut, refers to the Quest Airlock, "a pressurized space station module consisting of two cylindrical chambers attached end-to-end by a connecting bulkhead and hatch. The airlock is the primary path for International Space Station spacewalk entry and departure for U.S. spacesuits, which are known as Extravehicular Mobility Units, or EMU's" (Jerry Wright, "International Space Station: Quest Airlock," *NASA* 18 Oct. 2013: 1 <www.nasa.gov>). However, in this stanza, the crewmember that the speaker describes is Robonaut, "a state-of-the-art" android designed to "perform its tasks under the control of a *human* [emphasis mine] operator" (Peter Menzel and Faith D'Aluisio, *Robo sapiens: Evolution of a New Species* [Cambridge: MIT P, 2000] 129. *Station*

He clothes himself in the shape of a bell: This image underscores the design of the *chasuble,* the outer priestly vestment that, originally, "was a very full garment, shaped like a bell and reaching almost to the feet all the way round" (*Saint Joseph Daily Missal* [New York: Catholic Book, 1959] 10). *Dreaming in Code*

He enters like the flash upon a screen: i.e., probabilistically, like the beam of light in Thomas Young's famous two-slit experiment (c. 1801), since "the scientists don't know which slit [on card or *screen*] the photon really goes through" (Avery Thompson, "The Logic-Defying Double-Slit Experiment Is Even Weirder Than You Thought," *Popular Mechanics* 11 Aug. 2016: 2 <www.popularmechanics.com>). *Space*

He hitches a ride to Europa's site: The speaker anticipates NASA's multiple missions to Jupiter. See Tariq Malik, "Bold New Missions to Jupiter and Saturn Planned," *Space.com* 18 Feb. 2009: 2-3 <www.space.com>: "NASA and the European Space Agency (ESA) are pushing ahead with proposals to send ambitious new missions to explore Jupiter, Saturn[,] and the many [satellites] that circle both planets," including "Jupiter's ice-covered [moon] Europa and Saturn's shrouded moon Titan." Spacecraft "would launch in 2020 from different spaceports with the goal of reaching Jupiter by 2026." *Beyond Gender*

Height with strings / Embedded in matter: either the imaginary strings that keep the Space Shuttle aloft or the "tiny one-dimensional filaments" of string theory (Greene, *The Elegant Universe* 422). *Writing under Erasure*

He knew the shape of the sun as it was: The speaker refers not only to the biblical Job, but also to any ego-defeated nomad who, having shattered the metaphysical view of the world, presumed to penetrate "the mysteries of the sun and was therefore cursed by God and made blind" (Jung, *Mysterium Coniunctionis* 156). Commenting on the hubristic individual who supposed that "he knew the shape of the sun," Jung remarks that, psychologically, such a misstep would mean that "he knew about the transformation of consciousness, but that it was abortive, so that instead of being illuminated he fell into deeper darkness" (156n328). *The Exaltations of the Nettles*

He mounted his triangle in the square: In many Hermetic texts, the sign for Mercurius, as an analogue of Christ, was "a triangle set in a square," the latter an apt image, in the medieval mind, of the penultimate stage in alchemical transformation, spirit and soul having been "separated from its body and, after the purification of the latter, infused back into it" (Jung, *Psychology and Alchemy* 125). *The Spherical Glass Vessel*

He perturbs the orbit to Ceres' share: Like other scientists, the NASA astronaut seeks to steer the dwarf planet Ceres out of its stable *orbit* in order to transfer water from its seemingly vast "interior ocean" to the surface of Mars. Thus, in his online essay "How Do We Terraform Ceres?" Matt Williams suggests that, "being the largest body in the asteroid belt, Ceres could become the main base and transport hub for future asteroid mining infrastructure," thereby allowing mineral resources as well as water to be diverted not only to Mars but also to the moon and Earth. See *Universe Today* 5 May 2016: 1, 6 <www.universetoday.com>. *Terraforming Mars*

Hephaestan hybrid, I chain-link the world: an amatory image that expresses, ironically, the builder-astronaut's sublime embracement of the world. By contrast, Hephaestus, the cuckolded artisan of the gods, had "ensnared" Aphrodite, his wife, in a chain-link net, "when he caught her in the arms" of Ares, her lover (Michael Grant, *Myths of the Greeks and Romans* [1962; New York: Mentor-New American, 1964] 65). *Canadarm*

Hephaestus: in Greek literature, the lame god who presides over fire, metals, and metallurgy. In Homer's *Odyssey,* he is also the husband of Aphrodite, the Goddess of Love. *Bulk; Canadarm; Heracles Peeled; Mandragora's Dream; The Man Who Made a Copy of Himself; Outrider; Postmodern; Pushing Gravity; The Quilted Multiverse; Quintessence; Saturday; Serious Reader; Setting the Wheel on Fire; Swain; Symposium; Terraforming Mars; Travelling Forever in the Same Direction; Vas Bene Clausum; A Walking Man I; The Weight of History*

Hephaestus' ichor: in Greek mythology, the ethereal fluid of the gods, here prepared by Hephaestus, the deformed God of Fire no less than the honored "workman of the immortals" (Hamilton, *Mythology* 34-35). *Travelling Forever in the Same Direction*

He polar-aligns while She guides his hand: Under Gaea's tutelage, the wayfinder learns that, in order to track an object across the sky, he must point the rotational axis of his telescope's equatorial mount "precisely toward the North Celestial Pole," around which all the stars seen from the Northern Hemisphere appear to rotate. See Richard McDonald, "Polar Alignment of Your Equatorial Mount" 1-2 <www.themcdonalds.net>. Accessed on 8 May 2016. *The Limits of the Coded World*

He pressures the darkness out of its slot: In his essay "Pushing Gravity," Tom Rowan ponders a cosmological dilemma: "If dark energy surrounds us and makes up 75% of our known universe, then it is likely that the bodies of matter [like us] that make up the visible universe are merely trespassing in dark energy's space-time." Therefore, it is not unreasonable to assume that "Dark energy would pressure the matter to reclaim its [lost] space," since "'nature abhors a vacuum.'" In other words, "Dark energy would necessarily 'push' from all directions at an equal and constant pressure" (1). *Pushing Gravity*

he proffers a stone, / Upon it a name that aeons have known: / [. . .] Shown to me alone: Cf. Rev. 2.17: "I will give him [. . .] a white stone, and on the stone will be written a name, known to none but him that receives it." See also *Thru the Bible with J. Vernon McGee, Volume V: 1 Corinthians—Revelation* (Nashville: Thomas Nelson, 1983), where McGee weighs a startling interpretation of the latter passage: "the people of Asia Minor to whom John was writing had a custom of giving to friends a *tessera,* a cube or rectangular block of stone or ivory, with words or symbols engraved on it. It was a secret, private possession of the one who received it. [Thus,] Christ says that He is going to give to each of His own a stone with a new name engraved upon it. I do not believe that it will be a new name for you and me but that it will be a new name for *Him.* I believe that each name will be different because He means something different to each one of us. It will be His personal and intimate name to each one of us" (909). *Messenger*

Heracles peeled: *Heracles* (or Hercules) is the sun-hero "who submits to arduous labours and to the passion of self-cremation" and sublimation "culminating in divinity" (Jung, *Psychology and Alchemy* 381, 307n36). After Deianeira had unwittingly given *Heracles,* her husband, "a splendid robe" anointed with the poisonous blood of his enemy, the Centaur Nessus, "A fearful pain seized him, as though he were in a burning fire" (Hamilton, *Mythology* 171). Other versions of the myth indicate that, in his first agony, *Heracles* pulled at the cloak in order to tear it off, but to no avail. *Heracles Peeled*

Hercules in the vessel of the sun: According to Jung, symbolically, *Hercules* descended into "the dark world of the unconscious," even as he undertook "the perilous adventure of the night sea journey, [. . .] whose end and aim is the restoration of life, resurrection, and the triumph over death" (*Psychology and Alchemy* 329). See also 334, fig. 171: "Hercules on the night sea journey in the vessel of the sun," a design on the "Base of an Attic vase (5th cent. B.C.)." *Hercules in the Vessel of the Sun*

He rends the circle of the spheres: In *Psychology and Alchemy,* Jung remarks that the Cabalistic idea of the pneuma—the world-penetrating Spirit—as the Son of God "who descends into matter and then frees himself from it in order to bring healing and salvation to all souls, bears the traits of a projected unconscious content [. . .]." Thus, here, in the opening line, "He [the god-man] rends the circle of the spheres and leans down to earth and water" because "he is about to project himself into the elements" (301-02). *Something to Live For*

He retrofires at G the bird that stands; / With swollen knobs, hypnagogic his hands, / Procures from its drawplate its rays like strands: a description of NASA's future Space Launch System (SLS) rocket ride to Mars, including a fiery blast off here fused with

Jung's analysis of a patient's "hypnagogic visions"—i.e., of numinous primordial fantasies buried beneath the threshold of consciousness in "the state intermediate between wakefulness and sleep" ("Hypnagogic" [adj.], def. 2). See Jung, *Symbols of Transformation* 185: "a patient in a hypnagogic condition saw his mother painted on a wall, like a mural in a Byzantine church. She held up one hand, wide open, with splayed fingers. The fingers were very large, swollen at the ends into knobs, each surrounded by a small halo. The immediate association with this image was the fingers of a frog [. . .], then the resemblance to a phallus. The antiquated setting of the mother-image is also important. Presumably the hand in this fantasy had a spermatic and creative significance. This interpretation is borne out by other fantasies of the same patient: he saw what looked like a sky-rocket going up from his mother's hand, which on closer inspection proved to be a shining bird with golden wings—a golden pheasant, it then occurred to him. We have seen in the last chapter that the hand actually has a phallic meaning, and that it plays a corresponding role in the production of fire. Fire is bored with the hand [as in the twirling of an ancient firestick on its pointed end]; therefore fire comes from the hand; and Agni [the Vedic fire god of Hinduism] was worshipped as a golden-winged bird." *Heracles Peeled*

He rides upon an escalating floor: The speaker refers not only to the structure of the Earth, with layers that include crust, mantle, and core, but also to the rotation of the Earth on its own axis even as it revolves around the sun. *Something to Live For*

hermeneut: either an interpreter or a translator, especially of scriptural texts. *A User's Guide to Spacetime*

Hermes: In Greek mythology, *Hermes,* "the god who serves as herald and messenger of the other gods," is "generally pictured with wingèd shoes and hat, carrying a caduceus [. . .]" ("Hermes" [n.], def.). His Roman counterpart is Mercury. Significantly, Jung notes that, in alchemical literature, "Hermes or Mercurius possessed a double nature, being a chthonic god of revelation and also the spirit of quicksilver, for which reason he was represented as a hermaphrodite" (*Psychology and Alchemy* 65). Here, of course, the proper noun *Hermes* refers less to the herald of the gods who is also the "guide of departed souls" than it does to the "Feather-crowned" *human* speaker himself. *The Archivist; Beyond Gender; Body of Evidence; Carrier; Compass; Dreaming in Code; Electrospinlacing; Life Out There; Mandragora's Dream; Messenger; Peregrination; Plato's Cave; Postmodern; Pseudosphere; The Self-Thinking Thought; Serious Reader; Shapeshifter; Something to Live For; The Spherical Glass Vessel; Station; Techwed; Terraforming Mars; To Live and Work in Deep Space; To Mars in a Month; Travelling Forever in the Same Direction; A Walking Man I*

Hermes cultivates Ge's arsenic soul: In alchemy, "'Arsenic' originally meant 'masculine, manly, strong' [. . .] and was essentially an arcanum, as [Martin] Ruland's *Lexicon* [1622] shows. There arsenic is defined as [a Rebis or] an 'hermaphrodite, the means whereby Sulphur and Mercury are united. It has communion with both natures and is therefore called Sun and Moon.' Or arsenic is 'Luna, our Venus, Sulphur's companion' and the 'soul'" (Jung, *Mysterium Coniunctionis* 164). Here, the adjectival form of the word is pronounced ar-SEN-ik. *Carrier*

Her peacock feather placed upon His tray: In many civilizations, the *feather* is a symbol associated with the ritual of ascension as well as of sacrifice (Chevalier and Gheerbrant, *The Penguin Dictionary of Symbols* 373-74). Here, Gaea's *peacock feather* is *placed,* aptly enough, upon the paten, the small metal plate used to hold the Eucharistic bread, since "The peacock [itself] is an ancient symbol of resurrection, like the phoenix," and "annually renews" its plumage (Jung, *Mysterium Coniunctionis* 290-91). *Travelling Forever in the Same Direction*

He saves Admetus from his fear of ghosts: The speaker alludes to one of the definitive tales about Hercules, "the greatest hero of Greece" (Hamilton, *Mythology* 159), who was the son of Zeus, the "Lord of the sky" (27), and Alcmene, a mortal woman. After Alcestis, the wife of *Admetus,* had died, Hercules "went down to Hades," wrestled with Death, and returned Alcestis to her astonished husband, who thought at first that she was a ghost (170). Hamilton remarks that "no other story about Hercules [. . .] shows so clearly his character as the Greeks saw it"; in other words, "not even Death was his match." *Hercules in the Vessel of the Sun*

He scans at infrared: Since 2004, the Visual and Infrared Mapping Spectrometer (VIMS), an instrument onboard the Cassini Spacecraft, has helped scientists to obtain—among other images—"the glow of auroral emissions" in Saturn's polar regions; "carbon dioxide ice on Phoebe, a small moon very distant from Saturn"; "an ice volcano on the moon Titan and fresh ice along the 'tiger stripe' fractures on the moon Enceladus," as well as spectral variations in the regolith texture of Saturn's main rings. See "Visible and Infrared Spectrometer (VIMS)," *NASA Jet Propulsion Laboratory* 2-3 <saturn.jpl.nasa.gov>. Accessed on 24 Jan. 2017. *Mapping Celestial Terrains*

He secures a path to Hephaestus' pair: The nomadic astronaut—here, a surrogate Hermes: the herald of the gods—refers not only to the regimen of Mars and of Venus, alchemical procedures that represent cyclical death and renewal, but also to the planets that NASA seeks to terraform. *Terraforming Mars*

He sets His lancet upward in the air: Cf. the figures of the two Mithraic dadophors, the torch-bearers Cautes and Cautopates, "one with a raised and the other with a lowered torch," in Jung, *Symbols of Transformation* 200 and in pl. xxb. In the Persian solar myth, like the rising and setting suns, "One [brother] would stand for death, the other for life." *The Limits of the Coded World*

He shapes his egg: See Jung, *Psychology and Alchemy* 202: "In alchemy the egg stands for the chaos apprehended by the artifex, the *prima materia* containing the captive world-soul. Out of the egg—symbolized by the round cooking-vessel—will rise the eagle or phoenix, the liberated soul, which is ultimately identical with the Anthropos who was imprisoned in the embrace of Physis [. . .]." Elsewhere Jung reminds us that "It is the *punctum solis* [the sun-point] in the egg-yolk that grows into a chick" (*Aion* 220) and that, since the vessel is the *ovum,* "The egg is content and container at once" (239n53). *Vas Bene Clausum*

He sought to be neither woman nor man, / But both these sexes: a description of the *rebis,* "The dual being born of the alchemical union of opposites" (masculine/feminine) and recognized "as a symbol of the self" (Jung, *Aion* 268). See also Rabbi Mark Sameth's illuminating essay "Is God Transgender?" in *The New York Times* 13 August 2016: A17: "the Hebrew Bible, when read in its original language, offers a highly elastic view of gender. And I do mean *highly* elastic: In Genesis 3:12, Eve is referred to as 'he.' In Genesis 9:21, after the flood, Noah repairs to 'her' tent. Genesis 24:16 refers to Rebecca as a 'young man.' And Genesis 1:27 refers to Adam as 'them.' [. . .] And there are many other, even more vivid examples: In Esther 2:17, Mordecai is pictured as nursing his niece Esther. In a similar way, in Isaiah 49:23, the future kings of Israel are prophesied to be 'nursing kings.' Why would the Bible do this? These aren't typos. [The answer is that] In the ancient world, well-expressed gender fluidity was the mark of a civilized person. Such a person was considered more 'godlike.' [. . .] Counter to everything [that] we grew up believing," the God of Israel "was understood by its earliest worshippers to be a dual-gendered deity." (Even Rabbi Daniel Ross Goodman, a respondent who subsequently disagreed with the latter thesis, maintained that "Positing a transgender God is the kind of bold, imaginative thinking that we sorely need in contemporary theology" ["Gender Identity in Olden Times: Interpreting the Torah," *The New York Times* 19 August 2016: A20].) *Rebis*

He split them at the bottom of the stair: i.e., at the lowest rung of the Ladder of Love that Plato describes in the *Symposium,* a dialogue (c. 385-370 BC) in which Socrates shows how the true philosopher moves from the love of the beautiful body to the love of the beautiful soul and thereafter to the love of the immortal Form of Beauty itself; for, "in wanting the beautiful," Socrates tells Agathon, his misguided host, "love wants also the good"—in other words, wants God (Louise Ropes Loomis, ed., *Plato,* tr. B. Jowett [New York: Walter J. Black, 1942] 192). *Symposium*

Heterotic its patterns: The speaker refers to heterotic string, a fundamental component of matter: a closed string with two types of vibrations—the clockwise and the counterclockwise—"that [seemingly] live in two dimensions" of space. "That is why it is named after the Greek word for *heterosis,* which means '*hybrid vigor*'" (Kaku, *Hyperspace* 158). *Mandragora's Dream*

He undertook a journey to the sea: Like Joseph in the cistern, Christ in the sepulcher, and Jonah in the belly of the whale, Heracles descended into "the dark world of the unconscious," even as he actively pursued "the perilous adventure of the night sea journey [. . .], whose end and aim [in the archetypal solar myth] is the restoration of life, resurrection, and the triumph over death" (Jung, *Psychology and Alchemy* 329). *The Archivist*

He wandered like a wheel above the storm. / Ensconced in his bucket, salt in the swarm, / He capsuled the Spirit: a Hermetic variation on the twined themes of the glorified Jesus and of the indwelt believer-priest as the temple of God. See *Psychology and Alchemy* 380-81: "In the Manichean system the savior constructs a cosmic wheel with twelve buckets—the zodiac—for the raising of souls. This wheel has a significant connection with the *rota* or *opus circulatorium* of alchemy, which serves the same purpose of sublimation." *The Spherical Glass Vessel*

He wanders the hall where copies abound: The speaker navigates either a network of parallel universes—an illusory phenomenon not unlike a disorienting hall of mirrors—or a corridor of the spacious mind itself. *Serious Reader*

He wavers between the stone and the Son: i.e., between the Hermetic *lapis,* "the figure [of Christ] veiled in matter" (Jung, *Alchemical Studies* 247), and "the Spirit of the glorified Jesus," the *Son* of God (Murray, *The Spirit of Christ* 86). *Beyond Gender*

He wears his helmet like a feather-crest; / Silver-weaves the magus: In this stanza, the self-realized NASA astronaut, dressed in his spray-on, "second-skin" spacesuit, evokes Gaea's solar *rebis* even as he channels Gaea's coheir, His lunar *magus*. Cf. Jung, *Symbols of Transformation* 183: In the Native American culture, "the feather crest is a crown which is equivalent to the rays of the sun." In addition, see not only Jung, *Psychology and Alchemy* 244, fig. 125: "Mercurius as the sun-moon hermaphrodite (*rebis*), standing on the (round) chaos," but also Wisd. Sol. 5.16: "Therefore royal splendour shall be theirs, and a fair diadem from the Lord himself [. . .]." *Heracles Peeled*

Hidden or minimal, matter is dark: According to Brian Greene, "there is strong evidence, of both theoretical and experimental origin, that the universe is permeated with dark matter. This is matter that does not participate in the processes of nuclear fusion that powers stars and hence does not give off light; it is therefore invisible to the astronomer's telescope. No one has figured out the identity of the dark matter, let alone the precise amount that exists" (*The Elegant Universe* 235). *Mapping Celestial Terrains*

hierophant: either "a priest of a mystery cult," as in ancient Greece ("Hierophant" [n.], def. 1), or "a person confidently expounding, explaining, or promoting something mysterious or obscure as though appointed to do so" (def. 2). *Canadarm; Dreaming in Code; The Experiment of Eternity; Figure Skater; Herald; Life Out There; The Limits of the Coded World; The Man Who Made a Copy of Himself; Namespace; Prefigured; Pseudosphere; Pushing Gravity; The Quilted Multiverse; The Spherical Glass Vessel; Symbiote; A User's Guide to Spacetime; The Weight of History; The Whole Atlas*

the Higgs boson: the force-transferring particle that "generates symmetry breaking" (Kaku, *Hyperspac*e 183) and that helps to give other fundamental particles their mass. *Spherical*

His cyborg spectral or electrospun: The speaker alludes to the "spray-on" spacesuit that, in 2004, had been part of a study "on new mobility technologies for future astronauts." The project leader Dava Newman, an aerospace engineering professor at MIT, had argued that NASA's 300-pound (136 kilogram) spacesuit, though appropriate "for working in weightlessness," would be unwieldy for walking on Mars. As a result, her research group had considered "the possibility of spraying a layer of polymer fabric over an astronaut, in a booth much like those used for getting a spray-on suntan. The 'second-skin' suit could be augmented by temperature-control underwear, flexible joint attachments[,] and perhaps even an exoskeleton." See Alan Boyle, "NASA researchers investigate way-out ideas," *Space on NBC News.com* 20 Oct. 2004: 1 <www.nbcnews.com>. *Pushing Gravity*

His fingers large and swollen at the ends: a picture not only of the so-called "crepuscular rays"—the shafts of sunlight that occur during twilight hours, i.e., either at dawn or during dusk—but also of the moon's new or crescent phases, "when the sun is more or less behind the moon" (Daniel V. Schroeder, "The Moon and Eclipses," *Understanding Astronomy* 2010-11: 3 <physics.weber.edu>). Here, the image is phallic no less than astronomical. See also a fitting passage from *Alchemical Studies* 247, where Jung describes the dual form of the Son of God: In Christ, the second person of the Trinity, He is "the figure of light surpassing all lights," and in Mercurius, the analogue of Christ, "He is found in the vein swollen with blood." Equally germane is Jung's analysis, in *Symbols of Transformation,* of the fantasies of a patient who "saw his mother painted on a wall, like a mural in a Byzantine church. She held up one hand, wide open, with splayed fingers. The fingers were very large, swollen at the ends into knobs, each surrounded by a small halo. The immediate association with this image was the fingers of a frog [. . .], then the resemblance to a phallus" (185). *Pneumatic*

His hierophant tinctured: In this stanza, the speaker exalts the *tinctured*—i.e., the self-renewing—*hierophant:* the archetypal God-man of line 17, even as he compares His beatified soul to either a galactic star or the Eucharistic Host. For an incisive analysis of the astronaut's "alchemical dream language," see Jung, *Alchemical Studies* 297-302. *The Limits of the Coded World*

His labors form a cross by Clotho spun: In *Psychology and Alchemy,* Jung suggests that, as a sun-hero, Hercules is—like the Son of God in later Christian alchemy—"a sort of paradigm of sublimation," a myth-picture of the archetypal Redeemer "symbolized by the cross," a motif "often replaced by corresponding journeys" (368). Thus, "The Cretan bull led [Hercules] to the south; the man-eating mares of Diomedes to the north (Thrace); Hippolytus to the east (Scythia); and the oxen of Geryon to the west (Spain). The Garden of the Hesperides (the western land of the dead) leads on to the twelfth labour, the journey to Hades [. . .]" (369n75). *Hercules in the Vessel of the Sun*

His mother the moon, his father the sun: an excerpt from the exordium in the "Tabula Smaragdina," where the legendary first alchemist and emblematic magus Hermes Trismegistus describes "the 'sun-moon child' who is laid in the cradle of the four elements, attains full power through them and the earth, rises to heaven and receives the power of the upper world, and then returns to earth, accomplishing, it seems, a triumph of wholeness" (Jung, *Mysterium Coniunctionis* 219). The original article from Hermes' text reads as follows: "Its father is the sun, its mother the moon; the wind hath carried it in his belly; its nurse is the earth." *Siblings of the Sun*

His muscles pneumatic: In "High-Tech Spacesuits Eyed for 'Extreme Exploration,'" Leonard David reports that "Research is under way at the Massachusetts Institute of Technology (MIT) on a Bio-Suit System that incorporates a suit designed to augment a person's biological skin by providing mechanical counter-pressure. The 'epidermis' of such a second skin could be applied in spray-on fashion in the form of an organic, biodegradable layer. This coating would protect an astronaut conducting a spacewalk in extremely dusty planetary environments. Incorporated into that second skin would be electrically actuated artificial muscle fibers [designed] to enhance human strength and stamina" (*Space.com* 1 Jan. 2005: 2 <www.space.com>). *Pneumatic*

His *rebis* crowned, the Tree of Moon and Sun: In alchemy, the *rebis* is an androgyne, the "dual being born of the alchemical union of opposites" (masculine/feminine) and recognized "as a symbol of the self" (Jung, *Aion* 268). See also fig. 116 in Jung, *Psychology and Alchemy* 231: "Crowned hermaphrodite representing the union of king and queen, [standing] between the sun and moon trees." *Carrier*

His sapphirine *rebis:* a reference not only to the speaker as heavenly adept, but also to the "sapphire blue flower" of alchemy as birthplace of the spiritual hermaphrodite. See Jung, *Psychology and Alchemy* 80, fig. 30. *Mapping Celestial Terrains*

His scythe and His hourglass coated with rime: A curved cutting tool and a sandglass with upper and lower containers—traditional symbols of [Father] Time—are here covered with hoarfrost or icy crystals. *Plato's Cave*

His self-thinking thought: According to Aristotle, God, the Unmoved Mover, is also His own *self-thinking thought,* for "Mind thinks itself, if it is that which is best, and [then] its thinking is a thinking of thinking" (Aristotle, *Metaphysics,* vol. 2, section 1074b: 1, trans. Hugh Tredennick and G. Cyril Armstrong [1933; Cambridge: Harvard UP, 1989], *Perseus Digital Library* <www.perseus.tufts.edu>). *The Self-Thinking Thought*

holon: a whole embedded in larger wholes; hence, an entity—whether an atom or a universe—that is both a whole and a part. Arthur Koestler coined the term in *The Ghost in the Machine* (1967; New York: Arkana-Penguin, 1990) 48. *Bulk; Canadarm; The Möbius Strip; Platonic Riddles; Prefigured; Quintessence; Rebis; Saffron of the Metals; Saturday; Station; Stewards of Creation; To Mars in a Month; The Weight of History*

homunculus: "a little man; dwarf; manikin" ("Homunculus" [n.], def.). See also Jung, *The Archetypes and the Collective Unconscious* 293: "at the end of the *opus alchymicum,* the homunculus emerges, that is, the Anthropos, the spiritual, inner and complete man, who in Chinese alchemy is called the *chen-yen* (literally, 'perfect man')." Jung illustrates this concept vividly in *Psychology and Alchemy* 301, fig. 153, where the "artist" lifts "the homunculus, the 'son of the philosophers,' out of the Hermetic vessel." *Body of Evidence*

Horus' slot: the bony round *slot* or socket that contained the eye of Horus, the falcon-headed Egyptian sky god, the son of Isis and Osiris. His right eye represented the sun; his left eye, the moon. "His legendary battle with Set, whom he cut to pieces but who tore out one of his eyes [i.e., his moon-eye], is an example of the struggle [between] light and darkness [. . .]" (Chevalier and Gheerbrant, *The Penguin Dictionary of Symbols* 528). *Testing the Night of Pan*

Host in the mill: See Jung, *Psychology and Alchemy* 307, fig. 158: "The 'Mill of the Host.' The Word, in the form of scrolls, is poured into a mill by the four evangelists, to reappear as the Infant Christ in the chalice. (Cf. John 1:14: 'And the word was made flesh

. . . .')." *The Man Who Made a Copy of Himself*

Houseled, from Her brood-swarm, bees that yet buzz: The speaker refers not only to the precursor food of heroes—the meat and honey—that Samson had scraped from the carcass of a lion (Judg. 14.8-9), but also to the heavenly banquet—the bread and wine—that the priest dispenses to the faithful at the Lord's Supper. See also *The Bestiary of Christ,* trans. D. M. Dooling (1940; New York: Arkana-Penguin, 1992) 323, where Louis Charbonneau-Lassay indicates that "Christian symbolism, following that of the Ancients, accepted the bee as one of the emblems of resurrection and immortality," mainly because the honeybee disappears in the darkness of the hive during the winter season and then, like the risen Christ, "reappears in spring." *The Exaltations of the Nettles*

The House of Many Doors: a nod to the many-universes interpretation of quantum physics, an idea proposed by Hugh Everett in 1957 and developed later by Bryce DeWitt. Thus, in *Other Worlds,* Paul Davies concludes that "it is wrong to think of us as inhabiting one particular world of superspace: in the Everett theory, superspace itself is our home" (136). *Pneumatic*

How can he touch the earth when he is crowned? / [. . .] He concentrates till he reaches the ground: See Jung, *Alchemical Studies* 233: In alchemical texts, "the *filius macrocosmi* [the Son of the Macrocosm] starts from below, ascends on high, and, with the powers of Above and Below united in himself, returns to earth again." Thus, even in this poem, the indwelt Christian coheir—the NASA astronaut who is both "crowned" (l. 14) and "Quaternal as a precinct" (l. 10)—"has the circular nature of the uroboros [. . .]." *Precinct*

Hubble: i.e., the *Hubble* Space Telescope, named after Edwin Powell *Hubble* (1889-1953), an American astronomer who recognized, along with other astronomers, that the universe is expanding. Launched on the Space Shuttle *Discovery* on 24 April 1990, *Hubble,* the observatory, "is the first major optical telescope to be placed in space, the ultimate mountaintop. [. . .] Scientists have used Hubble to observe the most distant stars and galaxies as well as the planets in our solar system." See Rob Garner, "About the Hubble Space Telescope," *NASA* 2 <www.nasa.gov>. Last updated on 12 Dec. 2017. *Bellicose Ares; Blazar/Quasar; Hubble Ajar; Keeper of the Hubble; Life in a Mortal Universe; Saffron of the Metals; Wayfinder*

The humanoid wakens: Here, either an android rouses, or a cyborg, or even a being of our own species not yet fully human. *Heracles Peeled*

Hyades: the rainy stars, a galactic cluster located in the constellation Taurus (Engelbrektson, *Stars, Planets, and Galaxies* 28). In Greek mythology, the *Hyades* were the daughters of Atlas and the half-sisters of the Pleiades. They were also the nurses of Dionysus, the fertility god who "dared the terrible descent" to the underworld in order to rescue Semele, his mortal mother, from "the power of Death" (Hamilton, *Mythology* 56). *Hercules in the Vessel of the Sun*

A hybrid god, with hoofs instead of feet, / He fingers pipes of reed: i.e., Pan, in Greek literature, "a noisy, merry god [. . .], but he was part animal too, with a goat's horns, and goat's hoofs instead of feet." However, he "was a wonderful musician. Upon his pipes of reed he played melodies as sweet as the nightingale's song" (Hamilton, *Mythology* 40). *Testing the Night of Pan*

hylical water: in alchemy, a variant of the *prima materia,* "a dark sphere" of water that "the divine act of creation brought forth from the chaos" and that "contains a hidden elemental fire" (Jung, *Psychology and Alchemy* 325). *Serious Reader*

hyperbolic shell: i.e., a *hyperbolic* paraboloid *shell*—a "doubly curved" *shell* "with negative Gaussian curvature"—that is also called a Hypar *shell,* with a sub-class termed a Saddle-type *shell.* See M. Farshad, "Design of Hyperbolic Paraboloid Shells: Abstract," *SpringerLink* 1 <link.springer.com>. Accessed on 12 Feb. 2018. *Pseudosphere*

hypersee: to perceive visually with heightened knowledge and awareness. See Richard Werner's brief commentary on his own "construction" in plastic and wood titled "Meditations on $f(x,y) = (x^2)/2 + xy/2 - (y^4)/8$," the July entry in the *2011 Calendar of Mathematical Imagery* (Providence, RI: American Mathematical Society). Werner demonstrates that, in his work, "a myriad of delightful views of intersecting curves can be found," shapeshifting geometric forms that allow the observer "to hypersee the surface." *Tumbling Escher*

Hyperspace: "higher-dimensional space"—according to superstring theory, "the three dimensions of space (length, width, and breadth) and one of time [. . .] extended by six more spatial dimensions" (Kaku, *Hyperspace* vii-viii). *Blazar/Quasar*

hypnagogic: "designating or of the state intermediate between wakefulness and sleep" ("Hypnagogic" [adj.], def. 2). *Heracles Peeled*

I ascend to myself: In the *Liber de Spiritu et Anima,* Saint Augustine "attributes very great importance to self-knowledge, as being an essential condition for union with God. 'There are some who seek God through outward things, forsaking that which is in them, and in them is God. Let us therefore return to ourselves, that we may ascend to ourselves. . . . At first we ascend to ourselves from these outward and inferior things. Secondly, we ascend to the high heart. . . . In the third ascent we ascend to God'" (qtd. in Jung, *Alchemical Studies* 249n16). *Compass*

I become one with my kind: Cf. Tennyson, *Maud* 3: 55-56—"I have felt with my native land, I am one with my kind, / I embrace the purpose of God, and the doom assign'd." *Bystander Cyborgs*

I began to spin, then pulled in my arms / As if I were some cloud that formed the sun / Or newborn like a disk: The speaker compares his chance epiphany not only to the evolution of a protostar, but also to the rotational speed of a figure skater. To picture the phenomenon, see "Stars," *National Geographic* 3 <www.national geographic.com>: "Hydrogen is the primary building block of stars. The gas circles through space in cosmic dust clouds called *nebulae.* In time, gravity causes these clouds to condense and collapse in on themselves. As they get smaller, the clouds spin faster because of the conservation of angular momentum—the same principle that causes a spinning skater to speed up when [he] pulls in [his] arms." In effect, "Building pressures cause temperatures [to rise] inside such a nascent star, and nuclear fusion begins when a developing young star's core temperature climbs to about 27 million degrees Fahrenheit (15 million degrees Celsius)." Accessed on 10 Nov. 2016. *Figure Skater*

I board a mobile boom: i.e., the Orbiter Boom Sensor System, a 50-foot pole attached to the end of the Space Shuttle's robotic arm. Here, the speaker's climactic spacewalk may recall the famous EVA that occurred on 3 November 2007, during STS-120, "a highly complex space station assembly flight," when the NASA astronaut Scott Parazynski, "positioned by a 90-foot robotic boom," successfully repaired "a fully energized solar array wing." See "Bio," *Scott Parazynski* 2 <parazynski.com>. Accessed on 16 Jan. 2018. *Canadarm*

I carried it within me, like that stair, / Encoded in the chaos: The speaker alludes not only to DNA (deoxyribonucleic acid), the double-stranded molecule that carries "the chemical messages of inheritance from generation to generation" and that resembles "a sort of spiral staircase" (J. Bronowski, *The Ascent of Man* [Boston: Little, 1973] 90, 392), but also to the "icon that had disappeared" (l. 4)—i.e., the Spirit of Christ: the solar deity that dwells in the flesh—and to the astronaut's mystic identification with Him. See the pertinent passage in *Symbols of Transformation* 86-87, where Jung examines the "age-old" idea of "becoming a god": "To carry a god around in yourself means a great deal; it is a guarantee of happiness, of power, and even of omnipotence, in so far as these are attributes of divinity. To carry a god within oneself is practically the same as being God oneself. [. . .] Even Jesus proved his divine Sonship to the Jews" by citing Psalm 82.6: "'I said, You are gods'" (John 10.34). *Electrospinlacing*

I cross like a stone to the other side: See Jung, *Alchemical Studies* 101: "The connection of the lapis [the magical Hermetic stone] with immortality is attested from very early times." Thus, in a South African legend reported by the ethnologist Leo Frobenius (1873-1938), "the hero is left stranded by his pursuers on the bank of a river. He changes himself into a stone, and his pursuers throw him across to the other side. This is the motif of the *transitus:* the 'other side' is the same as eternity." *Something to Live For*

I don my spacesuit: See Gal. 3.27: "Baptized into union with him, you have all put on Christ as a garment," i.e., like a priest, but one vested for Mass, for "what is mortal must be clothed with immortality" (1 Cor. 15.53). Here, of course, the deployed NASA astronaut—the Keeper of the Hubble Space Telescope—functions as a symbol of the totalistic self. *Keeper of the Hubble*

I float in a jumble of spacesuit parts: In 1965, trials inside the cramped Gemini cabin involving the NASA astronaut's pressurized suit "left some engineers literally 'tangling' with the problem of a jumble of floating umbilicals, tethers, and jumper cables." See Ben Evans, "'A Finite Number of Heartbeats': The Trauma of Gemini VIII (Part I)," *AmericaSpace* 15 Mar. 2014: 2 <www.americaspace.com>. *The Weight of History*

I grieved an icon that had disappeared: The speaker laments the vanishing of the Sun, either because it had been momentarily eclipsed or, simply enough, because it had set. *Electrospinlacing*

I harness my cyborg to a gimbal: In 1960, the "gimbal rig, formally known as the MASTIF, or Multiple Axis Space Test Inertia Facility, was engineered to simulate the tumbling and rolling motions of a space capsule and train the Mercury astronauts to control" its pitch, roll, and and yaw "by activating nitrogen jets, used as brakes" ("Gimbal Rig in Motion," *NASA* 2 Aug. 2010: 1 <www.nasa.gov>). Of course, "NASA also used the [gimbal] rig" to calibrate its "physiological impact [upon] rapidly spinning astronauts" (Mika McKinnon, "NASA Tossed Astronauts with this Gimbal Rig Before Launching Them into Space," *Gizmodo* 1 Sept. 2015: 2 <gizmodo.com>). *Symposium*

I layer my body: an image of the vested astronaut that evokes the Cabalistic "formation of skins," the "inner consolidation" that "denotes a hardening or sealing off against the [unholy] outside" (Jung, *The Archetypes and the Collective Unconscious* 328). *Canadarm*

Imagination encircles the world: a statement attributed to Albert Einstein that exalts inspiration and intuition and that appeared in "What Life Means to Einstein: An Interview by George Sylvester Vierick," *The Saturday Evening Post* 26 Oct. 1929: 17. (See "Imagination Is More Important Than Knowledge," *Quote Investigator* 1 Jan. 2013: 2 <quoteinvestigator.com>.) *Pneumatic*

***I* measure gravity with an apple:** See Bronowski, *The Ascent of Man* 222: After Isaac Newton "conceived his idea of universal gravitation" in 1666, he "tested it by calculating the motion of the moon round the earth. The moon was a powerful symbol for him. If she follows her orbit because the earth attracts her, he reasoned, then the moon is like a ball (or an apple) that has been thrown very hard: she is falling toward the earth, but is going so fast that she constantly misses it—she keeps on going round because the earth is round." *Pushing Gravity*

I met my twin again: i.e., on a Möbius (MER-be-us) strip or band, one of the many strange topologies of hyperspace—a continuous, one-sided geometric surface "created by twisting a strip of paper 180 degrees and then gluing the ends together." In effect, "outside and inside are identical" (Kaku, *Hyperspace* 60-61). The "Möbius strip" was discovered by the German mathematician August Ferdinand Möbius in 1858. *The Möbius Strip*

Immersed, like His shaman, dreaming in code: The speaker would ascertain the meaning of the human psyche's "archetypal dreams," which—according to Jung—"have a peculiar numinosity" (*The Archetypes and the Collective Unconscious* 306). For a different take on the subject, see Adam Frank's trenchant review of Michio Kaku's *The Future of the Mind* (New York: Doubleday, 2014), where Frank describes Kaku as an advocate not only of the so-called "'connectome' [construct]—the explicit account of every neural connection in your head"—but also of "silicon minds" and "silicon self-consciousness, including a capacity to feel emotion." Thus, Kaku is especially excited about studying "the microscopic dynamics of the brain's wiring" through functional magnetic resonance imaging (fMRI), a technique that "tracks neural activity" and that can even enable scientists "to identify what people hooked to fMRI machines are dreaming about." However, according to Frank, "the internal luminosity—the 'being' of our being— [. . .] eludes Kaku's engineering-based perspective" because, in the final analysis, "simulations are not a self, and information is not experience" ("Dreaming in Code: Michio Kaku's 'Future of the Mind,'" *The New York Times* 7 Mar. 2014: 2-4 <www.nytimes.com>). *Dreaming in Code*

Impresses on Hermes his cosmic birth: The speaker identifies with the alchemical *Hermes* (Mercurius), who, in his role as hermaphroditic *rebis,* combines—i.e., *integrates*— paired opposites and thus "turns into a symbol of the unity of personality, [. . .] the distant goal of man's [and woman's] self-development" (Jung, *The Archetypes and the Collective Unconscious* 173-75). For a startling illustration of the alchemical hermaphrodite, see Jung, *Psychology and Alchemy* 244, fig. 125. *Station*

Incarnate the heart that Hephaestus nets: *Hephaestus,* the artisan of the gods, had "ensnared" Aphrodite, his wife, in a chain-link net, "when he caught her in the arms" of Ares, her paramour (Grant, *Myths of the Greeks and Romans* 65). *Postmodern*

In fibers of the dermis segments grow / Faster than a crosscut, as surgeons know: Cf. Nilsson, Lindberg, et al., *Behold Man* 105: "The dermis is a thin layer of connective tissue with elastic fibers arranged crosswise. They give the skin its elasticity. The arrangement of the fibers in segments creates natural cleavage lines in the skin. An incision along a cleavage line will heal faster than a crosscut, as all surgeons know." *The Skin That I Live In*

In melt or Kevlar: i.e., sealed either in the Shuttle's "bulky conventional 'balloon' spacesuit"—the Extravehicular Mobility Unit (EMU) made from numerous layers of material, including *Kevlar,* a heat-resistant, synthetic fiber—or in NASA's projected "sprayed-on" design: the customized, light-weight, "second-skin" Bio-Suit. Describing the latter model, Mark Wade explains that "the suit layers could be sprayed directly on the astronaut's skin prior to EVA [Extravehicular Activity]. Electrospinlacing, involving [the] charging and projecting of tiny fibers of polymer directly onto the skin, could be used. Melt blowing of liquefied polymer could [also] be used to apply thin elastic layers. Application could be made directly to the skin, or to advanced 3D forms generated by laser scanning." See "Bio-Suit," *Encyclopedia Astronautica* 1, 3. *Canadarm*

In mouths of the dead, the turquoise that chimes: See Jung, *Alchemical Studies* 100: In the Aztec cycle of legends, "The precious green stone was an animating principle and was placed in the mouth of the dead." Here, the speaker also alludes to Oriental wind *chimes* that maximize the flow of chi [CHEE], a life force that circulates in currents around the human body. *Kepler*

in pelican or goose: i.e., in an alchemical retort, the philosophical vessel also called, along with the stork, "the bird of Hermes [Trismegistus]" (Jung, *Psychology and Alchemy* 370n79). *The Spherical Glass Vessel*

in pileus and cape: During the alchemical process, the artifex—the refiner of ores and metals—wears "the queer little pointed hat, the pileus," associated not only with Attis and Mithras, majestic solar deities, but also with the Cabiri, misshapen dwarf gods. See Jung, *Symbols of Transformation* 126-27. *Siblings of the Sun*

Inscribes his footprint, the strength of his soul: In *The Grand Tour: A Traveler's Guide to the Solar System* (New York: Workman, 1981), Ron Miller and William K. Hartmann note that, on 20 July 1969, "Neil Armstrong and Edwin Aldrin, Jr., made the first human footprints on an unearthly landscape, while Michael Collins patiently orbited overhead in the command module. [. . .] they left this monument on the lava plains of Mare Tranquillitatis" (120). Elsewhere, in *Symbols of Transformation,* Jung explains that "The foot and the treading movement are invested with a phallic significance, or with that of re-entry into the womb." In other words, the "repetition of the infantile 'kicking'" (315) possesses "a magical generative power" (126). In addition, see *The Penguin Dictionary of Symbols* 400, where Chevalier and Gheerbrant emphasize that "the foot is a symbol of the strength of the soul, since it is the basis of the upright stance characteristic of human beings." *Footprint*

Inside a titanium vault we group / Infrared mappers: On 5 July 2016, after completing a five-year cruise to Jupiter, NASA's *Juno* spacecraft entered a polar orbit of the gas giant planet in order to make "scientific observations of gravity, magnetic fields[,] and the wetness of the Jovian atmosphere." Since belts of intense radiation surround Jupiter, infrared and microwave instruments carried by *Juno* were "housed [and shielded] inside [an electronically centralized] titanium vault." See Chang, "For NASA, Return Trip to Jupiter in Search of Clues to Solar System's Origins" 1, 4. *Figure Skater*

Inside a warp bubble: In his pertinent essay, "Mars, and Step on It," Michael Klesius explains that, in 1994, the "Mexican physicist Miguel Alcubierre offered a mathematical proof that faster-than-light travel is possible within the constraints imposed by Einstein's general theory of relativity. A spacecraft, Alcubierre theorized, would not dart across interstellar space; instead, it would ride a wave in the fabric of space-time, traveling inside a 'warp bubble' like a person standing on a moving sidewalk. Some not-yet-defined force would work to condense the space-time ahead of the spacecraft and stretch out the space-time behind" (1-2). *To Mars in a Month*

Inside the fiery furnace, pity me: Cf. Jung, *Symbols of Transformation* 167: "A hymn of Ephraem the Syrian says of Christ: 'Thou who art all fire, have pity on me.' This view is based on the apocryphal saying of our Lord: 'He who is near unto me is near unto the fire.'" However, Jung adds that "The fiery furnace, like the fiery tripod in *Faust,* is [also] a mother-symbol"—in effect, an emblem of the *maternal* depths of the unconscious. *The Archivist*

In situ sensors: here, on-site instruments that "could be attached to an orbiting spacecraft to search for bio-signatures" not only on Mars, but also on Europa and other planetary bodies. See "Mars rover could one day 'sniff' out life on red planet," *CBC News: Technology and Science* 3 Nov. 2016: 1-2 <www.cbc.ca>. *Techwed*

In skein of the tesseract: In this stanza, the speaker imagines that he enters, even as he unfolds, the four-dimensional, crosslike alternate world—a mathematical construct—that Michio Kaku describes in *Hyperspace* 71 and that Salvador Dali exploits in his 1954 oil-on-canvas painting *Crucifixion (Corpus Hypercubus),* where the artist depicts Christ "as being crucified on a tesseract," i.e., on an unraveled hypercube (72, fig. 3.7). *Something to Live For*

Insolate its surface: The NASA robonauts assist their human counterparts even as, teleoperated, they "expose [the face of Mars] to the rays of the sun" ("Insolate" [vt.], def.). Of course, in order to terraform Mars—to turn it into "a little Earth"—engineers would have to find a way not only to heat the Red Planet, but also to thicken its atmosphere. However, researchers maintain that, although it would take "decades" to complete the project, "both goals—heating and thickening—could be achieved [. . .]." Thus, one idea is "to build a large mirror, many miles in diameter, and place it in orbit above Mars," where it would be used "to focus the sun's rays onto a polar icecap," thereby melting the icecap and "releasing its frozen carbon dioxide contents." An alternative plan would be to generate "super-greenhouse" gases—i.e., "complex combinations of carbon, chlorine[,] and fluorine [that are] thousands of times more effective than carbon dioxide at trapping heat" and at raising global temperatures. See Robin McKie, "Now NASA looks to change Mars into a garden of Earthly delights," *the guardian,* 27 Mar. 2004: 1-2 <www.theguardian.com>. *Terraforming Mars*

In squashed elliptical orbits we swoop: In the voyage to Jupiter, NASA's *Juno* spacecraft traveled along "a squashed elliptical orbit, swooping within 3,100 miles of [Jupiter's] cloud tops" in order to "get a global view of the interior" and, at its north and south poles, "the first close-up looks at the bright auroras there" (Chang, "For NASA, Return Trip to Jupiter in Search of Clues to Solar System's Origins" 3-4). *Figure Skater*

Install the truss: Because the P6 *truss* segment generated electricity essential for the maintenance of the International Space Station (ISS), the NASA crew relocated it to its final position, bolted to the P5 truss segment, on 30 October 2007, during STS-120, i.e., during Mission 120 of The Space Transportation System (the official name for The Space Shuttle Program). See "Spaceflight Mission Report: STS-120," *Spacefacts* 4 <www.spacefacts.de>. Last updated on 8 Jan. 2018. *Canadarm; Swain; The Teleoperator's Dream*

In the ten-finger band that I have spanned: See "A mathematical theory proposed by Alan Turing in 1952," which explains an evolutionary advantage, i.e., "molecules for creating [ten] embryonic [human] fingers" (*Science Daily* 31 July 2014: 1-4 <www.sciencedaily.com>. *The Skin That I Live In*

Invest His globe with thunderbolt and rod: The speaker would endow the transfigured God-man with the "lightning shafts" of divine authority in 2 Sam. 22.15 and with the rod of miraculous power in Num. 20.11. *The Limits of the Coded World*

ions recombined— / Transparent site: an early stage in Big Bang cosmology. Thus, "about 380,000 years after the Big Bang," in "an epoch known as recombination, hydrogen and helium ions began snagging electrons, forming electrically neutral atoms. Light scatters significantly off free electrons and protons, but much less so off neutral atoms. So photons were now much more free to cruise through the universe. Recombination dramatically changed the look of the universe; it had been an opaque fog, and now it became transparent. The cosmic microwave background radiation [that] we observe today dates from this era." See Mike Wall, "The Big Bang: What Really Happened at Our Universe's Birth," *Space.com* 21 Oct. 2011: 9 <www.space.com>. *History's Thread*

ions that hiss: in Big Bang cosmology, relic radiation left over from the early universe. *A User's Guide to Spacetime*

I patch a thermal tile: During his spacewalk, the NASA astronaut, "using a device similar to a caulk gun," squirts "a rubberlike material into any cracks or holes in damaged thermal tiles" (Brittany Sauser, "NASA to Test Space Repairs," *MIT Technology Review* 1 Oct. 2007: 1 <www.technologyreview.com>. *Canadarm*

I reach beneath the syringe what lies hid; / [. . .] Electrospin its droplet: The speaker refers to an early version of NASA's projected "second-skin" Bio-Suit. Thus, before every EVA (Extravehicular Activity), "a layer of polymer fabric" could be sprayed over an astronaut, "in a booth much like those used for getting a spray-on suntan." Theoretically, "The 'second-skin' suit could be augmented by temperature-control-underwear, flexible joint attachments[,] and perhaps even an exoskeleton." See Alan Boyle, "NASA researchers investigate way-out ideas," *Technology & Science—Space / NBC News* 20 Oct. 2004: 2 <www.nbcnews.com>. (I must add, however, that this design has already been supplanted by another type of customized, "second-skin" spacesuit, one that would "plug into a spacecraft's power supply" and thereby trigger "tiny, musclelike coils [that line the spacesuit] to contract and essentially shrink-wrap the garment around the astronaut's body," as Jennifer Chu indicates in her update on the subject, "Shrink-wrapping spacesuits," *MIT News* 18 Sept. 2014: 1 <news.mit.edu>.) *Electrospinlacing*

I reach Gaea's wormhole; re-cut it; bend: Cf. Greene, *The Elegant Universe* 264, fig. 11.1: Theoretically, "In a 'U-shaped' universe, when the "fabric of space tears, and two ends of a wormhole start to grow," the "two wormhole ends merge together, forming a new bridge—a shortcut—from one end of the universe to the other." *Tearing the Fabric of Spacetime*

I rule my own spirit: In *Vital Dust: Life as a Cosmic Imperative* (New York: Basic Books, 1995), Christian de Duve argues that "In order to function, human society must set rules obeyed by its members. Hence we, the members of such a society, emerged with the feeling of responsibility and freedom [that enabled] society to function. We believe [that] we are free for the same reason [that] we believe matter to be solid and subject to the rules of causality, simply because such beliefs have helped our evolutionary success. They need in no way be true" (255). *The Exaltations of the Nettles*

I scaled my uncertainty, proofed my math, / Then, like an electron, crossed my own path: an idea enshrined in "the celebrated Heisenberg uncertainty principle." In essence, "The motion of an electron through space is [. . .] not a well-defined affair but more like a spread of possibility, with the available and possible paths spewing out after the fashion of a fluid" (Davies, *Other Worlds* 61, 63). *Hermes' Nested Spiral*

Isolated by a tectonic shift / Produced by the Afro-Syrian rift: The speaker refers to the movement of tectonic plates on the earth's surface—specifically, to a break in the earth's crust that extends from northern Syria to central Mozambique in East Africa. Because the Rift Valley has been "a rich source of [hominid] fossils," it is now viewed as the ancestral homeland of our species. See "Great Rift Valley," *New World Encyclopedia* 3 <www.newworldencyclopedia.org>. Last modified on 13 July 2017. *Herald*

I survive the shock / With wheels that lock: In this stanza, the speaker conflates details from NASA's first and last moonwalking missions: Apollo 11, at Tranquility Base, in July 1969, and Apollo 17, at Taurus-Littrow, in December 1972. For a partial yet pertinent description at close range of the *first* moon landing, which line 23 echoes, see Michael Collins, *Carrying the Fire* 404: Viewing the *Eagle,* the lunar module, from his post in the command module, Collins remarks that "It is the weirdest-looking contraption ever to invade the sky, floating there with its legs awkwardly jutting out above a body which has neither symmetry nor grace. Everything seems to be stuck on it at the wrong angle [. . .]. I make sure all four landing gear are down and locked [and] report that fact [. . .]." *The Self-Thinking Thought*

Iteration's void: repetition's nullity, a humanoid robot's emptiness. *Techwed*

It is not I who live: Cf. Gal. 2.19-20: "I have been crucified with Christ: the life I now live is not my life, but the life which Christ lives in me [. . .]." *Space*

Its source a giant star, its cohorts strewn: See "Siblings of the Sun" 31-32: "Simulations administered by Simon Portegies Zwart, a computational astrophysicist from Leiden University in the Netherlands, suggest that the sun was born in a cluster containing around 3,500 other stars," that the star cluster around the sun "dispersed long ago," and that "the stars are now scattered among millions of others formed in similar clusters." Portegies Zwart estimates that, today, "around 50 of the sun's cohorts are scattered across a half-circle [that follows] the sun's orbit around the center of the galaxy, at most 300 light-years away," while "another 400 are within 3,000 light-years." *Siblings of the Sun*

I twist a pseudosphere: Through gnuplot, a command-driven, interactive graphing program, the speaker creates a variant of Dini's surface, a twisted *pseudosphere* that is named after the Italian mathematician Ulisse Dini (1845-1918) and that, like the classic hyperbolic *pseudosphere,* has a constant negative curvature. See "Dini's Surface," a sample gnuplot-generated graph, in *Some Fun with GNUPLOT* 11-12 <soukoreff.com>. Accessed on 25 Jan. 2018. *Tumbling Escher*

I wake on Sunday: In *Alchemical Studies,* Jung reminds us that, in the *Confessions,* Saint Augustine (354-430), charting "the Christian transformation of the hylic into the pneumatic man" (233), states that the Sabbath "is the day on which a man returns to God and receives anew the light of the *cognitio matutina* [self-knowledge]. And this day has no evening." Jung adds that "From the symbological standpoint it may be not without significance that Augustine had in mind the pagan names of the days of the week." Thus, "The growing darkness [of human consciousness] reaches its greatest intensity on the day of Venus (Friday), and changes into Lucifer [the light-bringer, i.e., both the evening and the morning star] on Saturn's day." However, Saturday itself merely "heralds the light which appears in full strength on Sun-day" (249-50). See also 1 Thess. 5.5: "You are all children of light, children of day. We do not belong to night or darkness [. . .]." *Sunday*

I weave the tesseract: bead in the gland / Or sprout in the twill or star in the band: The speaker develops a textile metaphor—applicable to the cosmos as well as to the human body—which he extends throughout the poem. Thus, here, in his *tesseract*—the universe projected as a three-dimensional slice of a four-dimensional hypercube—the "outrider" chooses to *weave* together, even as he catalogs, a *bead* or droplet of perspiration that seeps from the human sweat *gland* (Nilsson, Lindberg, et al., *Behold Man* 110); a *sprout* or shoot of a plant that surfaces in the *twill* or doubled fiber of his design, and even a star that emanates from millions of disks located in the Milky Way Galaxy, "a hazy band of light" (Engelbrektson, *Stars, Planets, and Galaxies* 23). See also *The Body in Question* 266, where Jonathan Miller explains that "by the end of the eighteenth century biologists were confident that they had found a fundamental unit common to all the tissues of the body—a simple, irreducible element which could be put together in various ways to produce all the known textures. This unit was the fibre, a microscopic thread which could be woven into loose meshes or dense, impermeable sheets, tightly bound into tendons or loosely bundled to form muscles. By 1800 the body was seen as an elaborate textile, a garment of hemps, worsted and linens—the fact that the term 'tissue' was introduced at that time indicates the persuasiveness of the metaphor." Equally relevant is Clara Moskowitz's reminder—in "What Is the Smallest Thing in the Universe?" *Space.com* 17 Sept. 2012: 2 <www.space.com>—that, according to current superstring theory, "all particles, instead of being point-like, are actually little loops of string." *Outrider*

Jerusalem: the city where Jesus died and where he rose from the dead. *Hercules in the Vessel of the Sun*

Jerusalem laid / Even as hyperspace, jasper or jade: Jasper is a gemstone, light-green or yellow. See John's description of "the holy city of Jerusalem" in Rev. 21.11: "it had the radiance of some priceless jewel, like a jasper, clear as crystal." In Exod. 28.19, *jade* is one of the twelve gems that adorn Aaron's "breast-piece of judgement" (28.15), stones that "correspond to the twelve tribes of Israel engraved as on a seal" (28.21). *Carrier*

jinn: in popular usage, a single supernatural being that can assume either human or animal form. *Heracles Peeled; Made; The Teleoperator's Dream*

jollbot: "A robot that can jump like a grasshopper and roll like a ball" and that "might be the next best thing for space exploration," since its spherical shape "allows it to roll in any direction, giving it the maneuverability of wheels without the problems of overturning or getting stuck in potholes." In fact, its cagelike frame "is flexible and small—weighing less than two pounds," even as, in its "surface surveys of planets or moons," the *jollbot* can spring "upwards in the air to almost 20 inches." See Amelia Tomas, "Bizarre New Robot Jumps and Rolls," *Live Science* 10 Dec. 2008: 2 <www.livescience.com>. *History's Thread*

kenosis: in alchemy, a lunisolar symbol. Thus, "the 'waxing and waning' of the [lunar] bride [the Church] is based on the *kenosis*"—i.e., the emptying—"of the [solar] bridegroom [Christ], in accordance with the words of St. Ambrose" in his *Hexameron:* "'He emptied her that he might fill her, as he also emptied himself that he might fill all things. He emptied himself that he might come down to us. He came down to us that he might rise again for all'" (Jung, *Mysterium Coniunctionis* 35). *The Spherical Glass Vessel*

Kepler's cosmic census: NASA's Kepler spacecraft "was launched in 2009 to perform a kind of cosmic census, monitoring the brightness of 150,000 far-off stars in the Cygnus and Lyra constellations, looking for dips in brightness when planets pass in front of them" (Dennis Overbye, "Far-Off Planets Like the Earth Dot the Galaxy," *The New York Times* 4 Nov. 2013: 3 <www.nytimes.com>). *Kepler*

Kevlar: a brand name for a heat-resistant, synthetic fiber used in making the outer layer of the shuttle spacesuit. *The Archivist; Beyond Gender; Canadarm; History's Thread; Made; Pneumatic; Saffron of the Metals; Segway; Station; A User's Guide to Spacetime*

knapple: "To break off with an abrupt, sharp noise" ("Knapple" [vi.], def.). See *The Free Dictionary* <thefreedictionary.com>. *Pushing Gravity*

knot like a bow / Untethered: Even as he operates his Manned Maneuvering Unit (MMU), seemingly "a backpack with armrests," the NASA astronaut shuttlewalks, in his bulky suit, without a safety tether attached to his spaceship. See Joseph P. Allen and Russell Martin, *Entering Space: An Astronaut's Journey* (New York: Stewart, 1984) 113. See also Mark Prigg, "Radical figure hugging spacesuit shrinks itself to allow the first men on Mars to roam the surface easily," *Daily Mail.co.* 19 Sept. 2014: 6 <www.dailymail.co.uk>, an online essay that features a picture of a then-"current," but now-outdated, "balloon-like" spacesuit that resembles both a looping bowknot and a Celtic knot interlocked. *Mapping Celestial Terrains*

Kronos' child: in Greek mythology, Zeus, the Titan who dethroned Kronos, his father, "and seized the power for himself" (Hamilton, *Mythology* 24). *Shapeshifter*

the land of Nod: here, "the imaginary realm of sleep and dreams" ("Land of Nod" [n.], def. 2). *The Self-Thinking Thought*

The *lapis*: in alchemy, the philosophers' stone taken as a symbol of the unified self, i.e., "of the inner Christ, of God in man" (Jung, *Alchemical Studies* 96). *Herald*

leprous: an alchemical epithet—either impure, unclean, contaminated, or corrupt, like "metals, oxides, and salts" (Jung, *Alchemical Studies* 290n6). *History's Thread; Pneumatic*

leptons: "any of a class of light fermions that do not interact strongly with other particles or nuclei, including the electrons, neutrinos, muons, etc." ("Lepton[2]" [n.], def.). *Station*

light in a cone: The speaker refers to the space capsules that carried the NASA astronauts during flights to the moon "in the late 1960s and early 1970s." See Tim Sharp,

"Saturn Rockets & Apollo Spacecraft / The Most Amazing Flying Machines Ever," *Space.com* 23 July 2012: 4-5 <www.space.com>: "Sitting atop the Saturn V rocket was the Apollo spacecraft, which had three components: the service module, the command module, and the lunar module. [. . .] The [*cone*-shaped] command module housed the astronauts. It was 10.6 feet (3.2 m) tall and 12.8 feet (3.9 m) wide at its base. Inside, the astronauts had about 210 cubic feet (64 m) to move around in—about the space in a car's interior. The command module was the only part of the spacecraft that would return to Earth." Here, the allusion to *light* is Biblical: "For the same God who said, 'Out of darkness let light shine,' has caused his light to shine within us, to give the light of revelation—the revelation of the glory of God in the face of Jesus Christ" (2 Cor. 4.6). *Made*

like a globe I wind / Some netted omphalos: Like a satellite, the astronaut circles the Hubble Space Telescope, a rotating cylinder here compared to the *netted* or covered stone at Delphi that the ancient Greeks identified as the mid-point or navel of the Earth. Later, the Christians viewed the *omphalos,* the focal point of the Earth, as the hill at Golgotha where Adam, the first man, was buried and where Christ, the second and last Adam, was crucified. *Saffron of the Metals*

Like a pebble it falls; at its own pace, / Scatters Ge's trespass, then chastens its face: Here, the setting Sun intrudes or encroaches, even as, in dispersing its colors, the luminous star both "subdues" and "refines" its excess ("Chasten" [vt.], defs. 2, 3). *Pushing Gravity*

like a synchronized clock: In *Synchronicity,* Jung discusses Leibniz's view that, in a world defined by "an absolute synchronism of psychic and physical events," i.e., by a "pre-established harmony," soul and body relate to each other "like two synchronized clocks" (82). See also *Psychology and Alchemy* 120, where Jung remarks that "the life force that eternally renews itself" is like "the [cosmic] clock that never runs down." *The Self-Thinking Thought*

Like the handiwork of a moth on wool: In *The Elegant Universe,* Greene notes that, "If we could visualize six-dimensional geometry, we would see that, yes, the fabric [of space] is tearing, but it does so in a fairly mild way. It's more like the handiwork of a moth on wool than that of a deep knee bend on shrunken trousers" (280). In this stanza, the speaker also applies Greene's simile to the elusive image of Aldebaran even as the moon occults or blanks it out. Thus, in a recent online essay, the astronomer Bob King explains that, "If you've never seen a star in full daylight, the Aldebaran occultation presents a unique opportunity. Find the moon [and] point your telescope at it. [. . .] You just might catch a glimmering orange point of light minutes before it disappears in an instant behind the moon's bright western limb" ("Moon Hides Hyades, Occults Aldebaran Friday," *Sky & Telescope* 30 Sept. 2015: 2 <www.skyandtelescope.com>. *Tearing the Fabric of Spacetime*

Lion and unicorn: in Christian iconography as well as in alchemy, symbols of "the inner tension of opposites," since "The power of God reveals itself not only in the realm of the spirit, but in the fierce animality of nature both within man and outside him" (Jung, *Psychology and Alchemy* 464). *The Archivist*

locustae: "the tips of the branches" of the *arbor philosophica* (Jung, *Alchemical Studies* 287n16), the philosophical tree that "derives from the paradisal tree of knowledge" (240) and stands as a symbol for "the self depicted as a process of growth" (253). *Pneumatic*

The Logos is a dog: According to Hippolytus, a third-century Christian theologian who devised a Gnostic exegesis of the work of the Greek poet Aratus (c. 315 - c. 240 BC) in the *Elenchos,* "'The Logos [the Person of the Son as the Word of God] is a dog [. . .] who guards and protects the sheep against the wiles of wolves'" (Jung, *Mysterium Coniunctionis* 148). Thus, Jung notes that "The Gnostic parallel *Logos/canis* is reflected in the Christian one, *Christus/canis* [. . .]," i.e., Christ symbolized as watchdog of His flock (146-47n280). *Saffron of the Metals*

Lorentzian wormholes: See David Lewis Anderson, "Wormholes," *Anderson Institute* 2 <www.andersoninstitute>: Named after the Dutch physicist Hendrik Antoon Lorentz (1853–1928), "Lorentzian traversable wormholes would allow travel [either] from one part of the universe to another part of that same universe" or "from one universe to another." Accessed on 21 June 2017. *Full Circle*

Made of starstuff the universe is not: Cf. Frater Centaurus, "Testing the Night of Pan" 1: "Though we may be made of star stuff, the Universe is primarily not." In his online essay, the author explains that, according to quantum theory, "sixty-six percent of the Universe" is composed of Dark Energy; "another thirty-three percent" of Dark Matter; and, "astoundingly, only one-half of one percent" of visible matter. *Testing the Night of Pan*

The Magus: "a sorceror or [an] astrologer" ("Magus" [n.], def. 2)—here, Jesus Christ, the Son of God. In a "Diploma Thesis" completed for the C. G. Jung Institute in 1996, John Granrose observes that "Christ has often been viewed as a kind of magician." Thus, "many older illustrations show Jesus using a magic wand of some kind to perform his miracles. For example, [a] Fourth Century image from the Vatican library shows Jesus raising Lazarus from the dead by touching him with a type of wand" ("The Archetype of the Magician," 2 May 2017: 13 <www.granrose.com>). *Plato's Cave*

Mandragora's dream: The speaker refers to the mandrake, i.e., specifically to the forked root of the mandragora, a plant previously "thought to have magic powers because of its fancied resemblance to the human body" ("Mandrake" [n.], def. 2). In fact, in *Alchemical Studies,* Jung notes that "The idea that man is an inverted tree seems to have been current in the Middle Ages. [. . .] In Hindu literature the tree grows from above downwards, whereas in alchemy (at least according to the pictures) it grows from below upwards." However, "In East and West alike, the tree symbolizes a living process as well as a process of enlightenment" (312-14)—in fine, the work no less than the *dream* of both "[moral] transformation and [spiritual] renewal" (317). *Mandragora's Dream*

mandrake in the spud: the root of the mandragora, a medicinal plant, formerly thought to possess occult powers because of its seeming resemblance to the human body—specifically, to a man standing upside down (Jung, *Alchemical Studies* 312). Here, the "inverted tree" appears to spring from a *spud*—either a potato ("Spud" [n.], def. 2) or the small dimple "on the surface of [a] potato" planted in the womb of earth (Glen Vecchione, *Blue Ribbon Science Fair Projects* [New York: Sterling, 2005] 85). *Sunday*

manikin: in early biological theory, a fully-formed individual (the self-incubating homunculus) present in the sperm cell—in this poem, an emblem of transformation and resurrection. See Jung, *Psychology and Alchemy* 66, fig. 22: "Mercurius in the 'philosopher's egg,'" i.e., the alchemical vessel. "As *filius* he stands on the sun and moon, tokens of his dual nature." *The Limits of the Coded World*

Man in the mail: in the Middle Ages, a knight, the military servant of the king, covered with "flexible body armor made of small, overlapping metal rings, loops of chain, or scales" ("Mail" [n.], def. 1). *The Man Who Made a Copy of Himself*

mantic: "of, or having powers of, divination; prophetic" ("Mantic" [adj.], def.). *Bystander Cyborgs*

The Man Who Made a Copy of Himself: In 2006, "using silicone rubber, pneumatic actuators, powerful electronics, and hair from his own scalp," Hiroshi Ishiguro, a roboticist at Osaka University in Japan, constructed an android version of himself. "The robot, like the original, has a thin frame, a large head, furrowed brows, and piercing eyes that, as one observer put it, 'seem on the verge of emitting laser beams.' The android is fixed in a sitting posture" and "does a fine job of what it's intended to do: mimic a person" (Erico Guizzo, "Hiroshi Ishiguro: The Man Who Made a Copy of Himself," *IEEE [Institute of Electrical and Electronics Engineers] Spectrum* 23 Apr. 2010: 1 <spectrum.ieee.org>). *The Man Who Made a Copy of Himself*

The map of the brain is not drawn to scale: See Miller, *The Body in Question* 21: "The brain map is not drawn to scale. Certain parts of the body are represented over a much wider area of [the] brain than others, and not necessarily in proportion to their size. The face, especially the mouth, is allocated much more room than the leg; the hand, and especially the thumb, seem to have more than their fair share of space. It is like an electoral map as opposed to a geographical one. Because of their functional importance, the hand and the mouth have more sense organs per square inch than the leg or the trunk, and, since all of the parts of the body are clamouring for attention, they have many more Members representing them in their Parliament; that is to say, in the brain. This is what accounts for the strange anamorphic appearance of the felt image. The image that we see in the mirror reproduces the anatomical proportions of the body, whereas the image that we feel reproduces its Parliamentary proportions." In short, "The electoral map is not a *picture* of the body, it is a neurological *projection* of it [. . .]." *The Skin That I Live In*

mare: a dark plain on the Earth's moon. The word is pronounced MAH-ray. *Beyond Gender; Carrier; Heracles Peeled; Hubble Ajar; Made; Precinct; Prefigured; Quintessence; Rebis; Testing the Night of Pan; A Walking Man I; The Weight of History*

Maria's fettle: in Metallurgy, loose sand or crushed ore that lines the hearth of a reverberatory furnace before molten metal is poured. Here, the alchemist is the Maria of

Gnostic tradition, the legendary "Prophetissa" and "sister of Moses" (Jung, *Psychology and Alchemy* 401n169). *Bellicose Ares*

Maria's maxim: the axiom of Maria Prophetissa, the storied alchemist and sister of Moses: "'One becomes two, two becomes three, and out of the third comes the One as the fourth'" (Jung, *Psychology and Alchemy* 160). However, Jung observes that, in alchemical literature, since "Four signifies the feminine, motherly, [and] physical," while three represents "the masculine, fatherly, [and] spiritual [. . .], the uncertainty as to three or four" often amounts, in any definition of the holistic self, "to a wavering between the spiritual and the physical—a striking example of how every human truth is a last truth but one" (26-27). In fact, elsewhere, Jung describes "the triad" as "a mutilated quaternity" (*The Archetypes and the Collective Unconscious* 237). *Beyond Gender*

Maria's vase: For Maria Prophetissa, the reputed sister of Moses, "the whole secret of the [alchemist's] art lay in knowedge of the Hermetic vessel," which was both round and divine "and had been hidden from man by the wisdom of the Lord" (Jung, *Alchemical Studies* 85). *Pneumatic; Tumbling Escher*

Melissa: not only the Greek nymph who taught the use of honey and was transformed thereafter into a beautiful bee (Charbonneau-Lassay, *The Bestiary of Christ* 320-21), but also, in alchemy, an arcanum that Paracelsus had "singled out for special honour because in ancient medicine it was considered to be a means of inducing happiness, and was used as a remedy for melancholia and for purging the body [. . .]" (Jung, *Alchemical Studies* 153). *The Exaltations of the Nettles*

meninges (muh-NIN-jees): "the three membranes that envelop the brain and the spinal cord: they are the dura mater, arachnoid, and pia mater" ("Meninges" [n.pl.], def.). *Dreaming in Code*

Mercury's wight: Here, the *wight,* "a living being" ("Wight" [n.], def. 1), is Mercurius (or the alchemical Hermes), "who possessed a double nature, being a chthonic god of revelation and also the spirit of quicksilver, for which reason he was represented as a hermaphrodite" (Jung, *Psychology and Alchemy* 65). *Beyond Gender*

metaverse: in cosmology, a "spectrum" of possible universes. See Brian Greene, *The Hidden Reality: Parallel Universes and the Deep Laws of the Cosmos* (New York: Vintage-Random, 2011) 4. *Bystander Cyborgs*

mimic Gaea's eight: The spacewalking astronaut evokes not only the numinous figure of "Plato's Original [round] Man" (Jung, *Psychology and Alchemy* 84n38)—*Gaea's* own immortal, forever-flowing, upright, double-loop 8—but also, as in Goethe's *Faust 1,* the lowly chthonic eighth on Mount Olympus "'whom nobody thought of'" (67). *Keeper of the Hubble*

Minos: Hercules' seventh labor "was to go to Crete and fetch from there the beautiful savage bull that Poseidon had given" to King *Minos* and that Hercules eventually brought to

King Eurystheus, who had "devised a series of penances" for Hercules—all twelve of his labors (Hamilton, *Mythology* 164-65). *Hercules in the Vessel of the Sun*

Minuscule (mi-NUS-kyool) as seed-pearls: See Miller, *The Body in Question* 27: "Sensations or feelings are [. . .] distinguished by the fact that there is no intelligible answer to the question 'What do you recognise them with?' You recognise swellings or rashes with your eyes, but you don't recognise pain with anything. It is obvious that a sense organ must be involved at some point in the proceedings. Why aren't we aware of this? The answer is that the sense organs involved are very small and inconspicuous. The nerve endings which register these sensations are embroidered like millions of seed-pearls throughout the fabric of our body." *The Skin That I Live In*

mirror neurons twirled: brain cells that "respond equally when we perform an action and when we witness someone else perform the same action." In effect, *mirror neurons* may "explain how and why we 'read' other people's minds and [why we] feel empathy for them" (Lea Winerman, "The Mind's Mirror," *Monitor on Psychology* [Oct. 2005] 48). See also Richard Leviton's thesis that "Physical movement, especially spinning or twirling, can 'super-charge' your neurons [since] motion itself acts as a kind of brain nutrient" (*Brain Builders! A Lifelong Guide to Sharper Thinking, Better Memory, and an Age-Proof Mind* [Paramus: Prentice, 1995] 276-77). *A User's Guide to Spacetime*

Mithras' nubble: / Sapphire foetus in the eye of Hubble: some faraway infant sun, pictured as "a small knob or lump" in the Milky Way Galaxy ("Nubble" [n.], def.), an image captured by the Hubble Space Telescope (HST). Mithras was an ancient Persian sun-god. *Wayfinder*

Möbius' (MER-be-us) run: a possible universe in a higher-dimensional space; a continuous, one-sided geometric surface—i.e., a space warp "created by twisting a strip of paper 180 degrees and then gluing the ends together." In effect, "outside and inside are identical" (Kaku, *Hyperspace* 60-61). The "Möbius strip" is named after its deviser, the nineteenth-century German mathematician A. F. Möbius. *Beyond Gender; Canadarm; Carrier; Compass; Figure Skater; Hercules in the Vessel of the Sun; Life Out There; Made; Messenger; The Möbius Strip; Segway; Tearing the Fabric of Spacetime; Vas Bene Clausum*

Modular scaffolding: See "Building the International Space Station," *ESA* [European Space Agency] 1-2 <www.esa.int>: "The International Space Station weighs almost 400 tonnes and covers an area as big as a football pitch [soccer field]. It would have been impossible to build the Space Station on Earth and then launch it into space in one go—there is no rocket big enough or powerful enough. To get round this problem the Space Station was taken into space piece-by-piece and gradually built in orbit, approximately 400 km [248.5 miles] above the Earth's surface. This assembly required more than 40 missions. A partnership between European countries, Japan, Canada, and Russia, the International Space Station is the world's largest international cooperative programme in science and technology." Accessed on 20 Nov. 2017. *Writing under Erasure*

Moisture like an essence: a key ingredient of the microcosmic opus. See Jung, *Alchemical Studies* 86: "The prima materia, as the radical moisture, has to do with the soul because the latter is also moist by nature and is sometimes symbolized by dew." *Saffron of the Metals*

moles: tunnel-boring machines used to collect Martian scree—either loose stones or rocky detritus. See "Subsurface Explorers: Mars Exploration Program and Missions," *NASA* <mars.nasa.gov>: "A [British] lander [transported] on Mars Express [orbiter] called Beagle 2 will [. . .] carry the first robotic mole. Mimicking the behavior of the small furry earth-bound creatures that burrow into the ground, robotic moles will drill underground by pulverizing rock and soil, avoiding the need for a complex drill stem. [. . .] The samples sent up to the surface would be studied for scientific data such as mineral content and oxidation levels of subsurface soil." Accessed on 24 May 2017. *Techwed*

Monad: not only the indivisible point—"the jot of the iota"—viewed as a Gnostic emblem of the totalistic man or woman (Jung, *Aion* 218), but also a basic unit of matter—a microcosm—that, according to the German philosopher and mathematician Gottfried Wilhelm von Leibnitz (1646-1716), mirrors the universe. *Beyond Gender; Body of Evidence; Bystander Cyborgs; Compass; Electrospinlacing; Life Out There; Postmodern; Rebis; Saffron of the Metals; Saturday; Sunday; Writing under Erasure*

moonchild in the drum: "a prefiguration of the self"—in alchemy, "the spagyric embryo conceived by the sun in [the] womb and belly" of the moon (Jung, *Mysterium Coniunctionis* 175-76). *Terraforming Mars*

the Moon in its sulk: the Earth's satellite hidden in gloomy withdrawal either by cloud or by eclipse. *Bulk*

moon in the sun: In *Mysterium Coniunctionis* 35-36n104, Jung, quoting Professor Hugo Rahner [1900-68], refers to "the parallel *kenosis* [emptying] of Ecclesia—Luna," a key idea of the Christian theologians. Thus, "The closer Luna approaches to the sun, the more she is darkened until, at the conjunction of the new moon, all her light is 'emptied' into Christ, the sun. [. . .] The remarkable paradox of Luna, that she is darkest when nearest the sun, is a symbol of Christian asceticism: 'The more the inward man draws nigh to the sun, the more is the outward man destroyed, but the inward man is renewed from day to day' [a variation of 2 Cor. 4.16]. That is, the Christian dies like Luna and his life is 'hid with Christ in God' [Col. 3.3]. All this Augustine says in *Epistola* 55, v, 8. Afterwards he applies it to the Church and her destiny (*Epistola* 55, vi, 10)," for "she will vanish into Christ, the sun, at the end of time [. . .]." *Something to Live For*

Moonplant: In alchemy, "the moon itself is a plant" (Jung, *Mysterium Coniunctionis* 132). Thus, in the alchemical pictures, sometimes the prototype of the tree of paradise is "hung not with apples but with sun-and-moon fruit" (Jung, *Alchemical Studies* 302-03). *Compass; The Limits of the Coded World; Quintessence; Sunday*

Moonplant of the Adepts: See Jung, *Alchemical Studies* 308: In Arabian alchemy, "The secret moonplant of the adepts is 'like a tree [of coral] planted in the sea.'" In *Mysterium Coniunctionis,* Jung adds that "the tree of the sea" evokes not only the mandrake, with its roots of ore in the air and its summits in the earth, but also the tree of Zacchaeus in

Luke 19.4—i.e., the tree of faith that, according to the Flemish mystic John of Ruysbroeck (1294-1381), "'grows from above downwards, for its roots are in the Godhead'" (135n210). *Compass; The Limits of the Coded World*

Movement is mastery: Jung reminds us that, in *The Secret of the Golden Flower,* "it is said: 'Movement is only another name for mastery.' Psychologically, this circulation would be the 'movement in a circle around itself,' so that all sides of the personality become involved. 'The poles of light and darkness are made to rotate,' that is, there is an alternation of day and night. The circular movement thus has the moral significance of activating the light and dark forces of human nature, and together with them all psychological opposites of whatever kind they may be. It is nothing less than self-knowledge by means of self-brooding"—i.e., in the sacred language of Hinduism, the heat or glow of *tapas* (TUH-puhs). Jung adds that "A similar archetypal concept of a perfect being is that of the Platonic man, round on all sides and uniting within himself the two sexes" (*Alchemical Studies* 25-26). *Precinct; The Ultimate Fate of the Universe*

multiverse: a concept that derives from a cosmological theory advanced in 1957 by Hugh Everett, and later by Bryce DeWitt, both of whom argue that an infinite number of possible universes (including myriad copies of our local world) comprises but one part of physical reality (Kaku, *Hyperspace* 262-64). *The Experiment of Eternity; The Quilted Multiverse; The Ultimate Fate of the Universe; A Walking Man I*

The multiverse ***by way of life and mind*** **/ Reflects upon itself:** In *Vital Dust,* Christian de Duve suggests that "Conscious thought belongs to the cosmological picture, not as some freak epiphenomenon peculiar to our own biosphere, but as a fundamental manifestation of matter" (297). In fact, the very meaning of the universe is to be found in its structure, which produces thought "by way of life and mind" (301). *The Quilted Multiverse*

Musca: the Fly, a small constellation in the Southern Hemisphere near Crux, the Southern Cross. *Tumbling Escher*

my capsule His fane: either a space *capsule,* the "detachable, closed compartment designed to hold and protect [the astronaut] in a rocket" ("Capsule" [n.], def. 3b), or the sealed astronaut himself—the floating microcosm—enshrined as God's "temple" ("Fane" [n.], def.). See 1 Cor. 3.16: "Surely you know that you are God's temple, where the Spirit of God dwells." *Bulk*

Mylar: "a polyester made in extremely thin sheets of great tensile strength" ("Mylar" [n.], def.) and used for insulating the NASA spacesuit. The seven layers of Mylar insulation "make the suit act like a thermos" ("Learn about Spacesuits," *NASA* 13 Nov. 2008: 9 <www.nasa.gov>). *The Universe Speaks*

My mother in a sphere gave birth to me / That I might contemplate rotundity: These verses, translated from Sir George Ripley's *Cantilena,* appear in *Opera omnia chemica* (1649). See Jung, *Mysterium Coniunctionis* 278-79: In Ripley's alchemical allegory, written in the fifteenth century, "The secret content of the Hermetic vessel is the original chaos from which the world was created. As the filius Macrocosmi and the first man[,] the king is destined for 'rotundity,' i.e., wholeness, but is prevented from achieving it" because he has been corrupted by original sin. *An Oblate Spheroid*

My risen hierophant: rotund as awe, / Frequented as space, transcendent as law: the "round, original form" of "the spiritual, inner and complete man"—the "long-sought" or "sought-after" believer-priest of Isa. 62.12—taken either as Christ or as the bride of Christ, "the Ransomed of the Lord." See also Jung, *Mandala Symbolism* 9-10. *Herald*

myrtle that cools: a plant associated with Aphrodite, the Greek goddess of love and beauty. It has "evergreen leaves, white or pinkish flowers, and dark, fragrant berries" ("Myrtle[1]" [n.], def. 1). See also Jung, *Psychology and Alchemy* 286-87: The *myrtle* "keeps its green colour for a long time despite the alternations of heat and cold." *Space*

My silver scion: NASA's Robonaut, a "state-of-the-art humanoid" designed for space travel (Menzel and D'Aluisio, *Robo sapiens* 129). *Keeper of the Hubble*

mystagogue: the telepresent astronaut portrayed as "a person who interprets religious mysteries or initiates others into them" ("Mystagogue" [n.], def.). *Nothing; The Teleoperator's Dream*

Nain [NAY-in]: the village in Galilee where Jesus raised a widow's son from the dead (Luke 7.11-16). For an insightful analysis of the miracle, see Françoise Dolto and Gérard Sévérin, *The Jesus of Psychoanalysis: A Freudian Interpretation of the Gospels,* trans. Helen R. Lane (New York: Doubleday, 1979) 57: "the absence of his father to mediate between him and his mother had petrified [the son's] desire into impotence. Faced with his abandoned mother, guided and surrounded only by her, [the son] was unable to achieve his procreative destiny, for, unknowingly, she was barring his way." Thus, in the story of *his* resurrection, "it is a young man and not a child that Christ brings back to life" (91). *Hercules in the Vessel of the Sun*

Neither male nor female, the two as one: Cf. Gal. 3.28: "There is no such thing as Jew and Greek, slave and freeman, male and female; for you are all one person in Christ Jesus." *Carrier*

***A nested spiral* I circle the sun:** In his online essay "Patterns of Motion," Barry Carter explains that, according to "vortex-type forces" implied by spin-field theories, "A person standing on the earth would be describing a circle around the axis of the earth[,] while the earth itself would be circling the sun. At the same time, the sun would be circling the center of the galaxy" (3). However, because of "the additional motion of the earth and the sun, the motion of the person would not actually be a circle," but "a nested [or an embedded] spiral" instead (<www.subtleenergies.com>). *Hermes' Nested Spiral*

The Night of Pan: In an updated description of Thelema (the-LAY-ma), an occult religion developed in the early twentieth century by Aleister Crowley, *The Night of Pan* resonates not only as a symbol of the mystical state that leads to ego death and transmundane selfhood, but also as an emblem of Dark Energy and Dark Matter and "the Nightside of the Tree of Life." In effect, like *Pan* himself, a hybrid god, Thelema's redemptive *Night* evokes both subterranean magic and the Spirit-disturbing will to live. See Frater Centaurus, "Testing the Night of Pan" 2. *Testing the Night of Pan*

Nor even such moisture as stirs the spine: The speaker alludes to "'the [radical] moisture of the moon' [that] takes up the sunlight," since, according to such alchemists as Senior Zadith and Gerhard Dorn, "Luna draws near to the sun in order to 'extract from him, as from a fountain, universal form and natural life'" (qtd. in Jung, *Mysterium Coniunctionis* 129-30). In deep space, such light either dwindles or disappears. *Travelling Forever in the Same Direction*

The North Star: Polaris, the Pole Star, "a supergiant binary star" located in the constellation Ursa Minor and "used for navigation, since it is the closest star to the north celestial pole and remains nearly stationary throughout the night" ("Polaris" [n.], def.). See Jung, *Psychology and Alchemy* 188: "The Pole is the point around which everything turns—hence another symbol of the self." *The Teleoperator's Dream*

The North Star is white, an alchemist's phlegm, / Mystagogue's citrine, or rubedo's gem: In his analysis of the alchemical *opus* and the color stages in the creation of the Philosopher's Stone, Jung explains that, after the *nigredo* (the blackening), "The *albedo* (the whitening) is, so to speak, the daybreak, but not till the *rubedo* [the reddening] is it sunrise. The transition to the *rubedo* is formed by the *citrinitas* [the yellowing], though this, as we have said, was omitted later. The *rubedo* then follows from the *albedo* as the result of raising the heat of the fire to its highest intensity." In effect, "The red and the white are King and Queen, who may also celebrate their 'chymical wedding' at this stage" (*Psychology and Alchemy* 232-33). See also the definition of *phlegm* in the note given below. *The Teleoperator's Dream*

Nostoc: in alchemy, "a gelatinous alga that appears after continuous rain. These algae are still known as Nostocs in modern botany. It was earlier supposed that Nostocs fell from the air, or from the stars," like rays that light evinces. Thus, in the "Paracelsan process" of transformation, *Nostoc* "is a sublimating arcanum, because it comes from heaven" (Jung, *Alchemical Studies* 153n94). *Electrospinlacing; Precinct; Serious Reader; Space*

Nothing comes from nothing, Maria said: In *Perfect Symmetry: The Search for the Beginning of Time* (New York: Simon, 1985), Heinz R. Pagels remarks that, according to the 1984 Stephen Hawking-James Hartle model of the origin of the universe, "The nothingness 'before' the creation of the universe is the most complete void that we can imagine—no space, time or matter existed. It is a world without place, without duration or eternity, without number—it is what the mathematicians call 'the empty set.' Yet this unthinkable void converts itself into the plenum of existence—a necessary consequence of physical laws" (347). Here, the mathematical attribution to *Maria* Prophetissa, the legendary alchemist and reputed sister of Moses, although fanciful, seems apt, since the focus of her own Hermetic art is the life force, the "'glue of the world'" (Jung, *Psychology and Alchemy* 161). *Nothing*

Nothing else avails—the rest are details: Cf. Tom Rowan, "Pushing Gravity" 1: "Both Newton and Einstein knew for certainty that God created our universe." In fact, "Newton was such a devout Christian that he mathematically constructed a timeline for the return of Christ." Likewise, "Einstein summed up his mission in scientific discovery: 'I want to know God's thoughts; the rest are details.'" *Pushing Gravity*

Nothing has three variants: In his contentious *New York Times* essay "There's More to Nothing Than We Know," Dennis Overbye reports that, in a recent book, *A Universe from Nothing,* the cosmologist Lawrence M. Krauss "delineates three kinds of nothingness. First is what may have passed muster as nothing with the ancient Greeks: empty space. [. . .] Second is nothing, without even space and time. [. . .] There is a [third] deeper nothing in which even the laws of physics are absent." Overbye argues that, in order to explain the latter variant of *Nothing,* Krauss "resorts to the newest and most controversial toy in the cosmologist's toolbox: the multiverse, a nearly infinite assemblage of universes, each with its own randomly determined rules, particles and forces, that represent solutions to the basic equations of string theory"—in effect, to "the *alleged* [emphasis mine] theory of everything, or perhaps, as wags says, [of] anything" (2). Overbye adds that, according to Krauss, "If nothing is our past, it could also be our future. As the universe, driven by dark energy—that is to say, [by] the negative pressure of nothing—expands faster and faster, the galaxies will become invisible, and all the energy and information will be sucked out of the cosmos. The universe will revert to nothingness" (2). *Nothing*

nous: in alchemy, not only "the dyestuff or tincture" that "ennobles base substances," but also the pneuma [the life-giving Spirit] that purifies "the divine vessel" of transformation (Jung, *Psychology and Alchemy* 299). *The Spherical Glass Vessel*

novae: the plural form of *nova,* "a type of variable star that suddenly increases in brightness by thousands to hundreds of thousands of times up to 14 magnitudes, and then decreases in brightness over a period of months to years" ("Nova" [n.], def.). *Life in a Mortal Universe*

nubble: The speaker characterizes NASA's Robonaut, fraternally, as "a small knob or lump" ("Nubble" [n.], def.] and—with a bow to the source of the word—as "the point [. . .] or gist of the matter" ("Nub" [n.], def. 2). *Keeper of the Hubble*

Nudge Him at the cavern: The speaker supposes that, even as we narratize the history of the world, we might stir or rouse the Savior in His tomb and thereby reimagine not only the death of Jesus, but also the Resurrection of Christ. See Wijngaards, *Handbook to the Gospels* 245: "When we say that Jesus descended into hell we mean only (in the terminology of the Bible) that he was truly dead; he was no longer in the 'land of the living' but went down into the 'land of the dead.' He had taken upon himself everything that being man included, even death. When Jesus rose, therefore, he rose from among the dead. He is now the Lord of both the living and the dead, and shall come to judge both the living and the dead." In effect, "The descent into hell is not a geographical journey but theology in very human words [. . .]. Sheol, the prison of the dead, is now unlocked by Christ, who has the keys [. . .]." Thus, as Wijngaards adds, we are saved by the death of Jesus as well as by His Resurrection—in sum, by this "divine work" that we call "the pass-over mystery of our redemption" (249). *Platonic Riddles*

An oblate spheroid: Although it is often assumed that the Earth, Moon, and Sun are spherical, "In reality, because of their rotational properties they are each slightly flattened into shapes known as oblate spheroids, the northern hemisphere [being] a little thinner than the southern [. . .]" (Duncan Steel, *Eclipse: The Celestial Phenomenon That Changed the Course of History* [Wash., DC: Joseph Henry, 2001] 51). *An Oblate Spheroid*

Occam's razor: a rule named after William of Occam (c. 1285 – c. 1349), "who used it often in analyzing problems"—in short, "a philosophical or scientific principle according to which the best explanation of an event is the one that is the simplest, using the fewest assumptions or hypotheses" ("Occam's razor" [def.]). The alternate spelling is "Ockham's razor." *Plato's Cave*

Omega, Tucanae, Spirals that glow: In the cosmic journey that Patrick Moore rhapsodically envisions in *Travellers in Space and Time,* "We have left the centre of the [Milky Way] Galaxy in a direction which will take us to a particularly fine example of a globular cluster, M.13 [the Andromeda, another spiral galaxy] in the constellation of Hercules. It is not the closest of the globulars—that distinction belongs to the system in Ara—and neither is it the brightest; there are two in the southern sky, Omega Centauri and 47 Tucanae, which surpass it in size and brilliance, but M.13 is conveniently placed for observers in the Earth's northern hemisphere. With the naked eye it can just be seen as a dim patch; telescopes show that it is made up of stars, though near the middle of the cluster the stars are so packed that they merge into a general glow" (145). *Travelling Forever in the Same Direction*

Omicron Centauri: a supergiant star located in the constellation of Centaurus, the Centaur, the latter a mythical creature—half-man, half-horse—that the ancient Greeks identified with Chiron, "the wise tutor of Achilles" (Engelbrektson, *Stars, Planets, and Galaxies* 52). *Life in a Mortal Universe*

omniverse: in current physical cosmology, an infinity of universes—the conglomeration of all possible worlds. *Blazar/Quasar; Body of Evidence; Electrospinlacing; Mapping Celestial Terrains; The Möbius Strip; Plato's Cave; Postmodern; Rebis; Siblings of the Sun; Tearing the Fabric of Spacetime; The Universe Speaks; Vas Bene Clausum*

Omphale: In Greek mythology, *Omphale* is "a queen of Lydia in whose service Hercules, dressed as a woman, does womanly tasks for three years to appease the gods" ("Omphale" [n.], def.). Hercules had slain "a good friend in order to avenge an insult offered him by the young man's father, King Eurytus" (Hamilton, *Mythology* 168). *Kepler; Peregrination*

omphalos: the mid-point or navel of the earth—Golgotha; according to an ancient Christian tradition, both the hill where Adam was buried and the very spot where Christ was crucified. See Jung, *Mysterium Coniunctionis* 388-89. *Bystander Cyborgs; Saffron of the Metals; Siblings of the Sun; Stewards of Creation; Testing the Night of Pan*

The One and at the same time the Many: The speaker evokes the self-described, circular Ouroboros, the snake that bites its own tail, a symbol of "the One and All" and of "the union of opposites accomplished during the alchemical process" (Jung, *Alchemical Studies* 232). Cf. also *Mysterium Coniunctionis* 223-24, where Jung quotes a key section from the "Aurelia occulta" in the *Theatrum chemicum* (1603), a collection of alchemical essays: "'Many from one and one from many, issue of a famous line, I rise from the lowest to the highest. The nethermost power of the whole earth is united with the highest. I therefore am the One and the Many within me.' In these words the dragon makes it clear that he is the chthonic forerunner of the [unified and coherent] self." *Sunday*

the One called Immortal: In Hindu philosophy, "There is that ancient tree [like the mandrake], whose roots grow upward and whose branches grow downward, [. . .] that alone is called the Immortal. All worlds are contained in it, and no one goes beyond" (Jung, *Mysterium Coniunctionis* 135n211). *The Spherical Glass Vessel*

On tree or scaffold, Sophia descried, / His bed an altar, Bride and Groom elide: The speaker alludes not only to *Sophia,* the Greek embodiment of both Wisdom and the afflicted soul, but also to the Blessed Virgin Mary in her role as Mother of God. For a succinct overview of Mary's link to *Sophia,* see Anne Baring and Jules Cashford, *The Myth of the Goddess: Evolution of an Image* (New York: Viking, 1991) 609-11. See also *Alchemical Studies* 335-37, where Jung explores the Gnostic interpretation of Sophia's relation to wholeness: "Expressed in the language of myth, Christ (the principle of masculine spirituality) perceives the sufferings of Sophia (i.e., the psyche) and thereby gives her form and existence. But he leaves her to herself so that she should feel the full force of her sufferings. What this means is that the masculine mind is content merely to perceive psychic suffering, but does not make itself conscious of the reasons behind it [. . .]." In short, each participant in the agony of the Cross—the conscious Christ as well as the unconscious *Sophia*—must become aware of the other's suffering, since "There can be no [reunified] consciousness without this act of discrimination [. . .]." *Something to Live For*

open and shut: According to the Cambridge University physicist Stephen Hawking, "Combining real space-time with imaginary space and time [i.e., in a mathematical, not a fictive, sense] allows for both an open and a closed universe." Without a hint of irony, "Hawking [has] proposed that this open and shut universe comes into being from nothingness in the form of a pea instanton—a particle of space and time" that, "depending on how you look at it," is—even as the wave-particle duality of light, a classic example of quantum logic—"not so much a thing as an event." See K. C. Cole, "Hawking's Universe Is Open and Shut," *Los Angeles Times* 14 Mar. 1998: 1-2 <articles.latimes.com>. *Pushing Gravity*

orbweb: the gossamer network of the universe compared to a spider's (here, an orb-weaver's) web of silk. *Bulk; Life in a Mortal Universe; Life Out There*

Orion: in Greek mythology, a hunter whom the Moon goddess Artemis loves but accidentally kills. "After his death he was placed in heaven as a constellation" (Hamilton, *Mythology* 297). See also Engelbrektson, *Stars, Planets, and Galaxies* 24: Orion "consists of seven bright stars that outline the figure," three of which "represent his belt." *Techwed*

Orion's capsule: "a NASA spacecraft designed to take a crew of up to six Astronauts to destinations beyond low Earth orbit including the Moon, Mars and Asteroids." See "Orion Spacecraft Overview," *Spaceflight 101.com: Space News and Beyond* 1 <spaceflight101.com/spacecraft/orion>. Accessed on 31 Aug. 2016. *The Self-Thinking Thought*

Our eyes like cameras, we screen our trace: See the vivid photograph in Menzel and D'Aluisio, *Robo sapiens* 132-33: "By flexing his data-gloved hand, [the] robotics specialist Fredrik L. Rehnmark controls the NASA robonaut as it reaches for a battery-operated power drill on a test platform. Black goggles on Rehnmark's head give him the view from the twin digital cameras mounted in the robot's shiny carapace." *Terraforming Mars*

Ouroboros: "the self-devouring dragon that [. . .] begot and gave birth to itself," a symbol of alchemical transformation (Jung, *Alchemical Studies* 259). *Blazar/Quasar; The Exaltations of the Nettles; The Experiment of Eternity; Peregrination; Plato's Cave; Pushing Gravity; Quintessence; Segway; The Self-Thinking Thought; Siblings of the Sun; The Ultimate Fate of the Universe; Vas Bene Clausum*

Ouroboros, circling, devours its scales: *Ouroboros* is the snake that bites its own tail—in alchemy, not only a self-described circle, the *opus* that "proceeds from the one and leads back to the one" (Jung, *Psychology and Alchemy* 293, incl. fig. 147), but also a symbol of totality. *Pushing Gravity*

Overcomes Nessus: a myth that dramatizes the archetypal sun-hero's triumph over death. See Hamilton, *Mythology* 171: After Deianeira had unwittingly given Hercules, her husband, a robe "anointed with the [poisonous] blood" of the Centaur Nessus, "pain seized him, as though he were in a burning fire." However, "Since death would not come to him, he would go to death. He ordered those around him to build a great pyre on Mount Oeta and carry him to it. When at last he reached it he knew that now he could die and he was glad." In *Symbols of Transformation,* Jung interprets the meaning of this solar myth: "death with its cold embrace is the maternal womb, just as the sea devours the sun but brings it forth again" (218). *Hercules in the Vessel of the Sun*

paladins that chirr: knights or heroic champions ("Paladin" [n.], def. 2) that, as members of some species from another planet, might emit "a shrill, trilled sound" ("Chirr" [n., vi.], defs.), like insects or birds, or like the "breath-souls that blur" of line 6. *History's Thread*

Palapa: i.e., *Palapa B2,* a rogue communications satellite that the untethered Shuttle astronauts Joseph P. Allen and Dale A. Gardner retrieved from orbit in November 1984. See Kerrod, *Space Walks* 60-61. *Bellicose Ares; Prefigured*

Pallas in the star field: one of the largest asteroids discovered in the Solar System (the second after Ceres). Named after *Pallas* Athena, the Greek Goddess of Wisdom, 2 *Pallas* is now considered a protoplanet. For an arrowed photo of 2 *Pallas* "moving through a 25-arcminute-wide star field in Delphinus," a northern constellation, see Alan MacRobert, "Pallas in the Realm of the Galaxies," *Sky & Telescope* 17 June 2005: 1 <www.skyandtelescope.com>. *Heracles Peeled*

Papillary patterns that I have scanned: See Nilsson, Lindberg, et al., *Behold Man* 226: "The skin on the palm of the hand and at the fingertips has a characteristic papillary pattern, unique for every individual. The elements of the pattern are ridges and furrows formed by connective tissue fibers in the dermis. Sweat glands have openings on the ridges." *The Skin That I Live In*

parsecs: A parsec (*par*[allax] + *sec*[ond]) is a unit of astronomical length equivalent to 3.26 light years or to 206,265 times the distance from the earth to the sun ("Parsec" [n.], def.). *Blazar/Quasar; Stewards of Creation; To Live and Work in Deep Space*

The past is not lost, neither hers nor his— / Astarte's mysteries nor Mithras's: The speaker refers to the secret rites of Astarte, "a Semitic goddess of love, fertility, and war" ("Astarte" [n.], def.), and Mithras, "the ancient Persian god of light and truth" ("Mithras" [n.], def.). *Full Circle*

peacock: "an early Christian symbol for the Redeemer" (Jung, *Psychology and Alchemy* 419), since its "combination of all colors" signifies wholeness (223). *The Experiment of Eternity; Postmodern*

peacock flesh in the broth: In medieval literature, *peacock flesh* signifies the food of immortality (Jung, *Mysterium Coniunctionis* 292). Here, the speaker refers either to "the warm dilute broth" of the early oceans (Sagan, *The Cosmic Connection* 253) or to "a clear, thin soup" ("Broth" [n.], def.). *The Experiment of Eternity*

pelf: booty; here, any hidden spoil, reward, prize, or gift. *To Live and Work in Deep Space; Tumbling Escher; The Whole Atlas*

pelican: either the large, web-footed bird with a long, straight bill (a symbol of the salvific Christ) or—because of its resemblance to the *pelican*—an alchemical retort, the philosophical vessel also called, along with the goose [an avatar of the *swan*] and the stork, "the bird of Hermes [Trismegistus]." See Jung, *Psychology and Alchemy* 370n79. *The Universe Speaks*

A peloton of stars: A *peloton* is "A group of riders that clump together in a bicycle race on the open road"; hence, here—in the root sense of the French word *pelote* from which it derives—a ball or pack or platoon *of stars* (*The Free Dictionary* <www. thefreedictionary.com>). See also "Siblings of the Sun" 32-33, where the astrophysicist Simon Portegies Zwart calculates not only that our sun "'was born in a dense cluster with thousands of other stars,'" but also that, "After 27 Milky Way orbits, the cosmic peloton of stars has become quite dispersed." Nevertheless, "some 50 of the sun's siblings are still located within 300 light-years from the sun." As Portegies Zwart says, "'You can compare it with the racing cyclists in the Tour de France. Even though some of them break away from the pack, and others are left behind, they don't get far away, and they all go in the same direction.'" *Siblings of the Sun*

A pencil-thin bronze, a walking man I: The speaker compares the teleported astronaut to "Walking Man 1 [One]," Alberto Giacometti's bronze sculpture, a wiry, six-foot-tall "stick" figure, both a biped "whose limbs stretch out endlessly" and a nomad shaped "as a symbol of the human being." Giacometti's "walking man does not ask any questions; he simply comes from somewhere and is on his way elsewhere. His gaze fixed on the horizon, he strides decisively, [i.e.] forward[,] in order to discover [and] to understand, as if he has a goal to pursue. With an awakened conscience, he travels through time to observe the world. His feet, anchored in the ground, connect him inevitably to the earth with which he is one." See "Alberto Giacometti [(1901-66)], 'Walking Man 1, 1960,'" *The UNESCO Works of Art Collection* Dec. 1970: 1-2 <www.unesco.org>. *A Walking Man I*

pentagons: here, building blocks for a "near-miss" pseudosphere, each pentagon "a plane figure with five angles and five sides" ("Pentagon" [n.], def.). *Pseudosphere*

perchlorates: salts derived from perchloric acid, a colorless, toxic chemical prevalent in Martian soil. *Setting the Wheel on Fire*

perilune: the point nearest to the center of the moon in the orbit of a spacecraft. *Peregrination; Rebis*

Philosophic ambisexual man: In many alchemical texts, "Because of his united double nature Mercurius [the Roman messenger god] is described as hermaphroditic. Sometimes his body is said to be masculine and his soul feminine, sometimes the reverse. [. . .] He is also called husband and wife, bridegroom and bride, or lover and beloved" (Jung, *Alchemical Studies* 218-19). In addition, he "corresponds not only to Christ, but to the triune divinity in general." In effect, "Mercurius is the Logos become world" (222). In fact, here, as the "seed" of the shapeshifting Macrocosm, he is even named "the 'Philosophic ambisexual man'" (219), an archetype with whom the human speaker himself identifies. *Pseudosphere*

phlegm: "the residue, in the bottom of the vessel, of the evaporated wine" (Jung, *Mysterium Coniunctionis* 493), from which the quintessence—the image of God "imprinted in man" (478)—is "sublimed" (488). *The Teleoperator's Dream*

Phobos' pelf: detritus from a Martian moon. Evidently, "Phobos is close enough to Mars that it can collect debris kicked up by major impacts on the Red Planet. [. . .] These samples are likely embedded in the top meter or so of Phobos's surface—a difficult location for robots to sample, but easier for humans." See "Frequently Asked Questions about Humans Orbiting Mars," *The Planetary Society* 14 <hom.planetary.org>. Accessed on 13 May 2017. *To Live and Work in Deep Space*

phonemes: "a set of phonetically similar but slightly different sounds in a language that are heard as the same sound by native speakers and are represented in phonemic transcription by the same symbol." Thus, "in English, the phoneme *p* includes the phonetically differentiated sounds represented by *p* in 'pin,' 'spin,' and 'tip'" ("Phoneme" [n.], def.). Of course, here, according to the speaker, the *source* of the sounds may well be both immanent and transcendent, their effects but the offshoot of an empathetic subjective understanding. *Writing under Erasure*

photons: "messengers [. . .] between particles of matter" (Davies, *The Mind of God* 207), each of them, being "massless" (208), conveying the "smallest bundle of light" (Greene, *The Elegant Universe* 419). *Herald; Saffron of the Metals*

pine: In the worship of Cybele during the decline of the Roman Empire, "The pine symbolized the body of the god [Attis] who died and was restored to life again" (Chevalier and Gheerbrant, *The Penguin Dictionary of Symbols* 756). In the poem, the Aleppo (Syria) *pine* to which the speaker refers is also known as the Jerusalem *pine* and is often used as a Christmas tree, the evergreen that, even today, Christians associate with both the Son of God and the Tree of Life in Genesis 2.9. *Writing under Erasure*

the pinwheel pends: the Milky Way, our own spiral galaxy. *The Experiment of Eternity*

Pisces: the zodiacal Fishes, the astrological sign that augurs the coming of Christ's kingdom. See Jung, *Aion* 90: "to the extent that Christ was regarded as the new aeon, it would be clear to anyone acquainted with astrology that he was born as the first fish of the Pisces era, and was doomed to die as the last ram [lamb] of the declining Aries era." *Prefigured*

pi transcendental: The speaker means that *pi* is "the ratio [of the circumference of a circle to its diameter], equal to 3.14159265+ [. . .]" ("pi²" [n.], defs. 2a, b), and that it is *transcendental* because it is not a countable algebraic number. See Davies, *The Mind of God* 129: "pi can only be given to a particular approximation, because it has an infinite decimal expansion." *Tumbling Escher*

pixel: "the basic unit or picture element that makes up the image displayed on a video screen" ("Pixel" [n.], def.). *Life in a Mortal Universe; The Teleoperator's Dream*

plagioclase: i.e., *plagioclase* feldspar, a rock-forming mineral found mainly in the lunar crust. *Hercules in the Vessel of the Sun; A Walking Man I*

plantigrade: "walking on the whole sole, as a human or bear" ("Plantigrade" [adj.], def.). *Namespace*

Platonic solid: a mathematics-inspired, three-dimensional shape—e.g., the cube, since "each face is the same-sized square" and the same number of squares (3) "meet at each corner." *Tumbling Escher*

Plato's cave: in Book VII of the *Republic* (c. 380 BC), an allegory that demonstrates the difference between the material things that we perceive in the world—objects likened by Plato to shadows projected upon a *cave* wall—and the archetypal Forms from which they derive their essential reality. *History's Thread; Plato's Cave*

pneuma: either "a wind-breath or spirit" (Jung, *Symbols of Transformation* 316) or "the Son of God, who descends into matter and then frees himself from it in order to bring healing and salvation to all souls" (Jung, *Psychology and Alchemy* 301). "The cabalistic idea of God pervading the world in the form of soul-sparks (*scintillae*) and the Gnostic idea of the Spinther (spark) are similar" (301n26). *Dreaming in Code*

Pneumatic: "having to do with the spirit or soul" ("Pneumatic" [adj.], def. 3). See 1 Cor. 15.45: "Scripture [Gen. 2.7] says, 'The first man, Adam, became an animate being' [i.e., a living soul], whereas the last Adam [Jesus Christ, the all-inclusive Son of God] has become a life-giving spirit." *Life Out There; Pneumatic; The Ultimate Fate of the Universe*

Pneumatic as Hermes: *rebis* co-born: In medieval alchemy, *Hermes* (or Mercurius), in his role as hermaphroditic *rebis,* combines—i.e., integrates—paired opposites, like Sol and Luna. *Hermes,* "originally a wind god," is a forerunner of the alchemical Mercurius in his pneumatic or "aerial aspect": the "Philosophic ambisexual Man" who became both the "analogue of Christ" and the "breath-soul" of the body (Jung, *Alchemical Studies* 212-13, 219). *Life Out There*

point: According to Johann Christoph Steeb, a Renaissance alchemist, "The point is most akin to the nature of light, and light is a *simulacrum Dei*" (Jung, *Alchemical Studies* 151)—i.e., a trace or a semblance or an image of God. See also *Mysterium Coniunctionis* 45, where Jung quotes another alchemist, John Dee, Steeb's contemporary: "'Things and beings have their first origin in the point and the monad.'" *Figure Skater; Postmodern; Pushing Gravity; Wayfinder; The Weight of History*

The point that happened everywhere is One: in astrophysics, the big-bang singularity, the *point* of infinite compression from which the entire cosmos "erupted" (Greene, *The Elegant Universe* 83). In other words, at the first space-time moment, the matter of the universe was "squeezed into a single point" (Davies, *The Mind of God* 49). *The Weight of History*

Polaris: the Polestar, i.e., the North Star, "the point around which everything turns" and hence "a symbol of the self" (Jung, *Psychology and Alchemy* 188). *Blazar/Quasar; Herald*

Pollux' jot: Castor's immortal twin brother conceived as "'the emblem of [the] perfect and indivisible Man. . . . The Son of the Man is the one iota, the one jot flowing from on high, full and filling all things, containing in himself everything that is in the Man, the Father of the Son of Man.'" (Here, the Christian theologian Hippolytus translates Monoïmos' late-first-century Gnostic paraphrase of John 1, "a meaningful exposition of the psychological self" that Jung quotes in *Aion* 218.) *Tearing the Fabric of Spacetime*

Postmodern: a mode of thought characterized by ironic self-reference, culturally embedded discourse, deferred meanings, and self-amused complexity. Of course, the reader may decide that such subversive stylistic elements are tangential to the main point of this poem, since its basic theme underscores both the "universally binding" numinosity of the archetypes and their "eternal presence" (Jung, *Psychology and Alchemy* 36, 221). *Postmodern*

potter's wheel: See Dream 48 from a mandala dream series featured in Jung, *Psychology and Alchemy* 190-91: "The potter's wheel rotates on the ground [. . .] and produces earthenware ('earthly') vessels which may figuratively be called 'human bodies.'

Being round, the wheel refers to the self and the creative activity in which it is manifest." *Serious Reader*

Pour from the psyche, till the eye is full, / *Aldebaran* (al-DEB-uh-run), located in the Bull: *Aldebaran* is "the bright-orange [binary] star" situated in the constellation Taurus, the *Bull,* and representing, pictorially, "the eye of the Bull" (Engelbrektson, *Stars, Planets, and Galaxies* 28, 46). *Tearing the Fabric of Spacetime*

A precinct ubiquitous as a point: "the inner, sacred precinct, which is the source and goal of the psyche and contains the unity of life and consciousness" (Jung, *Alchemical Studies* 25). From its center emanates the suprapersonal self, a God-image that the alchemists represented by the "'indivisible point,' which is simple, indestructible, and eternal" (148). *Wayfinder*

Primordial Adam: The speaker refers to the archetypal first man and to his original androgyny; in Paradise, Adam and Eve "had no genitals" (Jung, *Alchemical Studies* 143). *Pneumatic*

the prison of the dun: the dungeonlike cosmic lockup. Thus, according to current data, "roughly 68% of the universe is dark energy. Dark matter makes up about 27%. The rest—everything on Earth, everything ever observed with all our instruments, all normal matter—adds up to less than 5% of the Universe." See Dr. Mamta Patel Nagaraja, "Dark Energy, Dark Matter," *NASA Science* 1 <science.nasa.gov>. Accessed on 5 June 2015. *Siblings of the Sun*

protoplast: Jung describes "the race of protoplasts" in *Alchemical Studies:* "The ancient teachings about the Anthropos or Primordial Man assert that God, or the world-creating principle, was made manifest in the form of a 'first-created' (*protoplastus*) man, usually of cosmic size. In India he is Prajapati or Purusha, who is also 'the size of a thumb' and dwells in the heart of every man, like the Iliaster of Paracelsus. In Persia he is Gayomart [. . .], a youth of dazzling whiteness, as is also said of the alchemical Mercurius. In the *Zohar* [the principal text of the Jewish Kabbalah] he is Metatron, who was created together with light. He is the celestial man whom we meet in the visions of Daniel, Ezra, Enoch, and also in Philo Judaeus. He is one of the principal figures in Gnosticism, where, as always, he is connected with the question of creation and redemption" (132) and with "the deathless Original Man, to whom the mortal man can be approximated by means of the alchemical opus" (166). *Pneumatic*

pseudosphere: the opposite of a sphere—hence, a "false" sphere. The surface of a hyperbolic *pseudosphere* has a constant negative curvature and can stretch out into such shapes as a saddle, a funnel, a horn, and a spinning top. For a related perspective, see Clifford A. Pickover, *The Math Book: From Pythagoras to the 57th Dimension, 250 Milestones in the History of Mathematics* (New York: Sterling, 2009) 254: "The pseudosphere is a geometrical object that resembles two musical horns glued together at their rims. The 'mouthpieces' of the two horns are located at the ends of two infinitely long tails, as if to be blown only by the omnipotent gods. The peculiar shape was first discussed in depth in the 1868 paper 'Essay on an Interpretation of Non-Euclidean Geometry' by [the]

Italian mathematician Eugenio Beltrami," a scholar also famous for his work in physics. Pickover adds that, "To produce the surface [of the *pseudosphere*], a curve called a *tractrix* is rotated about its asymptote" (AS-im-toht), the line that touches the curve without intersecting it. *Pseudosphere*

Purusha: the Hindu Cosmic Man, who embodies metaphysical consciousness even as Prakriti, his feminine counterpart, represents primal matter. See the note on "protoplast" given above. *A User's Guide to Spacetime*

The quantum collapses and is not done: According to the Everett-DeWitt many universes interpretation of *quantum* theory, our local world "is continually splitting into countless near copies of itself. [. . .] In addition to this ceaseless replication, our own bodies are part of the world, and they too are split and split again. Not only our bodies, but our brains and, presumably, our consciousness [are] being repeatedly multiplied, each copy becoming a thinking, feeling human being inhabiting another universe much like the one we see around us" (Davies, *Other Worlds* 136-37). *Hermes' Nested Spiral*

Quantum cosmic ray, I sense myself, shy: In his essay "Last Voyage for the Keeper of the Hubble," Dennis Overbye explains that "When the Space Shuttle passes through a zone in the orbit called the South Atlantic Anomaly, astronauts are exposed to large doses of cosmic rays, high-energy particles from the Sun or distant galaxies, which leave a wake of visible light as they pass through a dark-adapted human eyeball." Thus, the astronaut John Grunsfeld found that "he could identify the different kinds of particles zooming through his eyeball by how bright the flashes were." Simply put, "'In space you can get in touch with your quantum self,' Dr. Grunsfeld said. 'I was a human cosmic ray detector'" (4). *Keeper of the Hubble*

quasar [quas(i-stell)ar (radio source)]: "any of a number of starlike celestial objects that emit immense amounts of light and radio waves: quasars are thought to be the ancient, exploding origins of new galaxies and are probably the most distant and observable objects in the universe" ("Quasar" [n.], def.). *Life in a Mortal Universe; Spherical*

Quaternal as a precinct: an image of the total self, a psychologically quadratic figure (Jung, *Aion* 224) not unlike "the squared circle" of the crucified Christ (204), the latter icon, in Jungian texts, a symbol of *discriminated* wholeness, since it subsumes the four psychological functions: sensation and intuition; thinking and feeling. *Precinct*

Quaternal as Woman, triadic as Man: In alchemical literature, "Four signifies the feminine, motherly, [and] physical," while three represents "the masculine, fatherly, [and] spiritual [. . .]" (Jung, *Psychology and Alchemy* 26). *Messenger*

Quaternity's startlement: See *Aion* 224n7, where Jung remarks that "The circle has the character of wholeness because of its 'perfect' form; the quaternity, because four is the miminum number of parts into which the circle may be naturally divided." Thus "the quaternity of Christ [. . .] is exemplified by the cross symbol" (204). Here, of course, the speaker responds to an unexpected embodiment of the God-image: "Adam before the Fall" (39). *Rebis*

The Quilted Multiverse: an infinite universe composed, like a gigantic quilt, of patchwork parallel worlds (Greene, *The Hidden Reality* 355). *The Quilted Multiverse*

quintessence: not only an alchemical name for the ancient and medieval concept of the aether, a pure fifth element after earth, fire, water, and air—symbolically, "the ever-hoped-for and never-to-be discovered 'One'" (Jung, *Psychology and Alchemy* 124)—but also, in modern physics, a theoretical form of dark energy invoked to explain the accelerating universe. *Quintessence; Terraforming Mars*

Qwiff: a quantum wave function that describes "the probability of an observation and not the actual observation" (Fred Alan Wolf, *Taking the Quantum Leap* [New York: Harper, 1981] 170). An offshoot of wave-particle duality, qwiffs "are called functions because they are functional, which means [that] they depend on things for their operation"—on space and time (186). In effect, "Qwiffs represent what *could* take place in reality." Nevertheless, as ghostly, quantum-jumping particles, "Qwiffs predict with *uncertainty* [emphasis added] the behavior of matter" (219). Thus, according to Wolf, it is the human perceiver who activates the qwiff—i.e., turns it on and off—and, with each observation, collapses the wave of probability into reality. *The Experiment of Eternity; Keeper of the Hubble; Nothing; Symbiote; Tipler's Subset*

Qwiff like my *rebis:* According to Fred Alan Wolf, "in quantum physics all actions in the universe are governed by quantum wave functions," or qwiffs, that "govern the probabilities of events taking place." However, "When actions occur that follow a pattern of intelligent behavior[,] these qwiffs change abruptly from indicating probable or possible actions" to fostering a "meaningful," "single," and "actual" action ("Medical Questions and Quantum Physics," *The Yoga of Time Travel and Dr. Quantum's World* 22 June 2010: 1 <http://fredalanwolf.blogspot. com>). Of course, in this poem, the speaker discovers that he can further "reify"—i.e., concretize—his own illusive existence because, paradoxically, even as he dons his Kevlar spacesuit, he not only "distills" but also "inhabits" the Christ-centered symbol of the *rebis,* "one of the indefinite number of possibilities [that exist] within the mind, not outside of it" (Toben, Sarfatti, and Wolf, *Space-Time and Beyond* 95). Cf. also Wordsworth's "inward eye / Which is the bliss of solitude" in "I Wandered Lonely as a Cloud" (lines 21-22). *Keeper of the Hubble*

Rabboni's capes: The speaker alludes not only to the cloaks with which "Crowds of people carpeted the road" during Jesus' triumphant entry into Jerusalem (Matt. 21.8), but also to the Lord's "seamless" mantle, "woven in one piece throughout," for which the soldiers "cast lots" after the Crucifixion (John 19.24). See also John 20.14-16: Even later, on the Sunday morning after the Savior's death, Mary of Magdala "turned round and saw Jesus standing there, but did not recognize him. Jesus said to her, 'Why are you weeping? Who is it you are looking for?' Thinking it was the gardener, she said, 'If it is you, sir, who removed him, tell me where you have laid him, and I will take him away.' Jesus said, 'Mary!' She turned to him and said, 'Rabbuni!' (which is Hebrew for 'My Master')." Here, "Rabboni" is an alternate form. *Herald*

Raised to the sun, *albedo* in the spill: In the alchemical *opus,* "the silver or moon condition [. . .] still has to be raised to the sun condition. The *albedo* is, so to speak, the daybreak, but not till the *rubedo* is it sunrise" (Jung, *Psychology and Alchemy* 232). *Vas Bene Clausum*

raven: in chemical transformation, a symbol of the *nigredo* or blackness, the first stage of the *opus,* "which was felt as 'melancholia' in alchemy and corresponds to the encounter with the shadow in psychology" (Jung, *Psychology and Alchemy* 36). *Beyond Gender*

A reasoning soul ascends to the heart: In the *Liber de Spiritu et Anima,* a compilation of medieval views that flow from "the mainstream of Augustinian tradition," Alcher of Clairvaux, a twelfth-century Cistercian monk, "attributes very great importance to self-knowledge, as being an essential condition for union with God. 'There are some who seek God through outward things, forsaking that which is in them, and in them is God. Let us therefore return to ourselves, that we may ascend to ourselves. . . . At first we ascend to ourselves from these outward and inferior things. Secondly, we ascend to the high heart. . . . In the third ascent we ascend to God'" (qtd. in Jung, *Alchemical Studies* 249n16). *Sunday*

***rebis* (RAY-beese):** A basic alchemical symbol "compounded of two parts and therefore frequently hermaphroditic as an amalgam of Sol and Luna," the *rebis* depicts "the consciousness-transcending fact [that] we call the self" (Jung, *Psychology and Alchemy* 202). *The Archivist; Beyond Gender; Body of Evidence; Bystander Cyborgs; Canadarm; Carrier; Compass; Dreaming in Code; Electrospinlacing; The Exaltations of the Nettles; Figure Skater; Footprint; Heracles Peeled; Herald; Keeper of the Hubble; Life Out There; Made; The Man Who Made a Copy of Himself; Mandragora's Dream; Mapping Celestial Terrains; Namespace; Outrider; The Quilted Multiverse; Rebis; Saffron of the Metals; Siblings of the Sun; Space; Sunday; Techwed; Terraforming Mars; Tipler's Subset; The Universe Speaks; A User's Guide to Spacetime; Vas Bene Clausum; The Weight of History; The Whole Atlas; Writing under Erasure*

The *rebis* (RAY-beese) that springs from forebrain to brow: an androgyne, "the dual being born of the alchemical union of opposites" (masculine, feminine) and "recognized as a symbol of the self" (Jung, *Aion* 268)—here, either like the "flashing-eyed" battle-goddess Athena, the daughter of Zeus who, "Full-grown and in full armor, [. . .] sprang from his head" (Hamilton, *Mythology* 29), or else, having been sown, or constellated, in the human cerebrum, like any imagined god. *The Quilted Multiverse*

recursive: self-referential, like the perceiving human brain itself. See Harth, *Windows on the Mind* 225: The new laws of quantum physics not only "draw the observer onto the stage as an active participant in the spectacle [that] his senses pick up," but also suggest that "the dynamics of his consciousness may not be separable from the dynamics of the world." *The Self-Thinking Thought*

red quasars [quas(i-stell)ar (radio sources)]: "[S]tarlike celestial objects that emit immense amounts of light and radio waves," *quasars* "are thought to be the ancient origins of new galaxies and are probably the most distant and observable objects in the universe" ("Quasar" [n.], def.). However, extremely *red*-shifted *quasars* are another matter: Since they "are partially obscured by dust, which reddens their light in a way that is similar to the Sun [when] viewed during sunsets on earth," and since they are powered by super-massive black holes and therefore may be "involved in [driving] galaxy-wide blowouts of gas and dust," these phenomena may actually "inhibit star formation in the early universe." See Sean Nealon, "Do Extremely Reddened Quasars Extinguish Star Formation?" *UCR Today* 15 Nov. 2016: 1-2 <ucrtoday.ucr.edu>. *Life in a Mortal Universe*

Redshift: See Kaku, *Hyperspace* 196: "the fact that the stars are receding from us at fantastic velocities has been repeatedly verified by measuring the distortion of their starlight (called the red shift)." Kaku adds that "The starlight of a receding star is shifted to longer wavelengths—that is, toward the red end of the spectrum—in the same way that the whistle of a receding train sounds higher than normal when approaching and lower when receding. This is called the Doppler effect," a phenomenon named after C. J. Doppler, a nineteenth-century Austrian physicist. *A User's Guide to Spacetime*

Re-enters the cavern: In many cultures, although the *cavern* is a recurrent symbol of the world, "The characteristic 'centrality' of the cavern [also] makes it a place of birth and of regeneration"—in effect, a "womb" or "passageway" not unlike the cave where Jesus was born and where He was also buried. (See Chevalier and Gheerbrant, *The Penguin Dictionary of Symbols* 170-71). *Something to Live For*

Regimen of Venus: one in a series of alchemical procedures that represent cyclical death and renewal. Thus, at the end of the *Regimen of Venus,* the color "changes into a livid purple, whereupon the philosophical tree will blossom. Then follows the regimen of Mars [. . .]," during which the soaring colors of the rainbow and of the peacock appear (Jung, *Mysterium Coniunctionis* 288-89). *The Exaltations of the Nettles*

Regolith: here, a mixture of powdery gray moondust and pulverized rock. *Prefigured; Tumbling Escher*

Repairs the station: i.e., the International Space Station (ISS), both a habitable artificial satellite and a unique scientific laboratory. Its first component was launched into low-Earth orbit in 1998. *Station*

resin: i.e., the *resin* of the wise, "a synonym for the transforming substance," either the life force likened by the alchemists "to the glue of the world" or a red gum [originally gum arabic] fixed as "the medium between mind and body and the union of both" (Jung, *Psychology and Alchemy* 161). See also Chevalier and Gheerbrant, *The Penguin Dictionary of Symbols* 797: "Because it is incorruptible, because it is flammable, and because it is generally produced by evergreen trees [including such conifers as the spruce, the fir, the cedar, and the pine], resin is a symbol of purity and immortality." In fact, "The trees from which it comes have sometimes been taken as symbols of Christ." *Writing under Erasure*

Resorbed Her globe: According to Thomas Merton, not until he had eaten, and then metabolized, the Eucharistic Host, could the speaker—Gaea's restless drifter—know either "the soul of [his] own soul" or "the being of [his] own being" (*The Living Bread* [1956; New York: Dell, 1959] 120). *The Exaltations of the Nettles*

rhombi (ROM-bye): equilateral parallelograms, i.e., plane figures, each of them with four sides and each of them with the opposite sides parallel and equal. *Pseudosphere*

Rigel (RYE-jill): a supergiant double star in the constellation Orion. To read the star chart detailed in this stanza, see Engelbrektson, *Stars, Planets, and Galaxies* 46: "To the ancient Egyptians, Orion was identified with Osiris, who died periodically and was revived by the flooding of the Nile. [. . .] A line diagonally through Orion from the blue star *Rigel* to *Betelgeuse* and to the north locates *Gemini* with *Castor* and *Pollux*. Above Orion, the sky is dominated by *Auriga,* the *Charioteer.*" *The Limits of the Coded World*

the ring that curves: either any one of Saturn's seven icy rings or else a collapsing star—a spinning black hole—that "flattens" until eventually it "is compressed into a ring" (Kaku, *Hyperspace* 226). *Serious Reader*

Robonaut: NASA's robotic astronaut, a "state-of-the-art humanoid" designed for space travel. "Outside the spacecraft, it will perform its tasks under the control of a human operator at a tele-presence console" (Menzel and D'Aluisio, *Robo sapiens* 129). *Mapping Celestial Terrains; Travelling Forever in the Same Direction*

Robonaut's wand: a substitute magic *wand,* "the badge of an individual's power over material things" (Chevalier and Gheerbrant, *The Penguin Dictionary of Symbols* 1078)—here, the tether-hook that NASA's dexterous humanoid robot used during the construction of the International Space Station (Menzel and D'Aluisio, *Robo sapiens* 131). *Travelling Forever in the Same Direction*

A robot that looms by reel or by rite: In a line that contains multiple puns, the NASA robonaut that seems to 'take shape [. . .] indistinctly, as through a mist" ("Loom^2" [vi.], def.), either weaves at his loom ("Loom^1" [vt.], def.) or winds ("Reel^3" [vi.], def.), or else is wound, whether ceremonially, in some kind of religious ritual ("Rite" [n.], def. 3a), or fixedly in "a just claim" to power ("Right" [n.], def. 2a), on a spool of thread ("Reel^3" [n.], def. 1). *Segway*

the rock that at Horeb purled: See Exod. 17.6, where the Israelites drink a supernatural water that pours out of "a rock in Horeb," the latter a prefiguration of the *rock* that was Christ (1 Cor. 10.4). Here, the *rock at Horeb* moves "in ripples or with a murmuring sound" ("Purl" [vi.], def. 1). *Kepler*

Rooted in the torus: fixed or settled in a universe pictured as a hyperdoughnut, one of the "strange topologies" that Michio Kaku predicates in *Hyperspace* 94-98. *To Mars in a Month*

rotund as I tend: The speaker refers to "the spherical form of Plato's Original Man" (Jung, *Psychology and Alchemy* 84n38) as well as to the loops that generate wormholes. *Tearing the Fabric of Spacetime*

rotundum: in alchemy, the "round, original form" of "the spiritual, inner and complete man" (Jung, *Mandala Symbolism* 9-10). *The Möbius Strip; Rebis; Station*

RR Lyrae: globular cluster stars "that form a halo around the center of the [Milky Way] Galaxy" (Engelbrektson, *Stars, Planets, and Galaxies* 116). *Hercules in the Vessel of the Sun*

rubedo's gem: The rubedo [the reddening], the final stage in the alchemical *opus,* is "the continuation of [the] albedo," the whitening synonymous with the Light of Resurrection. "That is why they are often seen connected to each other, like the White Queen and the Red King. [. . .] In the eastern philosophies [the] rubedo corresponds with the formation of the 'diamond body,' [. . .] the pure and permanent Stone of the Philosophers" (Dirk Gillabel, "Alchemy 1.6: Rubedo-Redness," *Soul Guidance* 18 <www.soul-guidance.com>). Accessed on 17 Sept. 2017. *The Teleoperator's Dream*

Ruled by the light: i.e., by "the light of the discerning, conscious mind, a genuine *illuminatio* honestly acquired" (Jung, *Psychology and Alchemy* 91). *The Archivist*

rune: "any poem, verse, or song, esp[ecially] one that is mystical or obscure" ("Rune" [n.], def. 3b). *The Limits of the Coded World*

Saba's reveries: Saba (SAH-buh) is another name for the ancient kingdom of Sheba. Here, the word is used as a metonym for the Queen of Sheba, who visited King Solomon in order to experience his reputed wisdom (Kings 10.1-13). *Outrider*

saccades (suh-KAHDZ): "any of the rapid, involuntary jumps made by the eyes from one fixed point to another, as in reading" ("Saccade" [n.], def.). *Techwed*

A saffron clone: The speaker refers to the orange outer layer of the spacesuits that NASA astronauts wear "when they launch and land on the space shuttle." In fact, "that bright hue called International Orange was chosen for safety, because it stands out so well against a landscape" and is therefore a color highly apt for search and rescue. By contrast, the EVA (extravehicular activity) suits are white since they reflect "the strong heat of the sun" even as they offset "the black expanse of space." See Clara Moskowitz, "Why Are Astronauts' Spacesuits Orange?" *Live Science* 2 June 2010: 2-3 <www.livescience.com>. *The Weight of History*

Saffron of the metals: "the [yellow-orange] sun in the earth" (Jung, *Alchemical Studies* 225)—according to the alchemists, the philosophical gold taken as a symbol of eternity (149). *Saffron of the Metals*

salt in the swarm: not only the "arcane substance" hidden either in the primordial chaos or in the Hermetic vessel, but also Christ, "the salt of wisdom [. . .] given at baptism" (Jung, *Mysterium Coniunctionis* 241). *The Spherical Glass Vessel*

Salt of the metals, the lead of the air: symbols that integrate the male-female polarity of the hermaphrodite; the Rebis, and Christ as the *sal sapientiae* (the Salt of Wisdom). In fact, in alchemy, salt is an analogue not only of Christ, "the Word that is begotten from Eternity" (Jung, *Mysterium Coniunctionis* 241), but also of Christ (or Mercurius) in feminine form: the Queen of the South (377-78). Thus, "Johannes Grasseus says of the arcane substance: 'And this is the Lead of the Philosophers, which they also call the lead of the air. In it is found the shining white dove, named the salt of the metals, wherein is the whole magistery of the work. This [dove] is the pure, chaste, wise, and rich Queen of Sheba,'" the exemplar of wisdom and femininity ("Arca Arcani," *Theatricum chemicum* VI [Strasbourg, 1661] 314; qtd. in *Mysterium Coniunctionis* 245). See also Mark 1.10, where the Evangelist identifies Jesus with the dove, since "the Spirit, like a dove," descended upon the Savior. *Messenger*

Salt-sign: in alchemy, an analogue of the God-man, i.e., Christ. See Jung, *Mysterium Coniunctionis* 241: "the sign for salt was originally a double totality symbol: the circle representing non-differentiated wholeness, and the square discriminated wholeness." *Figure Skater; Wayfinder*

Salvific the blade that the Hebrew whets: Cf. "the Binding of Isaac" in Gen. 9-11: "Abraham built an altar and arranged the wood. He bound his son Isaac and laid him on the altar on top of the wood. Then he stretched out his hand and took the knife to kill his son [. . .]." *Postmodern*

Same Hermetic Name that Maria mimes: in the axiom of Maria Prophetissa (the Jewess also known as the sister of Moses), "the One as the fourth," a symbol of alchemy's quintessential Self, i.e., the Self as its own "container" (Jung, *Alchemical Studies* 87). *Kepler*

sapphire like a star: one of the precious stones that "adorned" the Garden of Eden (Ezek. 28.13). In *Alchemical Studies,* Jung emphasizes that "The special virtue of the sapphire is that it endows its wearer with chastity, piety, and constancy" (258-59). See also the note given below. *Postmodern*

Sapphirine as the Self: In *The Archetypes and the Collective Unconscious,* Jung states that, "As civilization develops, the bisexual primordial being [the hermaphrodite] turns into a symbol of the unity of personality, a symbol of the self. In this way the primordial being becomes the distant goal of man's self-development, having been from the very beginning a projection of his unconscious wholeness" (175). See also Jung's pertinent remark in *Psychology and Alchemy* 80, including fig. 30: "the golden flower of alchemy [. . .] can sometimes be a blue flower: 'The sapphire blue flower of the hermaphrodite.'" *An Oblate Spheroid*

The sapphirine planet: Earth, our home planet, "the pale blue dot" seen from outer space. (See the note above on *The blue dot wanders.*) *Prefigured*

Sapphirine satellite, capsule that pends / Above the mare—like a Sheetweb spends; / Secretes its silk; then, tabernacled, blends: the twelve-minute, computer-controlled descent of the *Eagle,* the Apollo 11 Lunar Module, compared to the silken movements of the *Sheetweb* Weaver, a spider that spins "a dome-shaped or flat web" (Herbert W. Levi and Lorna R. Levi, *A Guide to Spiders and Their Kin* [New York: Golden P, 1968] 44). The simile is, of course, fanciful. According to Michael Collins—the astronaut orbiting in the Command Module during the first moon-landing—the *Eagle* is "the weirdest-looking contraption ever to invade the sky, floating there with its legs awkwardly jutting out above a body which has neither symmetry nor grace. Everything seems to be stuck on at the wrong angle, which I suppose is what happens when you turn aeronautical engineers loose designing a vehicle which always flies in a vacuum and hence requires no streamlining" (*Carrying the Fire* 404). *Carrier*

Saturday: an Augustinian symbol: "Saturday heralds the [divine] light" that does not appear "in full strength" until Sunday (Jung, *Alchemical Studies* 249-50). See also Eph. 5.9: "Live like men who are at home in daylight, for where light is, there all goodness springs up, all justice and truth." *Saturday*

A Saturnine abstract being I mused: See Jung, *Alchemical Studies* 153: According to Paracelsus, when "the body has been purified by Melissa [an ancient arcanum] and freed from Saturnine melancholy, then the coniunctio [or 'chymical marriage'] can take place with the long-living inner, or astral, man." *Blazar/Quasar*

Saturn lidded tight: here, the *Saturn* V rocket that NASA used, during the 1960s and 1970s, to send Apollo astronauts to the moon. *Carrier*

the Saturn that peaks; / Cone that in the sky, mercurial, streaks: the 363-foot-tall Saturn V moon rocket that NASA used in its Apollo program. Here, the speaker describes the cone-shaped plume of fire and smoke that erupted from the Kennedy Space Center on Merritt Island, Florida, during a typical launch. *Writing under Erasure*

scales of the dace: "the thin, flat, overlapping, rigid, horny plates forming the outer protective covering" ("Scale"[2] [n.], def. 1) in the body of the *dace,* "any of various small, freshwater, cyprinoid fishes" ("Dace" [n.], def.). *Swain*

Scarab: in Egyptian mythology, the unicorned sun-beetle that symbolizes "both the Sun's cycle and, at the same time, resurrection" (Chevalier and Gheerbrant, *The Penguin Dictionary of Symbols* 833). See also *Psychology and Alchemy* 452, where Jung indicates that the scarab is "a creature born of itself." *Body of Evidence; Electrospinlacing*

scion: "a descendant; [an] offspring" ("Scion," [n.], def. 2)—here, of both Christ and Abraham. See Gal. 3.26: "For through faith you are all sons of God in union with Christ Jesus. Baptized into union with him, you have all put on Christ as a garment. There is no such thing as Jew and Greek, slave and freeman, male and female; for you are all one person in Christ Jesus. But if you thus belong to Christ, you are the 'issue' of Abraham, and so heirs by promise." *Keeper of the Hubble; Segway; Space; The Spherical Glass Vessel; The Weight of History; Writing under Erasure*

the scissors that twirled: the shears that move swiftly belong to Atropos, in Greek mythology the oldest of the Three Fates. After Clotho spins and Lachesis measures, Atropos cuts the thread of life to its appointed length. *The Universe Speaks*

Scoop in its scuttle: See "Collecting Moon Rocks: Sample Collection Tools," *Lunar and Planetary Institute* 1 <www.lpi.usra.edu>: During the Apollo (human spaceflight) program, "Scoops [spoonlike utensils] were used to collect soil samples." (Accessed on 8 May 2017.) Here, a *scuttle* is a pail or bucket that holds the lunar soil. *Station*

scree: a pile of loose stones or rocky detritus lying at the foot of a hill or at the base of a cliff. *Bulk; Compass; Life in a Mortal Universe; Serious Reader; Stewards of Creation; Techwed*

Secretes the foetus: The speaker refers to the spagyric *foetus,* equivalent in alchemy to the *filius philosophorum:* "the inner, eternal man [hidden] in the shell of the outer, mortal man" (Jung, *Alchemical Studies* 150). See the note on *The spagyric foetus* given below. *The Weight of History*

seed-pearls that glister: Cf. *The Body in Question* 27, where Jonathan Miller observes that "The nerve endings which register [our sensations or feelings] are embroidered like millions of seed-pearls throughout the fabric of our body." The word *glister* is an archaic variant of "glisten": "to shine or sparkle" ("Glisten" [vi.], def.), like the high-intensity illumination that fluorescence imaging allows. For an apt example of the latter technique, see John Farndon, "Nerve Signalling: Tracing the Wiring of Life," *Nobelprize.org* 16 Sept. 2009: 2 <www.nobelprize.org>. Equally pertinent—in light of "Saba's reveries" [line 16]— is the description of the pearl in *The Penguin Dictionary of Symbols,* where Chevalier and Gheerbrant indicate that "Pearls are rare, pure, and precious" and that "Their value makes them stand [not only] for the Kingdom of Heaven" (Matt. 13.45-46), but also for "the manifestation of God in the Cosmos" (743-44). *Outrider*

Segway: the Robotic Mobility Platform (RMP), both a "two-wheeled vehicle [that] can balance and hold position, while driving front to back and turning," and a lower body on wheels designed for Robonaut B. See Joe Bibby and Ryan Necessary, "Robonaut 1: RMP [Robotic Mobility Platform]," *NASA* 13 Mar. 2008: 1-2 <robonaut.jsc.nasa.gov>. *Made; Segway*

Selene's swain: the deployed Shuttle astronaut compared to Endymion, the androgynous shepherd-lover of Selene, the ancient Greek moon-goddess. *Symbiote*

Self's sun-and-moon tree: In *Alchemical Studies,* Jung reminds us that "Sometimes the prototype [of the *arbor philosophica*] is the tree of paradise, hung not with apples but with sun-and-moon fruit [. . .]" (302-03). Elsewhere, having analyzed the *coniunctio*—alchemy's "chymical wedding"—Jung features an apt illustration: the "Crowned hermaphrodite representing the union of king and queen" and "standing between the sun and moon trees," the entire scene a paraphrase of the alchemical *opus* (*Psychology and Alchemy* 231, fig. 116). *Space*

serpentine: supple, lithe, and curving, like the resurrected Savior, here projected as the crowned Ouroboros, "the snake that bites its own tail," the latter image both a self-described circle and a symbol of totality (Jung, *Aion* 190). *Something to Live For*

serpent of bliss: the healing serpent of Moses, a prefiguration of God's Chosen One, as Jesus himself indicates in John 3.13-15: "'No one ever went up into heaven except the one who came down from heaven, the Son of Man whose home is in heaven. This Son of

Man must be lifted up as the serpent was lifted up by Moses in the wilderness, so that everyone who has faith in him may in him possess eternal life.'" *The Universe Speaks*

Setting the Wheel on Fire: See Jung, *Aion* 137: In the fourth century the wheel of birth was in fact regarded as the horoscope, the symbolic *rota* of the heavens that "gives a picture first of the psychic and then of the physical constitution of the individual. [. . .] 'Setting fire to the wheel' is therefore a figurative expression for a catastrophic revolt of all the original components of the psyche, a conflagration resembling panic or some other uncontrollable, and hence fatal[,] outburst of emotion"—in effect, a veritable destruction of the soul that can be overcome only by spiritual conversion and "by the [Christ-centered] renewal of baptism" (136). So the speaker suggests in the last two lines of this poem: Despite the soul's defilement by leprous "matter that taints," an indwelling—*infilling*—"Essence that posits, [still] produces saints" (ll. 23-24). *Setting the Wheel on Fire*

the seven heavens: in various mythologies, the different levels of paradise that represent gradations of piety. *Bulk*

Seyferts (SEE-fertz): Named after the astronomer Carl K. Seyfert, who discovered them in the 1940s, *Seyferts* are spiral galaxies that are "known to have active nuclei" and, like quasars, are "thought to be powered by massive black holes at their centres." See Paul W. Hodge, "Seyfert galaxy," *Encyclopaedia Britannica Online* 1 <www.britannica.com>. Last updated on 9 Jan. 2018. *Life in a Mortal Universe; Plato's Cave*

Shaman: either a priest or a magus or a holy man with supernatural powers. *The Archivist; Carrier; Dreaming in Code; Electrospinlacing; The Exaltations of the Nettles; Figure Skater; Nothing; Pushing Gravity; Space; Writing under Erasure*

Shaman fixed like a peg in a sure spot: Cf. the Catholic translation of Isa. 22.23, where Eliakim receives from the Lord of Hosts the key of the House of David: "'I will fix him like a peg in a sure spot.'" See also *Thru the Bible with J. Vernon McGee, Volume III: Proverbs—Malachi,* where McGee asserts that "The Lord Jesus Christ is the nail in a sure place" (249). *Pushing Gravity*

the Shaman in her head, / Like the Zodiac, to the circle wed: Both the "round, original form" of "the spiritual, inner and complete man" (Jung, *Mandala Symbolism* 9-10) and the great *circle* of the ecliptic—along which the 12 constellations of the *Zodiac* lie—reflect an apparently fixed cosmic goal: archetypal wholeness. *Nothing*

Shard of plagioclase: Anorthosite, a fragment of moon rock collected by Apollo 15 astronauts, consists primarily of the triclinic feldspar mineral *plagioclase,* the latter component typically white, yellow, or reddish-gray, but also orange, pink, green, blue, brown, or even black. See not only Marc Norman, "The Oldest Moon Rocks," *Planetary Science Research Discoveries [PSRD]* 21 Apr. 2004: 4 <www.psrd.hawaii.edu>, but also Hershel Friedman, "The Plagioclase Mineral Series," *Minerals.net* 1-2 <www.minerals.net>. Accessed on 10 Nov. 2016. *Hercules in the Vessel of the Sun*

shell stars: The speaker refers to "a type of star [. . .] surrounded by a gaseous shell" ("Shell Star," *Dictionary.com* <www.dictionary.com>). *A Walking Man I*

Shem's outsiders: a prefiguration in the Old Testament of the "good stewards" who—as spiritual descendants of Shem, the son of Noah—shall dispense "the grace of God in its various forms" until the Rapture (1 Pet. 4.10). *Hermes' Nested Spiral*

The shirt of Nessus: in Greek mythology, the "splendid robe" that—being "anointed with the [poisonous] blood" of the Centaur *Nessus* and given unwittingly by Deianeira to Hercules—resulted in his torturous death (Hamilton, *Mythology* 171). Here, the infamous tunic is equivalent to the penitential hair shirt worn by Christian ascetics. *Setting the Wheel on Fire*

Should we harness a rocket, Fusion's pay, / Seconds of impulse confined in the bay: In his essay, "Mars, and Step on It," Michael Klesius indicates that, in order "to make a fusion-powered spaceship light enough to reach Mars in two weeks, propulsion experts will need a breakthrough in materials science." However, "If and when new materials make that possible, Mars may in fact be too close to Earth for a fusion rocket to truly show what it's got under the hood. A trip to Jupiter, on the other hand, 366 million miles away at its closest approach, would give the crew of a fusion-powered spacecraft almost 183 million miles of acceleration to the journey's midpoint. By then, a fusion engine delivering about 30,000 seconds of impulse would have gathered a speed of 50 miles per second—about 180,000 miles an hour. After decelerating for the next 90 days, it would slip into orbit around Jupiter; by then, the trip would have lasted 180 days, only six times as long as a one-way trip to Mars, despite covering 10.5 times the distance" (3). *A Walking Man I*

Should we leave the earth and track a straight line: a cosmic conundrum: "If you leave Earth and keep going in a straight line to the north or south in space, then you won't get to any planets in our Solar System. None of the planets of the Solar System ever stand to the north or south of the Earth; they are never more than about 25 degrees north or south of the equator." However, "If a spaceship [keeps] going north or south, then it may encounter planets around another star, but space is very empty, so the spaceship [will] have to travel thousands of lightyears before it encounters another star (unless the spaceship [adjusts] its course, [and] then it becomes easier)." In other words, "If we allow the spaceship to deviate a bit from the straight line (once it has left the Solar System), then it will be able to meet another planet more quickly"—yet still "about 15 million lightyears" before it reaches its destination. See *Astronomy Answers / AstronomyAnswer Book: Space Travel:* "Travelling Forever in the Same Direction" 16 <www.aa.quae.nl>. Last updated on 28 Dec. 2017. *Travelling Forever in the Same Direction*

Shriven hybrid: either the "scion" or offspring of line 23—a composite of body, soul, and spirit—or the Christian speaker himself heard and absolved by confessing ("Shrive" [vt.], 1, 2). *The Weight of History*

Sight's inverted bole: In *Alchemical Studies,* Jung notes that "The idea that man is an inverted tree seems to have been current in the Middle Ages. [. . .] In Hindu literature the tree grows from above downwards, whereas in alchemy (at least according to the pictures) it grows from below upwards." However, "In East and West alike, the tree symbolizes a living process as well as a process of enlightenment" (312-14)—in fine, the work of both "[moral] transformation and [spiritual] renewal" (317). *Space*

sigil: either "a seal" or "an image or [a] sign supposedly having some mysterious power in magic or astrology" ("Sigil" [n.], defs. 1, 2). *Messenger; Serious Reader*

Simulacra: the plural form of "simulacrum": not only "an image" and "[a] likeness," but also "a vague representation; [a] semblance" ("Simulacrum" [n.], defs. 1, 2). *Kepler; Testing the Night of Pan*

Skein of Golgotha reduced to a grain: The speaker regards *Golgotha,* the site of Christ's Crucifixion, as both Redemption's seed and the New Testament's narrative thread. *The Whole Atlas*

Sleeping, She slumbers for me in the stone: The speaker alludes to Nietzsche's metaphor in *Thus Spake Zarathustra,* "an image slumbers for me in the stone." Evidently Nietzsche "tried to wrest the secret of the superman from the stone in which it had long been slumbering. It was in the likeness of this slumbering image that he wished to create the superman, whom, in the language of antiquity, we may well call the divine man. But it is the other way about with the alchemists: they were looking for the marvelous stone that harboured a pneumatic essence in order to win from it the substance that penetrates all substances—since it is itself the stone-penetrating 'spirit'—and transforms all base metals into noble ones by a process of coloration. This 'spirit-substance' is like quicksilver, which lurks unseen in the ore and must first be expelled if it is to be recovered *in substantia.* The possessor of this penetrating Mercurius [. . .] can 'project' it into other substances and transform them from the imperfect into the perfect state. The imperfect state is like the sleeping state; substances lie in it like the 'sleepers chained in Hades' [. . .] and are awakened from death to a new and more beautiful life by the divine tincture extracted from the inspired stone" (Jung, *Psychology and Alchemy* 296-97). Of course, in this poem, even more pertinent than the transformation of matter in the alchemical *opus* is the "habitation" of God "in the heart of the believer" (Murray, *The Spirit of Christ* 6). Thus, "The eternal Son dwelt in the flesh in Jesus of Nazareth and prayed to the Father as man. In the same way, the eternal Spirit will dwell in us, sinful flesh, to train us to speak with the Father even as the Son did" (169). (Here, *She slumbers* because, implicitly, the transcendent Self "is androgynous and consists of a masculine and a feminine principle" [Jung, *The Archetypes and the Collective Unconscious* 364].) *Compass*

snow: In sundry Hermetic tracts, the mercurial Spirit of the Lord "flies [purified] like solid white snow" (Jung, *Alchemical Studies* 214). *Mapping Celestial Terrains; Travelling Forever in the Same Direction*

Sojourner immanent, artifex lame: The *Sojourner* is the Spirit of Christ that now indwells and infills His believer-priests (Murray, *The Spirit of Christ* 212), and the *artifex* is Oedipus, the archetypal suffering son who unwittingly killed his father [King Laius of Thebes] and married his own mother [Jocasta], and then, after "desolate wanderings, [. . .]

died rejoicing that he was no longer hateful to men, but welcomed as a benefactor" to humankind (Hamilton, *Mythology* (262). *The Whole Atlas*

Solar Max: the Solar Maximum Mission Satellite (SMMS). Launched into space on 14 February 1980, the satellite was designed primarily to investigate "the gamma-ray spectrum of solar flares." After it malfunctioned in January 1981, NASA astronauts recovered *Solar Max* with the Remote Manipulator System (RMS) in April 1984 and repaired the satellite in the aft-end of the space shuttle Challenger's payload bay. See "Solar Maximum Mission (SMM)," *NASA's HEASARC [High Energy Astrophysics Science Archive Research Center]: Observatories* 1 <heasarc.gsfc.nasa.gov>. Last modified on 10 May 2010. See also the picture of the astronaut George C. Nelson as he is "carried on a tour of inspection around *Solar Max* on the RMS 'cherry picker,'" in Kerrod, *Space Walks* 58-59. *History's Thread*

a solar sail: In 2011, a NASA team "embarked on the development of a Technology Demonstration Mission known as the Solar Sail Demonstrator [. . .], which intended to prove the viability and value of using a huge, ultra-thin sail unfurling in space," as well as "the pressure of sunlight itself to provide propellant-free transport, hovering and exploration capabilities." Among its goals, "solar sail technology could enable a host of versatile space missions," not the least of which is "flying an advanced space-weather warning system to more quickly and accurately alert satellite operators and utilities on Earth of geomagnetic storms caused by coronal mass ejections from the sun." See Jennifer Harbaugh, "Solar Sail Demonstrator ('Sunjammer')," *NASA: Tech Demo Missions* 1 <www.nasa.gov>. Last updated on 3 Aug. 2017. *Kepler*

Some Mayan sigil: See Jung, *Psychology and Alchemy* 353, fig. 190: "Mayan ritual tree with serpent." The Mayan civilization arose in the Yucatan area of what is now Mexico between 2600 BC and 1800 BC. *Serious Reader*

Some tumbling tessellation—like a sword, / The serpent rises back into the board: See the photograph of "Tumbling Escher," a quilt both designed and described by Mary Candace Williams as the November entry in *The 2011 Calendar of Mathematical Imagery,* a repeating geometric shape that helps us to visualize a higher-dimensional world: "If you look at the quilt at a perpendicular angle you have a traditional diamond tessellation known as Tumbling Block. From the side, however, it rises up and back into the quilt" and is "thus a nod to [the Dutch artist M. C.] Escher's 'Reptiles' in which the drawn lizard rises up and out and back into the drawing board"—not unlike [it might be added] Ouroboros, "the self-devouring dragon" that "begot and gave birth to itself" (Jung, *Alchemical Studies* 259). *Tumbling Escher*

So, Typhon pursuing him, Pisces shunts / In the wettest place that the foetus fronts: In Greek mythology, Typhon, the monster with a hundred heads, had pursued Leto when her son Apollo "was still in her womb; but she fled to the floating island of Delos on a 'night sea journey' and was there safely delivered of her child" (Jung, *Symbols of Transformation* 371). Here, of course, *Pisces,* who *shunts* or turns aside in order to conquer the serpent, represents not only Christ, both sun-hero and "Goat-Fish," but also His womb-entwining coheir, the speaker himself. In other words, the latterday galactic pilgrim, being reborn, has just emerged—like the Son of God—from "'the wettest place on earth,' [. . .] the maternal depths" (198). *Rebis*

soul-atoms: "a 'mythological' conception of smallest particles, which, as the smallest animated parts, [. . .] are known even to the still Paleolithic inhabitants of central Australia" (Jung, *The Archetypes and the Collective Unconscious* 57). *Dreaming in Code; Figure Skater; Made*

The souls of Hermes wrapped around this world: "In Neoplatonic philosophy the soul has definite affinities with the sphere." Thus, "The soul substance is laid round the concentric spheres of the four elements above the fiery heaven" (Jung, *Psychology and Alchemy* 83-84). See also Jung, *Mysterium Coniunctionis* 526: "Just as the air encompasses the earth, so in the old view the soul is wrapped round the world," and 358n386: "the individual has a plurality of souls." *To Live and Work in Deep Space*

Soul-spark: in Cabalistic texts, the spirit that descends into matter. *Beyond Gender; Canadarm; Dreaming in Code; Figure Skater; Kepler; Life Out There; Namespace; Postmodern; Precinct; Pseudosphere; Station; Tearing the Fabric of Spacetime; Techwed; Writing under Erasure*

the spagyric foetus: The word *spagyric* refers to an alchemical process that both separates and combines (Jung, *Mysterium Coniunctionis* 481n91). Thus, the *spagyric foetus* ascends into Heaven that it may become a spirit from a body and then descends to earth that it may become a body again. Cf. John 3.13: "'No one ever went up into heaven except the one who came down from heaven, the Son of Man whose home is in heaven.'" *Bellicose Ares; Beyond Gender; Body of Evidence; Carrier; Dreaming in Code; Figure Skater; Heracles Peeled; Hercules in the Vessel of the Sun; Kepler; Life Out There; The Limits of the Coded World; The Man Who Made a Copy of Himself; Mapping Celestial Terrains; Messenger; An Oblate Spheroid; Outrider; Pneumatic; Postmodern; Pushing Gravity; The Quilted Multiverse; Saffron of the Metals; Saturday; Space; Stewards of Creation; Sunday; Techwed; Terraforming Mars; The Universe Speaks; A Walking Man I; The Weight of History*

spagyric gum: gum Arabic, or "blessed" red gum, not only the "'resin of the wise'—a synonym for the transforming substance"—but also "the [alchemical] medium between mind and body and the union of both" (Jung, *Psychology and Alchemy* 161, 401). (In *Mysterium Coniunctionis* 481n91, Jung offers helpful *root* definitions of the word *spagyric:* either "to rend, tear, [or] stretch out" or "to bring or collect together.") *Terraforming Mars*

Spagyric paladins headed to Mars: Like knights or heroic champions ("Paladin" [n.], def. 2), the NASA astronauts will ride to Mars in Orion, "a next-generation spacecraft" carried atop the first Space Launch System (SLS) rocket; live and work on the Red Planet, and then return to Earth. See Kimberly Henry, "NASA's Space Launch System is the Rocket for the Ride to Mars," *NASA* 22 Sept. 2015: 1 <www.nasa.gov>. *Heracles Peeled*

spherical, chart / Then square the circle: In many alchemical texts, "the soul is a spiritual substance of spherical nature, like the globe of the moon, or like a glass vessel" that, according to Gerhard Dorn (c. 1530 – 1584), must be made 'by a kind of squaring of the circle'" (Jung, *Alchemical Studies* 86), the latter image but a "natural" symbol of totality (96). See also the note on *The Spherical Glass Vessel* given below. *Spherical*

The Spherical Glass Vessel: With this symbol, the speaker emphasizes that the realization of the self is always the work of God. Not surprisingly, then, in alchemy, the vessel of circular distillation "was 'hermetically' sealed (i.e., sealed with the sign of Hermes); it had to be made of glass, and had also to be as round as possible, since it was meant to represent the cosmos in which the earth was created. Transparent glass is something like solidified water or air, both of which are synonyms for spirit. The alchemical retort is therefore equivalent to the *anima mundi,* which according to an old alchemical conception surrounds the cosmos." Significantly, Caesarius of Heisterbach, the thirteenth-century Cistercian monk, "mentions a vision in which the [subsistent, individual] soul [itself] appeared as a spherical glass vessel" (Jung, *Alchemical Studies* 197-98), a sublime *vitrum* "that had eyes before and behind" (Jung, *The Archetypes and the Collective Unconscious* 295n4). *The Spherical Glass Vessel*

The spherical man that molecules flee: In *Psychology and Alchemy,* Jung observes that the form of "Plato's original man" is "spherical," like the world soul itself (84n38), because "The sphere is a [divine] whole that embraces all its contents [. . .]" (154). In fact, its round nature "suggests the lunar or feminine aspect of God" (325). *Serious Reader*

spheroid: "a body that is almost but not quite a sphere" ("Spheroid" [n.], def.). See also the note on *An oblate spheroid* given above. *The Archivist; Heracles Peeled; Setting the Wheel on Fire; Symbiote; Techwed*

spit that He spat: The speaker concludes his "platonic riddle" even as he underscores the miraculous sign—the manifestation of Jesus' divinity—in John 9.6-7. Thus, having met a man "blind from his birth," Jesus "spat on the ground and made a paste with the spittle; he spread it on the man's eyes, and said to him, 'Go and wash in the pool at Siloam.' (The name means 'sent.') The man went away and washed, and when he returned he could see." *Platonic Riddles*

a star like a hound: Sirius, also called the Dog Star and Sothis (SO-this), is the brightest star seen from Earth. In the ancient Egyptian story of Isis (EYE-sis) and Osiris (oh-SIGH-ris)—a "lunar mystery"—the rising of the Dog Star (i.e., of Isis manifest as the *star* Sothis) "brought Osiris back to life" (Baring and Cashford, *The Myth of the Goddess* 233-34). *The Limits of the Coded World*

stars like a spoon: the Little Dipper, a constellation in the Northern Sky. Its brightest star is Polaris, i.e., *Stella Polaris,* the Pole [or Polar] Star: the "point around which everything turns" and hence "a symbol of the self" (Jung, *Psychology and Alchemy* 188). *The Limits of the Coded World*

station: The International Space Station (ISS), a habitable artificial satellite launched into low-Earth orbit in 1998. *Station; A User's Guide to Spacetime*

a statue's oils: The speaker alludes to a familiar alchemical procedure: the extraction of the "stone-penetrating" spirit from matter. See Jung, *Psychology and Alchemy* 295n18: "'extract the oil from the hearts of statues.'" *Peregrination*

stave: "a set of verses, or lines, of a song or poem; [a] stanza" ("Stave" [n.], def. 3). *Space; Writing under Erasure*

The steersman in the Tree: the crucified Christ, like Heracles a sacrificial sun-god, but, here, hung upon the maternal *Tree*. *The Archivist*

a still / Born in the unconscious: A *still* is an alchemical vessel that both condenses and purifies. Here, of course, the reference is figurative. In other words, gripped by a series of numinous archetypes—Cross, *rebis,* omphalos, soul—the speaker distills even as he formulates them in the laboratory of the mind. See Jung, *Mysterium Coniunctionis* 524. *Siblings of the Sun*

the stinger: On 16 November 1984, in order to capture *Westar VI,* a rogue communications satellite, the astronaut Dale Gardner, flying a Manned Maneuvering Unit and riding the *stinger,* "a spear-like probe, [. . .] jetted over to the spinning satellite, [. . .] inserted the stinger and locked onto the motor nozzle. With bursts of his MMU jets, he stopped the satellite [from] spinning and then jetted back to the waiting orbiter. There, the RMS [the Remote Manipulator System] arm reached out and grasped a grapple pin on the stinger to capture the satellite. The satellite was then lowered into the payload bay. But the final stowing of the satellite had to be done by hand, proving once again the need for the human touch in space maneuvers" (Kerrod, *Space Walks* 50). *The Spherical Glass Vessel*

the stone in the mill: See Jung, *Psychology and Alche*my 307, fig. 158: "The 'Mill of the Host.' The Word in the form of scrolls is poured into a mill by the four evangelists, to reappear as the Infant Christ in the chalice. Cf. John 1:14: 'And the word was made flesh . . . .'" Equally pertinent is the note on *stone that is no stone* given below. *Vas Bene Clausum*

stone in the sea: i.e., either in the aquasphere or in the *sea* of infinity. In alchemical texts, "The chaos is a *massa confusa* that gives birth to the stone [. . .]. The definition of this spherical being as [. . .] 'the most serene God' sheds a special light on the perfect, 'round' nature of the *lapis,* which arises from, and constitutes, the primal sphere; hence the *prima materia* is often called *lapis* [. . .]" (Jung, *Psychology and Alchemy* 325). *Serious Reader*

The stone of the wise: in alchemy, the mysterious *lapis philosophorum,* the philosophers' *stone,* a symbolic "parallel of Christ" (Jung, *Alchemical Studies* 96, 320). See also 1 Pet. 2.5: "Come, and let yourselves be built, as living stones, into a spiritual temple; become a holy priesthood, to offer spiritual sacrifices acceptable to God through Jesus Christ." *Shapeshifter*

stone that, heated, dried: The speaker refers to "the motif of torture"—a crucial element in "the phenomenology of the individuation process as the alchemists experienced it" and to one "gruesome" recipe in particular: "the drying of a man over a heated stone" (Jung, *Alchemical Studies* 328-29). Jung notes that, ironically, it is the artifex himself who, having projected himself into the material substance—the "stone"—of the *opus,* "cannot endure the torments" (329). *To Mars in a Month*

stone that is no stone: in alchemy, the philosophers' *stone* taken as a symbol of the unified self, i.e., "of the inner Christ, of God in man" (Jung, *Alchemical Studies* 96, 291n9). *Space; Tumbling Escher*

the stone that transmutes inside me curled: The speaker refers to the transformational *lapis*—in effect, *the stone* that has a spirit: "the figure [of Christ] veiled in matter" (Jung, *Alchemical Studies* 247). *Kepler*

the stone that Trismegistus picked: "the secret stone," i.e., the philosopher's *stone:* the elixir of life sought by Hermes *Trismegistus,* legendary first alchemist and emblematic magus (Jung, *Psychology and Alchemy* 291n8). *The Ultimate Fate of the Universe*

Streams all colors: i.e., "the 'many colours' *(omnes colores),* or 'peacock's tail' *(cauda pavonis),* [that] lead to the one white colour that contains all colours" (Jung, *Psychology and Alchemy* 231), in alchemical texts a symbol of "indescribable" human wholeness (18, 223). *Made*

Streams like tesserae follow in my train: At lift-off, clouds of smoke and steam envelop the Saturn V rocket even as their repeated patterns mosaic the sky. *Bulk*

***Stretch a rubber membrane, and it will tear. / [. . .]* Likewise the fabric of Spacetime may snare:** an analogy that Brian Greene explores in *The Elegant Universe:* "If you relentlessly stretch a rubber membrane, sooner or later it will tear. This simple fact has inspired numerous physicists over the years to ask whether the same might be true of the spatial fabric making up the universe. That is, can the fabric of space rip apart, or is this merely a misguided notion that arises from taking the rubber membrane analogy too seriously?" In a chapter titled "Tearing the Fabric of Space," Greene proceeds to demonstrate that "a new formulation of physics that goes beyond Einstein's classical theory [of general relativity] and [that] incorporates quantum physics might [indeed] show that rips, tears, and mergers of the spatial fabric can occur" (263). *Tearing the Fabric of Spacetime*

string(s): In *The Whole Shebang: A State-of-the-Universe(s) Report* (New York: Simon, 1997), Timothy Ferris indicates that, according to superstring theories, "Subatomic particles are tiny strings made of space. [. . .] Strings are so small that when viewed from a distance—meaning at any wavelength of light or any other form of electromagnetic illumination—they 'look like' infinitesimal particles" (220). *Bystander Cyborgs; Postmodern*

strut: "a brace [or rod] fitted into a framework to resist pressure in the direction of its length" ("Strut" [n.], def. 2). *The Teleoperator's Dream*

Styrofoam: In the "cosmic census" conducted by the human race, *Styrofoam* appears as "an early trophy of Kepler's [satellite observatory]—a planet that is [. . .] half as large as Jupiter, but so puffed up by the heat of its star that it is only one-tenth as dense" (Overbye, "Gazing Afar for Other Earths, and Other Beings" 2). *Life Out There*

subclavian vein: here, "the left subclavian vein, which via the superior vena cava carries blood to the right atrium of the heart" (Nilsson and Lindberg, *Behold Man* 138). *Dreaming in Code*

such a beam as Hubble has set: / An accretion disk where positrons are, / *Gas and dust and the occasional star,* / Bulk speed of plasma, parsecs in a car, / Or toroid opaque or both near and far: The speaker pinpoints the birth of the blazar, a "blazing quasi-stellar object." Thus, blazars, like all Active Galactic Nuclei [AGN], "are thought to be ultimately powered by material falling onto a supermassive black hole at the center of the host galaxy. Gas, dust and the occasional star are captured and spiral into this central black hole, [thereby] creating a hot accretion disk which generates enormous amounts of energy in the form of photons, electrons, positrons and other elementary particles. This region is quite small, approximately 10-^{3} parsecs in size." However, "There is also a larger opaque toroid [a hyperdoughnut that extends] several parsecs from the central black hole [and that contains] a hot gas with embedded regions of higher density" ("Blazar," *Wikipedia* 1-2 <en.wikipedia.org>). Last edited on 7 Dec. 2017. *Blazar/Quasar*

such a concourse as I had neared: i.e., the Milky Way Galaxy, the "huge flat aggregation of stars" where Earth and the Sun are located (Engelbrektson, *Stars, Planets, and Galaxies* 73). *Electrospinlacing*

Such a homonym as Salmacis taught / To none but Hermes: A *homonym* is "a word with the same pronunciation as another [word] but with a different meaning, origin, and, usually, spelling ("Homonym" [n.], def. 1). It also refers to "either of two people with the same name" (def. 3). Here, the speaker suggests that *Salmacis,* the nymph who became united in a single body with Hermaphroditus, the son of *Hermes* and Aphrodite, was in fact an unconscious projection by *Hermes,* or by his mythologist, of a timeless archetype—i.e., the hermaphrodite, both his paired opposite and "His self-thinking thought." *The Self-Thinking Thought*

Such a play as magi electrospray, / Each droplet—plume or splay—become my kin, / A web of fibers carried to the skin / In seamless layers, melt beneath my shin— / Elastic, thin—embedded in my twin: The speaker describes the spacesuit of the future, a veritable epidermis "designed to augment [an astronaut's] biological skin" and "applied in spray-on fashion in the form of an organic, biodegradable layer." See Leonard David, "High-Tech Spacesuits Eyed for 'Extreme Exploration,'" *Space.com* 26 Jan. 2005: 2 <www.space.com>. See also the note on *Electrospinlacing* given above. *Body of Evidence*

such Cheshires as purr— / Swatches of tint on the retina—blur: See Jonathan Miller, *The Body in Question* 42: "our senses introduce us to a world, and not just to a kaleidoscope of sensations. The visual world, for example, is not just a patchwork of tints—although that is all there is on our retina. [. . .] In the very act of entering consciousness, sensations are somehow made up into scenery and we experience them as objects in the world. But this doesn't happen automatically. The mind has to make a guess about the identity of what it sees, hears, or feels, and the odds are determined by all sorts of hints and hot tips." In effect, each "imaginary picture" that we "improvise" appears to be—like the Cheshire cat in *Alice's Adventures in Wonderland*—both there and not there. *Outrider*

Sunday: In the New Testament, and "in the mainstream of Augustinian tradition," *Sunday,* or the Sabbath, is "the day on which man returns to God and receives anew the light of the *cognitio matutina,*" i.e., self-knowledge (Jung, *Alchemical Studies* 249). *Sunday*

The Sun in the scree: light that falls upon "a pile of rock debris at the foot of a cliff" ("Scree" [n.], def.], whether on Earth or on the Moon. *Bulk*

The Sun, unceasing, burns; it does not die: According to Frater Centaurus, a Thelemite, "science has helped us to understand" not only "that the Sun burns unceasingly, rather than dying daily," but also that light itself may yet prove to be the "invisible fifth dimension" ("Testing the Night of Pan" 3). Thus, beyond Dark Energy and Dark Matter, "the Nightside of the Tree of Life," lies "the star stuff of the 'Dayside,'" the precursor of "sentient consciousness" as well as the symbol of "spiritual divinity" (2). *Testing the Night of Pan*

the swain [. . .] / That patches his holon: The NASA astronaut describes himself as "a lover or suitor" of Spacetime ("Swain" [n.], def. 3) who repairs either a damaged solar panel of the International Space Station (ISS) or the broken world itself. Here, a *holon* is an entity—whether an atom or a universe—that is both a whole and a part. *Station*

Symbiote: a symbiont; "an organism living in a state of symbiosis" ("Symbiont" [n.], def.), i.e., in a relationship of mutual interdependence. See also John Thomas Riley, "How to Prevent a Robot Rebellion," *Tech Briefs: Create the Future Design Contest* 5 Mar. 2012: 2 <contest.techbriefs.com>: "We must clearly drop the master-slave concept we now have of humans over machines, and have a new vision. [. . .] Symbiotic relationships place very specific requirements on all involved. For one thing, symbiotes love each other devotedly. We certainly love our machines, like the car and the computer, but work has just started on getting our machines to love us. This then is our real challenge. One way to jettison our old way of thinking [. . .] would be to incorporate a robot, thus giving it the limited level of personhood that corporations now enjoy. Perhaps we could start with the Robonaut, who is currently occupying the International Space Station (ISS), for robot personification." *The Man Who Made a Copy of Himself; Symbiote*

Synergy: simultaneous or "cooperative action" of many separate agencies—here, an intrinsic "force" in the cosmos ("Synergy" [n.], def. 1). *Pushing Gravity*

syzygies (SIZ-uh-jeez): paired opposites that represent wholeness—e.g., Adam/Eve; Mars/Venus; male/female; the One/the Other. *Postmodern*

Talos congealed: See Hamilton, *Mythology* 127: "terrible to behold," *Talos* was "the last man left of the ancient bronze race." At the intervention of "dread" powers of the underworld, when *Talos* "lifted a pointed crag to hurl it at the *Argo,*" the ship that had sailed in search of the Golden Fleece, "he grazed his ankle and the blood gushed forth [and, here, coagulated] until he sank and died." *Heracles Peeled*

Teleoperator: See *YourDictionary* 2 June 2017: 1 <www.yourdictionary.com>: "One who operates (a robot, etc.) remotely" ("Teleoperator[2]" [n.], def.). In other words, in research and technical communities, teleoperation refers to "operation at a distance." By contrast, "Telepresence uses virtual reality display technology" in order to immerse the operator *visually* "in the robot's workspace" (Joe Bibby and Ryan Necessary, "Robonaut: Telepresence" <robonaut.jsc.nasa.gov>. *The Teleoperator's Dream*

Telepathic lace: the distribution of galaxies compared to the filamentary design of a *lace* tablecloth and, in this lyric, postulated as a paranormal cosmic phenomenon. *The Limits of the Coded World*

teleported: Teleportation is "the theoretical transportation of matter through space by converting it into energy and then reconverting it at the terminal point" ("Teleportation" [n.], def.). In *Space-Time and Beyond,* Bob Toben, "in conversation" with the physicists Jack Sarfatti and Fred Wolf, explains that, since "Every action in 'real' time is an indefinite sequence of materializations and dematerializations on the microscopic quantum level," and since the latter phenomena "occur faster than the speed of light and in such great numbers that perception of this action is continual," it is not inconceivable that "Teleportation could result from a giant quantum jump" (80). *A Walking Man I*

Telepresent: The speaker refers to a sophisticated form of teleoperation—in effect, to an experience that resembles virtual reality. Thus, wearing a Helmeted Mounted [Stereo] Display (HMD), along with force and tactile feedback gloves, a human teleoperator senses—even as he simulates—the programmed actions of NASA's Robonaut. *Segway; Techwed; A Walking Man I*

temenos (TEH-meh-NAHS): in Greek mythology, a sacred place; "a taboo area" where one can "meet the unconscious" (Jung, *Psychology and Alchemy* 54). *Outrider*

terabyte: "a unit of digital information storage used to denote the size of data. It is equivalent to 1,000 gigabytes," or one trillion [10^{12}] bytes. See "Terabyte (TB): Definition—What does *Terabyte (TB)* mean?" *Technopedia* <www.technopedia. com>. Accessed on 25 Jan. 2018. *The Whole Atlas*

tessellation: the arrangement of one or more geometric shapes in a repeated pattern without gaps or overlaps in the covered surfaces. Only three regular polygons can tessellate the plane: squares, [equilateral] triangles, and hexagons. *Tumbling Escher*

tesseract: a four-dimensional hypercube "that has been unraveled," or unfolded, as a series of "ordinary three-dimensional cubes [. . .] arranged in a three-dimensional cross"—in these poems, a symbol as well as a manifestation of our own "harrowing," unknown, "reassembled," and "seemingly impossible" universe. See Kaku, *Hyperspace* 70, 77-78, and also 72, fig. 3.7: Salvador Dali's 1954 oil-on-canvas painting *Crucifixion (Corpus Hypercubus),* where the artist depicts Christ "as being crucified on a [crosslike] tesseract." *Beyond Gender; Canadarm; The Exaltations of the Nettles; Hercules in the Vessel of the Sun; Outrider; Prefigured; Saturday; Something to Live For; Stewards of Creation; Symbiote; Testing the Night of Pan; Tumbling Escher; A Walking Man I*

Tethys: in Greek mythology, both a Titan goddess and—as the wife-sister of Oceanus, the world-encircling river-god—a personification of the sea. *Hercules in the Vessel of the Sun*

Theonomous: "controlled by God" ("Theonomous" [adj.], def.). *Serious Reader*

thermosphere: "the atmospheric zone or shell located above the mesopause beginning at an altitude of *c.* 85 km (53 mi.) and characterized by a great rise in temperature with increasing altitude" ("Thermosphere" [n.], def.). *Swain*

Thetis' shield: Thetis was the Mother of the Greek warrior Achilles. After she had beseeched Hephaestus, the lame blacksmith of the gods, to replace her son's lost armor, he forged and crafted for Achilles—in addition to a breastplate, "brighter far than fire light"; and "a massive helmet, measured for his temples," and "greaves [i.e., shin armor] of pliant tin"—a glittering yet subtle *shield* that depicted the history of the world and that Thetis delivered to her ill-fated son at Troy. See Homer, *The Iliad* 454:18.581-85. *Heracles Peeled*

Though man is heaven, and woman the key, / Castor, *all joy still wants Eternity:* The latter clause echoes the last line in the repeated "roundelay" from Nietzsche's *Thus Spake Zarathustra*: "Woe implores: Go! / But all joy wants eternity." *Kepler*

***The Three Laws* defined:** The speaker refers to *The Three Laws* that govern the behavior of robots and that Isaac Asimov introduced in "Runaround," a short story published in 1942: "(1) A robot may not injure a human being or, through inaction, allow a human being to come to harm; (2) A robot must obey orders given to it by human beings, except where such orders would conflict with the First Law; (3) A robot must protect its own existence as long as such protection does not conflict with the First or Second Law." Later, Asimov enunciated "a fourth or zeroth law that outranked the others: [0] A robot may not harm humanity, or, by inaction, allow humanity to come to harm." See Ulrike Barthelmess and Ulrich Furbach, "Do We Need Asimov's Laws?" *MIT Technology Review* 16 May 2014: 1-2 <www.technologyreview.com>. *The Teleoperator's Dream*

The Three plus One: See the note on *Maria's maxim* given above. *Compass*

Through alienation of instinct, errs: In *Psychology and Alchemy,* Jung suggests that the separation of "rational present-day consciousness" from "the collective unconscious," although inevitable, "leads to such an alienation from that dim psyche of the dawn of mankind that a loss of instinct ensues. The result is instinctual atrophy and hence disorientation in everyday human situations." Jung adds that the individual can recover from this cramped and dessicated "lack of soul" only if "the conscious mind will suffer itself to be led back to the 'children's land,' there to receive guidance from the unconscious as before" (58-59). *Footprint*

Through its spherical shell: "The possibility of traversable wormholes in general relativity was first demonstrated by Kip Thorne and his graduate student Mike Morris in a 1988 paper; for this reason, the type of traversable wormhole [that] they proposed, held open by a spherical shell of exotic matter, is referred to as a Morris-Thorne wormhole." However, in the pure Gauss-Bonnet theorem (1848), "exotic matter is not needed in order for wormholes to exist—they can exist even with no matter" (Anderson, "Wormholes" 2). *Full Circle*

Through recombination photons that kiss: In "Capturing the birth of the universe," an online essay, Abigail Beall reminds us that, in the standard cosmological model, "photons mediate electromagnetic interactions between particles" (*Daily Mail.com* 22 Apr. 2016: 5-6 <www.dailymail.co.uk>). See also the note on "ions recombined— / Transparent site" given above. *A User's Guide to Spacetime*

thumbling: a creative dwarf—a personification of "the hidden [or subterranean] forces of nature" (Jung, *The Archetypes and the Collective Unconscious* 158). *Bellicose Ares; The Ultimate Fate of the Universe*

thus we advance / In pulses or packets: i.e., in *pulses or packets* that contain "a given [fixed] quantity of energy" (Davies, *Other Worlds* 32) and that, in the strange domain of the quantum, "behave like waves [of probability] as well as particles" (63). Matthew W. Browne upholds this theory in "Physicists Confirm Power of Nothing, Measuring Force of Quantum Foam," *New York Times* 21 Jan. 1997: C6: "We are all quantum fluctuations. [. . .] That's the origin of us all and of everything in the universe, not just dark matter." *Hermes' Nested Spiral*

Till, crowned in the caul above Adam's grave: Here, the figurative *caul* is the foetal membrane that encloses the still-gestating Christian astronaut. (See Jung, *Aion* 221n157: "'Jesus is still in the making.'") See also the allusion to *Adam's grave* in the note on the *omphalos* given above. *The Experiment of Eternity*

Till in the Mind's eye the Shaman revolts: / [. . .] REM's hierophants carry His thunderbolts: Although "actual manned flights to Jupiter must be ruled out" because "Jupiter is surrounded by zones of intense radiation which would be fatal to any astronaut unwise enough to venture too close" to the gaseous planet (Moore, *Travellers in Space and Time* 5), the speaker insists, whether nostalgically or perversely, that, in his rapid-eye-movement imaginings, sublime solar priests still transport the *thunderbolts* of the masterful Roman deity. See also Chang, "For NASA, Return Trip to Jupiter in Search of Clues to Solar System's Origins" 4, where the writer indicates that, on the voyage to Jupiter, *Juno* (the spacecraft named after the wife of the god of light) "would be carrying a commemorative plaque of Galileo Galilei, the scientist who first looked at Jupiter through a telescope, as well as three aluminum Lego figures: of Galileo [balancing his telescope and a model of the planet Jupiter], Juno [holding a magnifying glass], and [the sky-god] Jupiter carrying His thunderbolts." *Figure Skater*

Tipler's Subset: a variant of the Everett-DeWitt or many-universes interpretation of quantum mechanics. See Davies, *The Mind of God* 126: Frank J. Tipler, a professor of Mathematical Physics at Tulane University, "believes that all possible universes that can support consciousness [are] experienced" and that "The set of programs capable of generating cognizable [i.e., knowable] universes will be a small subset of the set of all possible programs." Our subset "can be regarded as typical." *Tipler's Subset*

To conquer fear, I build a pseudosphere / Complete with panels; upon rhombi peer; / Invert my pentagons, yellow for clear: Cf. PolyClare, "Pseudosphere from Geomag Box," *Fandom* 22 Jan. 2009: 5-7 (<geomag.wikia.com>, where the artisan had knowingly crafted a "near-miss" pseudosphere from Geomag Box, a construction set with assorted panels: "First I built the Augmented Truncated Dodecahedron CT2T. [Next,] I popped out and replaced the neighboring triangles with yellow rhombi. I also replaced the central pentagon with a yellow pentagon, just for fun. [. . .]. While the model was still relatively strong, I inverted the model, so that the yellow panels were on the bottom. I then proceeded to *gingerly* replace the rest of the triangle pairs with rhombi, also replacing the clear pentagons with yellow pentagons as I went along. I would never lift the model, just twist it as I worked to complete all the replacements." *Pseudosphere*

To Hermes corresponds or to His sign: In this stanza, the speaker links the caduceus, the wingèd staff with two serpents coiled about it, not only to *Hermes,* in Greek myth the divine herald and messenger of the other gods, but also to the Ouroboros, the snake that bites its own tail, a self-described circle (Jung, *Psychology and Alchemy* 293), and, even earlier, to the revolving NASA astronaut of line 21. *Mandragora's Dream*

To mystery, Castor, cyborg I bow: Cf. Christian de Duve, *Vital Dust* 301—"The human mind may be only a link—perhaps even a side branch—in an evolutionary saga that is far from completed and may well some day produce minds much more powerful than ours. According to the predicted lifetime of the sun, on our planet alone the thinking biosphere has another five billion years to go, one thousand times the duration of the step from ape to man. We must bow to mystery." *The Quilted Multiverse*

torus: the universe pictured as a hyperdoughnut, one of the "strange topologies" that Michio Kaku predicates in *Hyperspace* 94-98. *Bulk; The Man Who Made a Copy of Himself; Messenger; Namespace; Outrider; Precinct; Quintessence; Segway; Something to Live For; Symbiote; Tearing the Fabric of Spacetime; To Live and Work in Deep Space; To Mars in a Month; A User's Guide to Spacetime*

torus and square: not only a hidden topological conceit—the universe shaped as a toroidal polyhedron—but also a muffled allusion to the squaring of the circle, an apt symbol of the alchemical *opus,* since the latter process "breaks down the original chaotic unity into the four elements and then combines them in a higher unity. Unity is represented by a circle and the four elements by a square." In other words, "The spirit (or spirit and soul) is the *ternarius* or number three which must first be separated from the body [the fourth] and, after the purification of the latter, infused back into it" (Jung, *Psychology and Alchemy* 124-25). See also 126, fig. 60: "Squaring of the circle to make the two sexes one whole." *Quintessence*

To scale the planet and in the moon sit / Alembicated, he goes round with it: The astronaut journeys to the moon in order to "beget" himself, i.e., to be born—by the synthesis of male and female—whole again. See *Mysterium Coniunctionis* 140, where Jung notes that "in Plutarch [c. 46-120] Hermes [god of revelation and guide of souls] sits in the moon and goes round with it (just as Heracles does in the sun)." In effect, the moon is the white "receptacle of souls" (140n240). Thus, "with her moisture," Luna "brings the slain dragon to life." Indeed, in alchemy, "The idea that the dragon or Sol must die is an essential part of the mystery of [his moral and spiritual] transformation" (142). However, psychologically, the moon, like the sun, "must [also] be contained in the dragon" and in its voluntary [shared] death, since "consciousness (Sol)" cannot exist without "the unconscious (Luna)," its feminine counterpart (144). Here, of course, the astronaut is "alembicated" because "the coniunctio [the union of opposites] takes place in the retort" (460). In effect, through the rite of the circular distillation, "He who ascends unites the powers of Above and Below and shows his full power when he returns again to earth" (227). *Beyond Gender*

Transcerebral substance, inborn, divined, / The Psyche that observes us: In *Synchronicity: An Acausal Connecting Principle,* Jung argues that "we must ask ourselves whether there is some other nervous substrate in us, apart from the cerebrum, that can think and perceive" (93) and that, being either uncanny or "transcerebral" (95), exists over and above or even prior to consciousness. Here, *The Psyche* is both "the mind considered as a subjectively perceived, functional entity, based ultimately upon physical processes but with complex processes of its own" ("Psyche" [n.]. def. 3), and "the human soul" itself (def. 1). *Wayfinder*

Transit, without dips, as real in its squirm / As Aphrodite's mold or Ares' herm: The speaker refers to "the repeated dips caused by planet crossings, or 'transits,'" in the field of view of the Kepler Space Telescope (Overbye, "Gazing Afar for Other Earths, and Other Beings" 4). However, at times, even without Kepler's telltale "dips," the passage of such celestial bodies proves as *real,* i.e., as *palpable,* as the clay form of Aphrodite, the Greek Goddess of Love, or the carved head of Ares, the Greek God of War. In other words, for those clear-sighted seers who "dwell" in the light, "phantoms" become facts (Arthur Zajonc, *Catching the Light: The Entwined History of Light and Mind* [New York: Oxford UP, 1993) 184, 195), like "metaphors of the eye" (Jacob Bronowski, *The Origins of Knowledge and Imagination* [New Haven: Yale UP, 1978] 21). *Life Out There*

Transparent as crystal: In the literature of the Church Fathers, Christ is often compared to a crystal. Thus, in his *Homiliae in Ezechielem (Homilies on Ezekiel),* Saint Gregory the Great (c. 540-604) explains that, through the "glory" of His resurrection, Christ "'hardened after the fashion of a crystal from water, so that there was one and the same [immaterial] nature in it and in [H]im [. . .]'" (qtd. in Jung, *Mysterium Coniunctionis* 449n345). *An Oblate Spheroid*

Travel full circle *in a single day:* In *Other Worlds,* Paul Davies remarks that "The topology of the universe might be much more complicated than either the simple 'torus' or 'sphere,' and contain a whole network of holes and bridges. [. . .] Space and time would then be connected to themselves in a bewildering way. It would be possible, for instance, to go from one place to another by a variety of routes—each apparently a straight path—by threading through the labyrinth of bridges. The idea of a space bridge giving almost instantaneous access to some distant galaxy is much beloved of science fiction writers. The possibility of avoiding the long route through intergalactic space would be most appealing if giant wormholes really do thread the universe" (98). See also Jung, *Alchemical Studies* 79n64: Ouroboros, the self-devouring, self-fertilizing dragon, "brings itself forth in a single day." *Full Circle*

The Tree of Life burled: here, not only Jesus Christ, the wounded Savior, but also "the outward and visible sign of the realization of the self" (Jung, *Alchemical Studies* 196). *The Weight of History*

the tree of the sea: in the alchemical *opus,* the *arbor philosophica,* "which, if it has any meaning at all, symbolizes spiritual growth and the highest illumination" of the individual (Jung, *Alchemical Studies* 89), and "which in turn has parallels with the Cabalistic tree of the Sefiroth and with the tree of Christian mysticism and [of] Hindu philosophy" (Jung, *Mysterium Coniunctionis* 134-35). *The Spherical Glass Vessel*

Trepan the skull and ascend to the heart: The speaker suggests that, in order to achieve self-knowledge, "an essential condition for union with God," the reasoning soul must bore into the brain as with a crown saw ("Trepan[1]"[vt.], def. 1) and, "after a night during which consciousness slumbered, wrapped in the darkness of the unconscious," *ascend* to the [high] *heart.* According to Saint Augustine in the *Liber de Spiritu et Anima,* "the high heart" is nothing less than "the *imago Dei,* or self" (Jung, *Alchemical Studies* 249&n16). See also the note on *I ascend to myself* given above. *Spherical*

Trismegistus: i.e., Hermes Trismegistus, both the legendary first alchemist and emblematic magus. *The Ultimate Fate of the Universe*

troll: a fabulous creature, either dwarf or giant. *Footprint*

Turin's cloth: a Catholic icon—the linen shroud that bears the image of the crucified Savior. *The Experiment of Eternity*

turpentine: here, an organic solvent derived from the resin found in pine trees. *Writing under Erasure*

The undertaking seemed so vast at first: i.e., the fulfillment of the New Covenant, the heaven-sent promise that we may be "made new in mind and spirit, and put on the new nature of God's creating, which shows itself in the just and devout life [centered in the Spirit of the glorified Jesus] called for by the truth" (Eph. 4.23-24). See also Andrew Murray, *The Spirit of Christ* 84-85. *Saturday*

unfolds like a scroll: Here, the astronaut steps from his moonship in a "space-time landscape [that] unfolds like a scroll with all moments and events co-existing within it, though we view these sequentially, one by one, as the scroll unfolds" (Shalini Asha Bhaloo, *Oneness: How to Live with Joyous Expansion, Ease, and Lightness* [Bloomington: Balboa P, 2012] 112). See also Rev. 5.7, where "the Lamb went up and took the scroll from the right hand of the One who sat on the throne" and broke the seven seals. *Footprint*

uniped: not only Robonaut, NASA's one-footed robotic astronaut, but also the alchemical Monocolus, the one-stemmed, semi-castrated, androgynous version of Mercurius. See Jung, *Mysterium Coniunctionis* 500n135, 505-10, and also Pl. 4: "The Two Unipeds." *Station; The Whole Atlas*

unit: the MMU (Manned Maneuvering Unit), a now-defunct propulsion device, couched here as a metonymy for the helmeted (and hence glass-encased) NASA astronaut. The term evokes the image of the astronaut as a wandering microcosm. See also Jung's assessment of the Monad (the indivisible point) conceived by the Gnostics as an emblem of the "perfect Man" (*Aion* 218-19). *Precinct*

Unravel the torus: See Davies, *Other Worlds* 136: According to the many-universes interpretation of quantum theory, "the world is continually splitting into countless near copies of itself." However, "it is wrong to think of us as inhabiting one particular world of superspace," since "superspace itself is our home." *Something to Live For*

Until we clear a moon without a skin: i.e., Europa, Jupiter's smallest moon, in this poem a magnet for the NASA astronaut and his crew. Cf. Moore, *Travellers in Space and Time* 51-52: "Drawing towards it we search for the usual craters and hills, but this time the landscape is completely different. Nothing can be made out except for a bright background and a medley of darkish lines which form an intricate maze [. . .]. Craters are absent; so are any well-defined features—nothing but these curious lines, and a closer look shows that the lines are very shallow. [Covered with a layer of ice,] Europa is as smooth as a snooker ball." *Tipler's Subset*

Upborne by my Saturn or hung with strands: The speaker imagines that his surrogate Apollo astronaut has been carried to the moon by NASA's Saturn V rocket or else lifted there by invisible rope or thread. *Bulk*

upon a stair, / Venus locked in the arms of Mars: The scene shapeshifts to the gnu-generated graph of a trefoil knot (i.e., a knotted loop) that evokes a floating *stair* wound around itself like interlocking *arms*. See "Trefoil Knot," the wry geometric skein featured, along with a "top-down view" of its intersecting lines, in *Some Fun with GNUPLOT* 9. Accessed on 25 Jan. 2018. *Tumbling Escher*

Vas Bene Clausum: "The *vas bene clausum* (well-sealed vessel) is a precautionary measure very frequently mentioned in alchemy, and is the equivalent of the magic circle. In both cases the idea is to protect what is within from the intrusion and admixture of what is without, as well as to prevent it from escaping" (Jung, *Psychology and Alchemy* 167). *Vas Bene Clausum*

The vas is a phial of spherical shape: See Jung, *Psychology and Alchemy* 236n15: The Hermetic vessel is "a circular instrument, a [well-sealed] phial of spherical shape." *Siblings of the Sun*

vassal: the cyborg (the astronaut) no less than the android (the robonaut) conceived as "a subordinate, subject, [or] servant" of God ("Vassal" [n.], def. 2). *Station*

veer / With six degrees of freedom: The speaker refers to the Space Shuttle's peculiar module, the Manned Maneuvering Unit (MMU)—seemingly "a backpack with armrests"—that "has enabled astronauts, for the first time, to orbit for brief periods without any umbilical line or safety tether [attached] to their spaceships" (Allen and Martin, *Entering*

Space 113). Thus, "Unconstrained by a surface of any kind," the astronauts may move "in all six degrees of freedom: three linear and three rotational" (Joseph P. Allen, "Physics at the edge of the earth," in *Pictorial Communication in Real and Virtual Environments,* ed. Stephen R. Ellis, with Mary K. Kaiser and Arthur C. Grunwald [1991; Bristol, PA: Taylor & Francis, 1993] 17). *Wayfinder*

Velcro strip: *Velcro* is "a nylon material made with both a surface of tiny hooks and a complementary surface of a clinging pile, used, as in garments, in matching strips that can be pressed together for easy fastening and unfastening" ("Velcro" [n.], def.). Not surprisingly, *Velcro* figured significantly "in many contexts" during Project Apollo. Thus, "On the lunar surface," astronauts used it "to keep suit pockets closed or open, to secure Sample Collection Bags (SCBs) and other gear" to the PLSS [Portable Life Support System] tool harness, and even to hang "the Cosmic Ray Experiment from a convenient landing gear strut [. . .]" (Eric Jones, Ken Glover, and Ulli Lotzmann, "Fastenings: Velcro," *Working on the Moon* 1 <www.workingonthemoon.com>). Last revised on 4 Oct. 2007. *Dreaming in Code*

verbena: "of plants of the verbena family, with spikes or clusters of showy red, white, or purplish flowers, widely grown for ornament" ("Verbena" [n.], def.). *Techwed*

Warm secretions from some sebaceous gland: "Sebaceous glands are found around the hair follicles. These glands excrete sebum, a fatty substance which when distributed on hair and epidermis [the upper or outer layer of the skin] makes them water-repellent, more elastic, and better able to endure cold" (Nilsson, Lindberg, et al., *Behold Man* 105). *The Skin That I Live In*

We are the subset of some other set: In *The Physics of Immortality: Modern Cosmology, God and the Resurrection of the Dead* (New York: Doubleday, 1994), Frank J. Tipler argues that a "person" is "a computer program that can pass the Turing test" (210)—i.e., can behave in every way like a person. However, Tipler adds that, as "an entity that codes information," each of us may be but a "subsimulation"—in effect, a simulation "embedded inside a larger simulation that does not stop" (211). *Tipler's Subset*

We become a child and a fish at once: See Jung, *Symbols of Transformation* 198: "The fish in dreams occasionally signifies the unborn child, because the child before its birth lives in the water like a fish"; within weeks, during its fetal phase, "becomes child and fish at once"; and, like the astrological Christ, the first *fish* of the Pisces era, "is therefore a symbol of renewal and rebirth." *Rebis*

We bring our own atmosphere: The speaker broaches a subject as controversial as it is exciting—the terraforming of Mars: i.e., the transformation of the Red Planet "into a little Earth" by "thickening its atmosphere" through the growth of oxygen-rich "plants and trees imported from Earth" and by generating heat-trapping, "super-greenhouse" gases. See McKie, "Now [NASA] looks to change Mars into a garden of Earthly delights" 2-3. *To Mars in a Month*

We build a craft predestined as a spear— / A rocket to Centauri: In 2014, Dr. Harold "Sonny" White—the head of NASA's Advanced Propulsion Team—unveiled his version of an advanced spacecraft based on the concept known as the Alcubierre "warp drive"—the idea that faster-than-light travel might be implemented by distorting spacetime. Yet, in a recent essay, Deborah Byrd states that the creation of such a spaceship is "highly speculative, to say the least." In fact, with "current technologies" it is not even possible. However, Byrd does concede that, "if it could be accomplished, it would reduce the travel time to Alpha Centauri from thousands of years to *just days.*" See "How long to travel to Alpha Centauri?" *EarthSky* 16 May 2017: 8-9 <earthsky.org>. *To Mars in a Month*

We build a star shade for our telescope: NASA's Kepler spacecraft, "seeking out the shadows of planets circling other stars, has spotted hundreds, and more and more of these other worlds look a lot like Earth—rocky balls only slightly larger than our own home, that with the right doses of starlight and water could turn out to be veritable gardens of microbial Eden." However, "if we want to know what the weather is like on these worlds, whether there is water or even life, more powerful instruments will be needed." Thus, Dr. Sara Seager, a planet theorist at MIT, "is heading a NASA study investigating the concept of a starshade, which would float in front of a space telescope and block light from a star so that its much fainter planets would be visible" (Dennis Overbye, "So Many Earth-Like Planets, So Few Telescopes," *The New York Times* 6 Jan. 2015: 1, 3 <www.nytimes.com>). *Kepler*

We could simulate Spacetime as we spend: In *The Physics of Immortality,* Tipler argues that, "if the physical universe can be put into one-to-one correspondence with some mutually consistent subcollections of all mathematical concepts," then "the universe can certainly be simulated," because "the physical universe [itself] is a concept"—in effect, "the collection of all mathematical objects" (209). Furthermore, even "*we shall be emulated in the computers of the far future*" (220), since "a 'living being' is any entity [that] codes information [. . .] preserved [not only] by natural selection" (124), but also by the universal "cogitative layer"—the *noosphere*—that will eventually coalesce into the "supersapient being" [the Tillich-Pannenberg God] that Tipler calls the Omega Point (113). *Life in a Mortal Universe*

We enter the funnel; ravel each ray / Through its spherical shell; propel the stray / To Alpha Centauri: In other words, astronauts would navigate a wormhole in order to reach Alpha Centauri's triple star system. However, astronomers offer an even more viable solution. See Sarah Lewin, "What Do We Know About Alpha Centauri?" *Space.com* 13 Apr. 2016: 4 <www.space.com>: "because of their nearness, the Alpha Centauri twins and Proxima Centauri offer a promising location to look for planets at a distance—especially using direct imaging—if researchers can filter out the complexities of the double star. And they also seem a good place to visit. The distance may be vast, but it could be relatively easy for Starshot's nanocraft or other interstellar [light sail] travelers to blast through and beam back information to Earth about the system with a bit more than a four-year delay. While planets orbiting those stars would see a starscape that is quite different from Earth's, the stars' similarity to the sun would make their habitable zones an intriguing place to look for Earth analogues." *Full Circle*

We find Him in dust clouds swollen with blood: Before his spiritual conversion, the hyphenated god-man—like the alchemical Mercurius, the archetype of the unconscious—

"is found in the vein swollen with blood," even as "he tempts us out into the world of sense" (Jung, *Alchemical Studies* 247). *Sunday*

We hitch a ride on a computation: In his essay "God Is the Machine," Kevin Kelly remarks that, according to "nearly every mapper of [the] new digitalism," the ultimate computer—one that supersedes "the natural universal computer"—is bound to be "human-made." Kelly notes that Tommaso Toffoli, a quantum computer researcher, advocates the latter goal even as he clarifies its execution: Since "nature has been continually computing the 'next state' of the universe for billions of years[,] all [that] we have to do—and, actually, all [that] we can do—is [to] 'hitch a ride' on this huge, ongoing Great Computation" (*Wired* 1 Dec. 2002: 8 <www.wired.com>). *Nothing*

We host the blazar, observe down its jet: "Blazars are thought to be active galactic nuclei, with relativistic jets oriented close to the line of sight with the observer." In effect, we *observe down* the *jet* of plasma, or virtually so. See "Blazar," *Wikipedia* 4. *Blazar/Quasar*

We intuit the Garden that we glean / In the eye: an irreducible green: Cf. Psalm 23.2: "He makes me lie down in green pastures," a place of bliss and plenty. *Spherical*

We pass through crystal clouds: In his rocket ship, as the astronaut bypasses Jupiter, "the giant of the Sun's family," he observes, as Moore emphasizes in *Travellers in Space and Time,* that "Clouds are in rapid motion; [that] Jupiter is never calm" (50-51). In fact, photos taken by the Narrow Angle Camera (NAC) onboard NASA's Cassini spacecraft on 29 December 2000 have revealed multiple layers of clouds. Almost everywhere clouds proliferate. Thus, "The visible surface of Jupiter is a deck of clouds of ammonia crystals [. . .]. At levels below the deck of ammonia clouds, there are believed to be ammonium hydrosulfide (NH_4SH) clouds and water crystal (H_2O) clouds, followed by clouds of liquid water." See "Jupiter," *All about Jupiter* 2 <zebu.uoregon.edu>. Accessed on 22 Sept. 2016. *Tipler's Subset*

We penetrate the planet: In this poem, the speaker charts a timeline for human spaceflight. Thus, in the first stanza, NASA astronauts help to construct The International Space Station (ISS), a laboratory that orbits 220 miles above the ground; in the second stanza, they paraterraform Phobos, a Martian moon; in the third stanza, having developed "a transport system for human travel beyond the Earth-Moon system," they reach the Red Planet itself. See Eric Berger, "Finally, some details about how NASA actually plans to get to Mars," *ars technica* 28 Mar. 2017: 2-3 <arstechnica.com>, and also Robert Walker, "Is it possible to terraform just a portion of Mars by enclosing it in a dome?" *Quora* 22 July 2015: 3 <www.quora.com>. *To Live and Work in Deep Space*

we reach a ring, and it is thin: i.e., Jupiter's *ring* formation: the halo ring, the main ring, the Amalthea gossamer ring, and the Thebe gossamer ring. Discovered in 1979 by the Voyager 1 spacecraft, Jupiter's ring system "is thin, and the particles making it up are dark [. . .]" (Moore, *Traveling in Space and Time* 54). Elsewhere Holly Zell explains that Jupiter's rings are "faint and tenuous" because "they are formed from dust particles hurled up by micro-meteor impacts on Jupiter's small inner moons [Amalthea and Thebe] and captured into orbit." In fact, "The rings must constantly be replenished with new dust [in order] to exist." See "Jupiter's Ring Formation Confirmed," *Goddard Space Flight Center* 1-2 <www.nasa.gov>. Last updated on 24 Sept. 2009. *Tipler's Subset*

We ride on the cloud where soul-sparks once flowed / Inside the bucket, each coheir that stowed— / Attached to the wheel that His *rebis* rode—: See Jung, *Psychology and Alchemy* 380-81: "In the Manichaean system the savior constructs a cosmic wheel with twelve buckets—the zodiac—for the raising of souls. This wheel has a significant connection with the *rota* or *opus circulatorium* of alchemy, which serves the same purpose of sublimation." In other words, "The wheel turns into the wheel of the sun rolling round the heavens, and so becomes identical with the sun-god or [sun]–hero who submits to arduous labours and to the passion of self-cremation, like Herakles [and Christ], or to captivity and dismemberment at the hands of the evil principle, like Osiris. [Another] well-known parallel to the chariot of the sun is the fiery chariot in which Elijah ascended to heaven" [2 Kings 2.11]. *Dreaming in Code*

We rise in the east and sink in the west; / Coil like a serpent; circle like a quest / Ge's shining clay: the foetus in the chest: See Jung, *Psychology and Alchemy* 382-83: "The circle described by the sun is the 'line that runs back on itself, like [Ouroboros,] the snake that with its head bites its own tail, wherein God may be discerned.'" The alchemist Michael Maier (1568-1622) "calls it 'the shining clay moulded by the wheel [*rota*] and hand of the Most High and Almighty Potter' into that earthly substance wherein the sun's rays are collected and caught. This substance is the gold," i.e., either Maier's "joyful giant" of Psalm 18.6-7 (Vulgate; D.V.) or, here, the Spirit of the glorified Christ: *the foetus in the chest.* *Dreaming in Code*

We secure the House, then forget the key: The speaker refers either to the first astrological House, ruled by Aries and associated with the self, or to the ninth House, ruled by Sagittarius and associated with both religion and philosophy. *Blazar/Quasar*

We seek such a heaven as coheirs hymn / [. . .] A zodiacal cloud that we yet skim: The speaker anticipates the archetypal journey through the planetary houses—a *peregrinatio chymica* that "repeats the old 'heavenly journey of the soul'"—even as he broaches the theme of ascent and descent (Jung, *Mysterium Coniunctionis* 224-26). Thus, in the myth of Hercules, "the cross formed by his journeys (labours 7-10) lead South-North-East-West, while labours 11-12 lead upwards" and culminate thereafter in self-cremation, *sublimatio,* and divinity (Jung, *Psychology and Alchemy* 307n36). See also the note on *We secure the House, then forget the key* given above. *Spherical*

we shape His sod: Having evaluated the future trajectory of humankind, and the cultural codes by which we choose to define, or even to re-define, religious and moral values, William Egginton, quoting a famous "dictum" from the twentieth-century French existentialist Jean-Paul Sartre, declares that "I am condemned to freedom. I am not free because I *can* make choices, but because I *must* make them, all the time, even when I think [that] I have no choice to make" ("The Limits of the Coded World," *The New York Times* 25 July 2010: 6 <opinionator.blogs.nytimes.com>). Eggington maintains that "our reason always strives to know more" (4). *The Limits of the Coded World*

Westar: i.e., *Westar VI,* an errant geosynchronous communications satellite that Shuttle astronauts (Dale A. Gardner and Joseph P. Allen) "plucked" from orbit and returned to Earth on 16 November 1984 (Kerrod, *Space Walks* 46). *The Spherical Glass Vessel*

We swing around and point the other way; / Cut the transit time: To get us to Mars, Bill Emrich, a propulsion engineer at NASA's Marshall Space Flight Center in Huntsville, Alabama, has recommended "a nuclear thermal rocket. It would produce thrust the way chemical rockets do: by heating a propellant—in this case, hydrogen—and ejecting the expanded gas through a nozzle. Instead of heating hydrogen through combustion, however, the nuclear rocket vaporizes it through the controlled fission, or splitting of atomic nuclei, of uranium. Because nuclear fuel has a greater energy density, it lasts a lot longer than chemicals, so you can keep the engine running and continue to accelerate for half the trip. Then, with the speedometer clicking off about 15 miles per second—twice the speed reached by returning Apollo astronauts—you'd swing the ship around to point the other way and use the engine's thrust to decelerate for the rest of the trip. Even when factoring in the weight of the reactor, a nuclear engine would cut the transit time in half" (Klesius, "Mars, and Step on It" 2-3). *To Mars in a Month*

What *he* shall be has not yet been revealed: The speaker refers either to the vague, unfinished humanoid robot of line 18 or to the ever-evolving, archetypal hero—the sun-god Heracles—of line 23. See also 1 John 3.2-3: "Here and now, dear friends, we are God's children: what we shall be has not yet been disclosed, but we shall be like him, because we shall see him as he is. Everyone who has this hope before him purifies himself, as Christ is pure." *Heracles Peeled*

When spectrographs fail: The Space Telescope Imaging Spectrograph (STIS), which was installed on the Hubble Space Telescope during Servicing Mission 2 in 1997, stopped functioning in August 2004, but was repaired by Shuttle astronauts during Servicing Mission 4 in May 2009. See "Repair of Space Telescope Imaging Spectrograph," *Hubble Space Telescope* <www.spacetelescope.org>. Accessed on 26 Jan. 2018. *Keeper of the Hubble*

where Leto gave birth: In Greek and Roman mythology, *Leto gave birth* to Apollo (the Sun) and his twin sister Artemis (the Moon) "under a palm-tree in Delos" (Jung, *Mysterium Coniunctionis* 71n195). In effect, "the protecting tree [. . .] is the mother" and, as Jung emphasizes, "is therefore a source of life" (71). *Shapeshifter*

Where s-waves ripple and where p-waves roam: See David Wood, "Seismic Wave: Definition, Types & Frequency," *Study.com* 3 <study.com>: "The first thing you feel when an earthquake happens is the P-wave, or primary wave," which "moves faster and arrives first. It's a longitudinal wave, meaning [that] it vibrates the ground parallel to the direction of motion—it basically shakes the ground up and down and side to side," yet causes "relatively minor damage." The S-wave, or secondary wave, "is pretty much the exact opposite of the P-wave: [. . .] it's slow-moving, but it causes far more damage. Imagine it as a ripple through the ground." Accessed on 11 May 2015. *Full Circle*

Where the fir tree may yet supplant the gorse: Cf. the Wycliffe Bible translation of Isaiah 55.13: "A fir tree shall go up for a gorse." According to J. Vernon McGee, "This verse looks forward to the Millennium when the earth will be redeemed from the curse of sin. [. . .] When Christ died, He not only redeemed sinners. He also redeemed a sin-cursed earth" (*Thru the Bible with J. Vernon McGee, Volume III: Proverbs—Malachi* 321). Here, the "curse and sin" are expressed by the *gorse,* a prickly or thorny evergreen shrub, and redemption and undying life by the *fir tree,* an evergreen now associated with Christ, the Cross, the Tree of Life, and Christmas. *Station*

Whether closed, like the surface of a sphere; / Open, the curve of the horn that we clear; / Or flat, the fixed line of Archytas' spear: See Nola Taylor Redd, "What is the Shape of the Universe?" *Space.com* 15 Jan. 2014: 3 <www.space.com>: "The shape of the universe depends on its density. If the [actual] density is more than the critical density, the universe is closed and curves like a sphere; if less, it [is open] and will curve [horn-shaped] like a saddle. But if the actual density of the universe is equal to the critical density, as scientists think [that] it is, then it will extend forever like a flat piece of paper." Here, the speaker also refers to the *horn* antenna with which, in 1965, Arno Penzias and Robert Wilson "detected the cosmic fireball radiation"—a *horn* "built like an over-sized ear trumpet" and "sensitive to faint radio whispers that travel through the Universe" (Robert Jastrow, *God and the Astronomers* [New York: Norton, 1978] 20). Elsewhere, Carl Huffman broaches the riddle of *Archytas' Spear.* Thus, the Greek philosopher Archytas of Tarentum [fourth-century BC] "asks anyone who argues that the universe is limited [rather than unlimited] to engage in a thought experiment [. . .]: 'If I arrived at the outermost edge of the heaven, could I extend my hand or staff into what is outside or not? It would be paradoxical [given our normal assumptions about the nature of space] not to be able to extend it.'" In other words, "The end of the staff, once extended[,] will mark a new limit. Archytas can advance to the new limit and ask the same question again, so that there will always be something, into which his staff [or, as in this poem, his spear] can be extended, beyond the supposed limit, and hence that something is clearly unlimited" and—overall, on a large scale, as Taylor Redd reports—*flat* ("Archytas," *Stanford Encyclopedia of Philosophy* 23 Aug. 2016: 19 <plato.stanford.edu>). *The Ultimate Fate of the Universe*

A whirlpool in chaos: In the philosophy of Anaxagoras (c. 500 - c. 428 BC), "the nous [the Universal or Divine Mind] gives rise to a whirlpool in chaos," a vortex in the *massa confusa* that, in this poem, "gives birth to the stone" (Jung, *Psychology and Alchemy* 325). *Serious Reader*

Who knows and understands? – It is myself: The speaker refers to Saint Augustine's view that "self-knowledge is the *scientia Creatoris* [the knowledge of the Creator], a morning light revealed after a night during which consciousness slumbered, wrapped in the darkness of the unconscious. But the knowledge arising with this first light finally and inevitably becomes the *scientia hominis,* the knowledge of man, who asks himself: 'Who is it that knows and understands everything? Why, it is myself'" (Jung, *Alchemical Studies* 249). *Tumbling Escher*

wight: "a living being; [a] creature" ("Wight[1]" [n.], def. 1). *Segway*

wired in the brane: a climactic pun; hence, programmed not only in the human forebrain (specifically, the parts of the cerebrum associated with thought and reason), but also in the D-*brane*—dimensional space into which energy can flow once it leaves its quantum string. In *brane* cosmology, since elementary particles may be neither more nor less than vibrational states of quantum strings, conservation of energy demands that each open string must have its unjoined endpoint attached to a D-*brane*. *Life on Mars*

within the gate: Cf. Christ's Sermon on the Mount, in Matt. 7.13.14: "Enter by the narrow gate. The gate is wide that leads to perdition, there is plenty of room on the road, and many go that way; but the gate that leads to life is small and the road is narrow, and those who find it are few." *Precinct*

Without a moon, the blue dot that we seize / Would yet stabilize, see-saw with us, tease, / The tilt of Earth's axis precess with ease, / Its motion vary by just ten degrees: In "The Odds for Life on a Moonless Earth," Nola Taylor Redd reminds us that "Scientists have long believed that, without our moon, the tilt of the Earth would shift greatly over time, from zero degrees, where the Sun remains over the equator, to 85 degrees, where the Sun shines almost directly above one of the poles." However, Taylor Redd adds that "new simulations show that, even without a moon, the tilt of Earth's axis—known as its obliquity—would vary only about ten degrees." In short, "The influence of other planets in the solar system could have kept a moonless Earth stable" (*Astrobiology Magazine* 4 Aug. 2011: 1-2 www.astrobio.net). For a less sanguine view of this subject, see Ira Flatow and Jason Barnes, "Is A Moon Necessary For A Planet To Support Life?" *NPR* 18 Nov. 2011: 6-7 <www.npr.org>. *Compass*

Without a suture: The speaker refers to the visible seam or portion of thread with which the opposites (e.g., light/darkness; consciousness/unconsciousness) are united, as in the symbol of the *rebis*. By contrast, in the higher Adam, "the opposition is invisible" (Jung, *Aion* 248). *The Archivist*

wobble like a gnome: In "Gazing Afar for Other Earths, and Other Beings," Overbye reminds us that "It was only in 1995 that a team of Swiss astronomers led by Michael Mayor of the Geneva Observatory discovered the first planet of another Sun-like star [by] using what is now known as the 'wobble' method. A planet gives its star a little gravitational tug as it goes around, causing the star to go back and forth, or wobble, a little as both star and planet circle the same center of gravity." Thus, the Swiss team "detected a wobble in the motion of the star 51 Pegasi as an object half the mass of Jupiter whipped around it every four days." However, Overbye emphasizes that there is a "hitch" to finding exoplanets—in particular, the presence of "Earth-size planets in habitable zones"—mainly because "Such planets would not exert enough of a gravitational tug on their suns to be detectable by the 'wobble' method." As a result, "Instead of 'confirming' such planets, Kepler astronomers talk about 'validating' them by using high-powered telescopes to make sure, for example, that there is only one star [in sight] and not a pair of eclipsing stars or some other phenomenon that could mimic a planet's shadow" (2-3). *Life Out There*

The world does not happen; it simply is: Cf. Hermann Weyl, *Philosophy of Mathematics and Natural Science,* trans. Olaf Helmer (1949; Princeton: Princeton UP, 2009)

116: "The objective world simply is; it does not happen. Only to the gaze of my consciousness, crawling upward along the life line of my body, does a section of this world come to life as a fleeting image in space which continuously changes in time." *Full Circle*

the world-egg cracked: "the philosophical egg of the medieval natural philosophers, the vessel from which, at the end of the *opus alchymicum,* the homunculus emerges, that is, the Anthropos, the spiritual, inner, and complete man [. . .]" (Jung, *The Archetypes and the Collective Unconscious* 293). *Prefigured*

The world-soul draws him like an aquasphere: "The idea of the rotating aquasphere reminds us of the Neopythagoreans: in Archytas, the world-soul is a circle or sphere; in Philolaos it draws the world round with it in its rotation. The original idea is to be found in Anaxagoras, where the nous [the cosmic Mind] gives rise to a whirlpool in chaos" (Jung, *Psychology and Alchemy* 325). See also the note for *hylical water* given above. *Serious Reader*

wormhole: in hyperspace, amid endlessly spawning universes, a crosscut from one place and time to another. *Bulk; History's Thread; Outrider; Serious Reader; Tearing the Fabric of Spacetime; A User's Guide to Spacetime*

wormhole that you comb: a hypothetical passageway; here, a tunnel that connects Mind and Body in both the speaker and the reader. In the quoted adjective clause, the verb means "to search thoroughly; [to] look everywhere in" ("Comb" [vt.], def. 3). *A User's Guide to Spacetime*

Yahweh's sun-and-moon trees: In alchemy, "the moon itself is a plant" (Jung, *Mysterium Coniunctionis* 132). Thus, in the alchemical pictures, sometimes the prototype of the tree of paradise is "hung not with apples but with sun-and-moon fruit" (Jung, *Alchemical Studies* 302-03). For an apt illustration, see Jung, *Psychology and Alchemy* 231, fig. 116: the "Crowned hermaphrodite representing the union of king and queen, [standing] between the sun and moon trees." *Station*

yew berries that brood: Against a backdrop of lanceolate, dark-green leaves, the sumptuous, bright red fruit of the female *yew* tree appears to "hover or loom" ("Brood" [vi.], def. 3) or hang in an enveloping manner. The *yew* tree itself is associated with both rebirth and immortality. In fact, according to a current online essay, the *yew* "is the only creature biologically capable of living indefinitely." Oddly enough, the *yew* is a "very poisonous [tree] except for the fleshy part of the berry [. . .]. Even the seed inside the berry is deadly." However, in the past, the poison of the *yew* tree was widely regarded as a "cardiac stimulant" ("Yew," *The Goddess Tree* 2 <www.thegoddesstree.com>). Accessed on 12 Oct. 2016. *Electrospinlacing*

You are Here: See "You-Are-Here Maps for International Space Station: Approach and Guidelines," *SAE International Conference on Environmental Systems* 19 July 2004: 1-7 <mvl.mit.edu>, where J. J. Marquez, C. M. Oman, and A. M. Liu review terrestrial as well as micro-gravity YAH maps, even as they discuss "spatial disorientation" and "wayfinding problems" in new environments. *Wayfinder*

Your capsule but a body made of foam: The speaker refers not only to a deployed spacecraft and to the self-contained form of a human being, but also to the *prima materia: foam,* "the spongelike structure of the world canvas" (Davies, *Other Worlds* 96). *A User's Guide to Spacetime*

zero-g: a popular term for zero gravity, the condition of weightlessness that "results from a balance between the earth's gravitational pull and the inertia of a spacecraft [. . .]. Zero gravity is floating without having to pay the consequences—a strange and sublime experience that is at once bizarre and immensely enjoyable, a relaxed, slow-motion state in which all of the earth-bound rules have been broken" (Allen and Martin, *Entering Space* 65). *Life in a Mortal Universe*

Zion: Mount *Zion,* the site of "that new Jerusalem which is coming down out of heaven" after End-time and the second creation of Heaven and Earth (Rev. 3.12). *A Walking Man I*

www.ingramcontent.com/pod-product-compliance
Lightning Source LLC
Chambersburg PA
CBHW081720100526
44591CB00016B/2442
* 9 7 8 1 9 4 3 6 9 1 1 6 6 *